KU-707-896

THE ITINERARY

OF

JOHN LELAND

IN OR ABOUT THE YEARS

1535—1543

PARTS IX, X, AND XI

WITH

TWO APPENDICES, A GLOSSARY, AND
GENERAL INDEX

EDITED BY

LUCY TOULMIN SMITH

PUBLIC LIBRARY

JUN. 1920

READING

LONDON

G. BELL AND SONS, LTD.

1910

CLASS 942.052

ACC. No. R/7059

9 9 4 85 887

CHISWICK PRESS: CHARLES WHITTINGHAM AND CO.
TOOKS COURT, CHANCERY LANE, LONDON.

LELAND'S ITINERARY IN ENGLAND AND WALES

LONDON : G. BELL AND SONS, LTD.
PORTUGAL ST. LINCOLN'S INN, W.C.
CAMBRIDGE : DEIGHTON, BELL & CO.
NEW YORK : THE MACMILLAN CO.
BOMBAY : A. H. WHEELER & CO.

PREFACE

OF the three parts comprised in this concluding
volume only one, and that the shortest, viz. Part X,
is consecutive narrative, written in the personal style
of those in vol. i. Taking up the tale in Oxfordshire it
moves about Berkshire, Wilts, Somerset, and Gloucestershire, ending abruptly near Shaftesbury in Dorset.
Some of the places had been visited before, but this
may have been a separate tour, as is indicated by the
route in blue on Map II. The building of the bridge
between Culham and Abingdon in 1457, noted by
Leland, gave Hearne the occasion for an interesting
addition from a local record detailing the manner of
the whole work, worthy of attention from an economic
point of view; this will be found in the appendix to
Part X. Part IX consists of many notes better classified
than usual, chiefly in the more northern counties;
while Part XI,[1] which we owe to Stow's copy, contains
many miscellaneous matters, topographical, personal,
and historical, some of which formed the foundation of
narrative in parts of vols. i and ii. Leland's route to the
northern counties and back, partly drawn from these
notes, is shown in blue on Map III. The bishops and
bishoprics of Lincoln, Durham, Hereford, Canterbury

---

[1] No omissions have been made ; it was found better to print
the whole part. See vol. i, Introd., p. vi.

and Worcester, are dealt with pretty fully—how far
the lists are accurate must be judged by special study.
I have endeavoured to point out a few errors. An
interesting series of notes from the lives of English
saints is taken from John of Tynemouth's "Sanctilogium," and I am glad to have identified another set
of lengthy extracts as taken from the "Mappa Mundi"
by Gervase of Canterbury. These extracts give with
varying fullness the lists of religious houses in England, and we may take it that Leland regarded them
as still of some authority in his day. They might be
compared with the long particulars of religious houses
gathered together by Leland in the first MS. volume
of his Collectanea (second edition by Hearne, 1774,
vol. i, 25-123), and with other material at Cheltenham
(see my vol. ii, p. 118 *note*), all being of additional
interest in view of Professor Savine's recent study of
the "Valor Ecclesiasticus."

Stow's copy of Part XI has itself lost eight leaves
(*see* p. 136 *note*). While we are grateful for what he has
preserved, it must be said that his careless Latin
has given his editors much trouble. Frequent want
of concord, and much mis-spelling,—partly due, no
doubt, to his not understanding contractions in the
MS., partly to his very casual use of vowels, and
occasionally to his following the mediaeval spelling,—
offended the modern scholar's sense, and Hearne took
immense pains to remedy this by means of numerous
little foot-notes; but even his meticulous eye grew
tired and towards the end he dropped his correcting
pen, or occasionally made alterations in the text without indicating them. This treatment seemed unneces-
sarily tedious; I have therefore embodied most of

Hearne's corrections in the text without foot reference, placing a selection only of the MS. readings at the foot of the page, which serve as specimens of Stow; and giving all cases where there is any question of meaning or identification. Comparison with the original works quoted by Leland, where identified, has been also of much assistance. Though a few errors may occur, it is hoped that all requirements are thus fairly satisfied.

A final appendix of Welsh matter (Glamorganshire) from the manuscript of Collectanea, vol. iii, closes the volume. It should be noted that all the extracts from Collectanea which belong to the Itinerary and are printed in this edition—except that found in the Cheltenham MS.—are taken from the MS. vol. iii; the most important are the " New Year's Gift," the notes and map of the Channel Islands, a large portion on Kent (vol. iv, pp. 47-70), the curious description of Anglesea, and further notes on Wales, the last of which I regret are not all gathered together in the volume on Wales owing to my imperfect knowledge of the Collectanea at the beginning of this undertaking. Reference to the General Index, which has been prepared with care and revision, and to the tables of counties, will, it is hoped, supply the needed links.

For the third edition of Hearne's print of the Itinerary, 1768, Dr. Charles Lyttleton, bishop of Carlisle, sent a few emendations which were inserted by Mr. Pote the publisher; three of these referring to names of places I add to the list of errata in the present volume; others had been already made in the course of my collation.

Leland is a valuable writer for the English philo-

logist, quotations from his expressive Tudor language
are scattered up and down the pages of the New
Oxford Dictionary. A short glossary of disused or
difficult words and senses is here appended to be near
at hand for the reader.

Regarding Leland himself two additions since my
Introduction to vol. i have arisen. Thinking that the
" commission " given him by King Henry VIII, under
power of which he made his researches and journeys,
might be now attainable, I have had a thorough
search made once more among all the likely sources
in the Public Record Office, but still without result.
It does not appear on the Patent or the Close Rolls
from 1533-1543, and Anthony Wood was perhaps mistaken in affirming that it was under the " broad seal "
(Introd., p. ix).—The interesting fact has been shown
me by Dr. James Gairdner that John Leland in 1546
was holding from the Court of Augmentations a tene-
ment in the parish of St. Botolph without Aldersgate,
London, within the site of the late Charterhouse
(Letters and Papers, Henry VIII, vol. xxi, Part i,
p. 767). We may conjecture, therefore, that he set-
tled in this house, and not in St. Michael's parish, at
the end of his travels to write his works, and may
have sent his " New Year's Gift " of 1546 thence to
the King; further, that it may have been his brother
John, who took charge of him during his insanity
until he died, who actually lived in the parish of
St. Michael le Querne, a supposition to which colour
is lent by the fact that our John, the younger brother,
was buried in the church of that parish. These con-
jectures seem probable, but there being the two Johns
we cannot tell with certainty (see Introd., pp. xiv, xv).

In conclusion it may be useful to give a note of the Leland manuscripts, or parts of manuscripts, in the British Museum [1] beyond those mentioned in vol. i, Introd., pp. xxviii-xxx, and in my Comparative Table in the same volume (p. xxxvi; see also vol. ii, p. 117). Some of these now indicated contain various extracts from the Itinerary; the first two are notable on account of the eminent antiquaries William Camden and Francis Thynne, who made the respective collections. The third is a large folio, chiefly valuable because the first ninety leaves are in Leland's autograph hand; judging by size, shape, and contents they must probably have once formed part of his Collectanea; the rest of the volume contains copies from various detached portions of the Itinerary (printed in our vols. iii, iv, v), including some of those culled from the third volume of Collectanea, and a copy of the whole of Part I; ending with ten leaves copied by William Burton from Collectanea and a letter. Perhaps the most interesting manuscript as regards the Itinerary is the Harl. 842, a small paper folio containing a number of selected extracts relating to thirty-five counties, also including the Itinerary passages from the third volume of Collectanea. The Leland portion of No. 5, one of the latest in date, is entirely devoted to extracts from the Itinerary, copied by several hands.

I add references to the manuscripts containing similar extracts from Leland's general Collectanea, apart from the Itinerary. One of these also contains a small portion in autograph (No. 10).[2]

[1] Up till April, 1909; I do not know of any later acquisitions.
[2] Except for No. 5, in referring to the folios of manuscripts the old numeration is used.

1. Lansdowne 229; "W. Camden Miscellanea," dated 1573. Fos. 83-87*b*, notes from Parts IV, VI, and others of the Itinerary; fos. 88-98, or perhaps 99, "ex aliis diversis Collectaneis Johanni Leilandi."

2. Cotton MSS., Cleopatra C. iii ; catalogued, "Collections of Mr. Fras. Thynne." Fos. 67*b*-87*b*, extracts from Part II of the Itinerary, copied 17 Dec., 1589, and signed F. Thynne. Fos. 179*b*, 199*b*-201, a few miscellaneous notes from Itinerary; fos. 301-319*b*, extracts copied apparently by John Stow (judging by the hand and ink) from parts of Collectanea.

3. Cotton, Julius C. vi. Folio. Nearly the whole is occupied by Leland. Fos. 1-90, truly described by a later hand, "Johannis Lelandi collectiones ex antiquissimi authoribus desumptæ quæ ad Britanniam spectant manu ejusdem Lelandi scriptæ." Among the writers quoted are Priscian, Polybius, Tacitus, Politian, Paulus Diaconus, Diodorus Siculus, Antonini Itinerarium, and John Boscatius De stagnis et paludibus: these leaves, like those in the Phillipps MS. 12111 at Cheltenham, have been at some time separated from Leland's Collectanea: so far, I do not find them printed by Hearne, but this would require more investigation. After fo. 90 follow many extracts from the third volume of Collectanea, as well as some from the Itinerary, in a late sixteenth-century hand. Fos. 192-232 contain the whole of Part I copied by another (?) seventeenth-century hand. Fos. 233-243 are copies "Ex Collectaneis," and a letter to Selden, all in the hand of William Burton.

4. Harleian 842, a small folio, of 93 leaves, paper Written by a hand of the late sixteenth or early seventeenth century. Consists of extracts from the Itinerary,

orderly arranged according to the counties of England and Wales.

5. Lansdowne 940, 4to, of 190 leaves. Fos. 122-154 (pencil numbering); a collection of extracts from various parts of the Itinerary, written by various hands of seventeenth century.

6. Lansdowne 825, fos. 19-21. Two leaves contain a partial list of names of counties and the towns along Leland's routes, taken from the parts of the Itinerary, in a large loose hand; they are endorsed on an outside sheet, "An account of Leland's Itinerary." (Of no special value.)

7. Harleian 6193, a square folio of 290 pages, written in a fine bold hand, titles rubricated; title on p. 1, "John Leland's Commentarys of England," that on the fly-leaf, "Johannis Lelandi Collectanea," expresses the contents of the volume, which is filled with copies entirely, I believe, from the Collectanea.[1]

8. Lansdowne 963 (from Bishop Kennett's collection). A small 8vo. MS. of 139 leaves, written in small hand of seventeenth century; fos. 15b-16b have a few extracts "ex Collectaneis Johannis Lelandi, MS., 4to, vol. 2," a reference which appears to point to a lost volume of Leland's notes (the known MSS. of his Collectanea being all in folio), or it may be intended for Part II of the Itinerary, in which, as well as in Part III, one or two of the items occur (vol. i,

---

[1] Hearne wished to borrow all the "pieces of Leland" from Lord Harley's library, among which he notes some "originals" in Leland's hand. See Hearne to Humphrey Wanley, 23 Oct., 1714, in Ellis's "Letters of Eminent Literary Men," Camden Soc., 1843, p. 355. I have not found any originals of the Itinerary in the Harleian collection.

READING FREE PUBLIC LIBRARY

pp. 129, 265). Further extracts from the folio Collectanea, vol. i, occur on fos. 177 to about 186.

9. Cotton, Vespasian B. xv, fo. 40. A page containing lists of witnesses from eight or nine old charters, copied " ex Lelando," probably from Collectanea.

10. Cotton, Vitellius C. ix. Fos. 234-239*b* contain a copy from Leland's extracts from several old writers and his notes thereon, including the Sibilline verses on the Day of Judgment. Fos. 240-245 are in Leland's own hand, consisting of extracts from several Latin poets. It seems possible that these leaves, like others, may have dropped out of some quire of Leland's great collections.

11. Stowe 305, fo. 296. Contains an extract from Collectanea, vol. i.

12. Stowe 1048, eighteenth century. Fo. 12*b*, a page containing small notes from Collectanea, vol. iii.

In drawing to a close a work full of details which has occupied the spare time of many years, while I am conscious of some errors or mistakes, I can truly say I have done my best to avoid them; the further knowledge gained in the course of editing might have improved the earlier volumes had it been possible. I hope, too, that I have omitted little of importance. It is a pleasure to acknowledge my obligations and thanks for kind help to Messrs. F. Madan of the Bodleian Library, C. E. Doble, Professors Adam Kirkaldy and A. J. Herbertson, for the long loan of working books and maps; to the Rev. Travers Herford, Mr. A. S. Buxton of Mansfield, Mr. Francis Harrison of Bath, C. L. Kingsford, Esq., Mr. R. Blair of South Shields, Mr. W. H. Stevenson, the Hon. Miss

Bruce, Miss Fell Smith, for suggestions and assistance in some identifications of places; to Sir Edw. Maunde Thompson, Sir John Rhys, Dr. Craigie, and especially my old friend Sir James Murray, for valued help in explanation of certain words. Other acknowledgements have been made in the sections on Wales and the Channel Islands. Nor must I forget to own my gratitude to the patience and considerate friendliness of my kind publisher, Mr. Edward Bell, without whose encouragement I could not have carried through the work.

L. TOULMIN SMITH.

OXFORD, *July* 9, 1910.

CONTENTS

v.   *b*

ERRATA, VOL. V

Page 8, note a, *for* " Amphtill " *read* " Ampthill."

   ,,   10, line 8 from bottom, *for* " Hampton Court " *read* " Westwood in Hampton Lovet." (Bishop Lyttleton.)

Page 15, note c, *for* " Wumbridge " *read* " Wombridge."

   ,,   28, *for* " Lestewich " *read* " Leftwich."

   ,,   29, *for* " Letewich " *read* " Leftwich."

   ,,   32 in margin, *transfer* " Lincolnshire " *opposite* " Market-Kesten."

Pages 35, 36, *for* " Hutetost " *read* " Hutetoft."

Page 46, line 5 from bottom, *for* " Kenne nuage " *read* " Kenne ? village."

Page 72, note b, *for* " Besils " *read* " Bessels."

   ,,   117, line 28, *after* " Abendon " *insert note* " A verb is omitted here, the line should read ' The good lord of Abendon *gave* of his londe.' "

Page 155, line 1 margin, *for* " Warwicks " *read* " Gloucester."

   ,,   211, line 22, *for* " Deus dedit " *read* " Deusdedit " [proper name].

Page 223, line 25, *for* " parre " *read* " Parre."

   ,,   298, item Clothiers, *insert* " Trowbridge, i, 136 " *before* " Bath."

ADDITIONAL ERRATA

VOL. I

Page xviii, note 2, line 4, *for* " p. x, note " *read* " p. xxiv, note 2."

Page xxxvi " Comparative Table," in *note* 3, instead of the last clause *read* for pages 126-145, 149-152; 161, 204, see vol. iv, pp. 47-71, 164-167; 180-182.

Page 6, line 14, *for* " Thor[pe water mill " *read* " Thor[pe Waterville."

Page 25, line 6, *to word* "Marteres" *insert note*, "Marmonstier Abbey, at Tours."

Page 136, line 3 from bottom, *to word* "Alexandre" *insert note*, "Mr. Francis Harrison of Bath suggests that Leland omitted the name Langford, no clothier surnamed Alexander being found in Wilts. Alexander Langford was a well-known clothier of the time and was ancestor on the mother's side of Edward Hyde, Lord Clarendon."

Page 188, line 3, *to word* "Godolcan" *insert note*, "Godolphin."

Page 189, line 1, *to word* "Ludewin" *insert note*, "Ludgvan."

  „   189, line 8 from bottom, *to word* "Revier" *insert note*, "? Godrevy"; line 3 from bottom, *to word* "Treheddy" *insert note*, "Tehidy."

Page 237, line 11 from bottom, *for* "Tregor" *read* "Tregoz."

  „   324, note *, *for* "Penpoll" *read* "Polperro."

VOL. II

Page vii, Counties, Essex, *insert* "p. 25."

  „   25, margin, *under figure* "fo. 44" *insert* "Essex."

  „   25, note *b*, *for* "Henham" *read* "Castle Hedingham."

  „   52, line 6, *to word* "Coukfeild" *insert note*, "Cookhill." (Bishop Lyttleton.)

Page 62, line 10, *to word* "Hertlebury" *insert note*, "Hartpury."

Page 90, line 20, *to word* "Bloxham" *insert note*, "Blocklcy." (Bishop Lyttleton.)

Page 168, line 20, *for* "sundator" *read* "fundator."

VOL. III

Page 16, note *g*, *for* "Dyvodwg" *read* "y Vodwg."

VOL. IV

Page 54, note *a*, *for* "Estree" *read* "Eastry."

  „   70, line 9 from bottom, *to word* "Cantuariæ" *insert note*, "That is, the Mappa Mundi by Gervase of Canterbury. See our vol. v, p. 191 *n*."

Page 97, margin, *for* "Derby" *read* "Cheshire."

CONSPECTUS OF ENGLISH AND WELSH
COUNTIES IN THE FIVE VOLUMES

Anglesea, vol. III.
Bedfordshire, I, IV, V.
Berkshire, I, II, IV, V.
Buckinghamshire, I, II, V.
Brecknockshire, III.
Cambridgeshire, I, II.
Cardiganshire, III.
Carmarthenshire, III, IV.
Carnarvonshire, III.
Channel Islands, IV.
Cheshire, III, IV, V.
Cornwall, I, IV, V.
Cumberland, V.
Denbighshire, III.
Derbyshire, I, II, V.
Devonshire, I, IV, V.
Dorsetshire, I, IV, V.
Durham, I, II, IV, V.
Essex, II, IV, V.
Flint, III.
Gloucestershire, I, II, III, IV, V.
Glamorganshire, III, IV, V.
Hampshire, I, II, IV.
Herefordshire, II, III, IV, V.
Hertfordshire, I, IV.
Huntingdonshire, I, II.
Kent, II, IV, V.

Lancashire, II, IV, V.
Leicestershire, I, II, IV, V.
Lincolnshire, I, II, IV, V.
Merionethshire, III.
Middlesex, I, II.
Monmouthshire, II, III, IV.
Montgomeryshire, III, IV.
Norfolk, I, II, IV.
Northamptonshire, I, II, IV, V.
Northumberland, IV, V.
Nottinghamshire, I, II, IV, V.
Oxfordshire, I, II, III, IV, V.
Pembrokeshire, III.
Radnorshire, II, III.
Rutlandshire, I, IV, V.
Shropshire, II, III, IV, V.
Somersetshire, I, IV, V.
Staffordshire, II, IV, V.
Suffolk, II, V.
Surrey, II, IV.
Sussex, II, IV.
Warwick, II, IV, V.
Westmorland, IV, V.
Wiltshire, I, II, IV, V.
Worcestershire, II, III, V.
Yorkshire, I, II, V.

MAPS AND ILLUSTRATIONS IN THE FIVE VOLUMES

CONCORDANCE OF THE PRESENT EDITION OF LELAND'S ITINERARY WITH HEARNE'S PRINTED TEXT, SECOND EDITION, 1744

Thomas Hearne	*L. Toulmin Smith*
New Year's Gift, Vol. I, p. xviii.	Vol. I, p. xxxvii.
Itinerary:	
Vol. I, pp. 1-76, 84-116.	Vol. I, Part I.
Vol. I, p. 76, line 8 from bottom-83.	Vol. I, Appendix I.
Vol. II, 1-85.	Vol. I, Part II.
Appendix to Vol. VII, 105-114.	Vol. I, Appendix II, pp. 315-326.
Vol. III, 1-119.	Vol. I, Part III.
Vol. IV, 133, 134.	Vol. I, Appendix III, 327, 328.
Vol. IV, Part I, 1-31.	Vol. II, Part IV.
Vol. IV, Part I, 31-55.	Vol. III, Part VI (Wales), 12-38.
Vol. VII, Part I, 2, last line-7.	Vol. II, Part V, 33-38, line 20.
Vol. IV, Part II, 57-124.	Vol. II, Part V, 38, line 21-114.
Vol. IV, Appendix.	Vol. II, Appendix.
Vol. V, 1-84.	Vol. III, Part VI, 38-126.
Vol. VII, 14-18.	Vol. III, Part VI, 9-12, 53-57.
Vol. V, 84-105, 108-118.	Vol. IV, Part VII.
Vol. VI, 1-36, 83-88.	Vol. IV, Part VIII, 37-47, line 4, and 71, line 7 from bottom-143.
Vol. VI, 36-83.	Vol. IV, Appendix I.
Vol. VII, Appendix, 115-137.	Vol. IV, Part VIII, 47-71.
Vol. VII, Appendix, 137-143.	Vol. IV, Appendix II.
Vol. VII, Part I, 1-14, 19-63.	Vol. V, Part IX, 1-56, 60-68.
Vol. V, 105, line 15-109.	Vol. V, Part IX, 56, line 18-60, line 23.
Vol. VII, Part II.	Vol. V, Part X and Appendix.
Vol. VIII, Part II.*	Vol. V, Part XI.
Hearne's "Collectanea," ed. 1774	*Itinerary, L. T. Smith*
Vol. IV, p. 94.	Vol. III, p. 127, Appendix A.
Vol. IV, pp. 85-90.	Vol. III, 129-134, Appendix B.
Vol. IV, 90-94.	Vol. V, Appendix, 237-242.
Vol. IV, Plate of Channel Islands.	Vol. IV, Appendix III.

* Part I consisted of the fragments bound in the MS. Vol. VIII, which were in this second edition distributed into the text.

GLOSSARY

OF THE PRINCIPAL ARCHAIC WORDS AND SENSES IN THESE VOLUMES

NOTE.—*The references are intended for illustration; they do not necessarily include every example of a word. N.E.D. indicates that a definition is taken from the New English Dictionary.*

Accustumer, the, of Bridgewater, collector of customs or dues, i, 163.
Achelei stones, acheler or ashlar, hewn stones, v, 94.
Adcertenid, assured, i, 167.
After, afterwards, "after, he was redemed," iv, 141.
Al-to, all, quite, "al to minischyd and torne," iii, p. 43.
Arere, to raise; the way was raised with the earth cast up out of the dykes, v, 117.

Baches, beach or shingle, iv, 67.
Bal, Celtic word, ton or town, v, 52.
Balinger, a small sea-going vessel, apparently a kind of sloop, N.E.D., i, 317.
Balissed, balasted, i, 50.
Balkynge ground, a ridge left at the end of furrows?, ii, 109.
Barnes, children, v, 116.
Batable ground on one side the Esk river, debatable or disputed land on the Scottish border, v, 51, 53.
Beche, beach, iv, 48.
Bekyn, beacon, i, 59.
Berall, crystal or glass used for glazing windows, v, 155.
Bid, *verb,* to pray, v, 118.
Boote, probably here signifies boat, iv, 64; the form *boote* is found in i, 51.
Bord clothes, table cloths, v, 117.
Boteres, buttresses, i, 167 (*cf.* Old French *bouterez,* plural).
Bowys, arches of a bridge, v, 116.
Braye, a fals braye, "an advanced parapet surrounding the main rampart," N.E.D., i, 316.
Breed, breadth, v, 117.
Bremely, clearly, distinctly, v, 155.

Bullatike (French *bullatique*) hand, writing like that used in Papa bulls, iv, 94.

Bunks, perhaps an error for banks, which makes better sense, v, 117.

Burbolt-shot, an estimate of distance, from bird-bolt, a blunt-headed arrow used for shooting birds, i, 131.

But shot, *i.e.*, a butt-shot, a measure of distance, "a good but shotte off," iii, 109; v, 90.

Bygge, bigge, barley, iv, 12, 32.

Cantref, or hundred, a division of a county in Wales, iii, 1-9. *See* Commote.

Car, carre, a pond or pool, sometimes in moorish land, i, 51; iv, 32 v, 144.

Carnary, a charnel vault or house, i, 184, 270.

Caryke, carrack, a large ship of burden or warfare, iv, 48.

Causey, cawsey, a causeway, a raised way formed on a mound across low wet ground, bog or marsh, N.E.D., ii, 101; v, 110, 144.

Causey, *verb*, bridge "well cawsied with stone at both ends," ii, 109.

Champaine, champayne ground, plain, open country, without hills or woods, perhaps unenclosed, i, 27, 130; ii, 52; iii, 102; v, 81, 97.

Chart, a map, iv, 125; v, 44.

Cheping-, Cheaping or Chipping, as prefix to the name of a town, indicates a market town, Cheping-Faringdon, i, 125; Chipping-Sodbury, i, 130; Chiping-Norton, ii, 38.

Chisil, gravel or shingle, The Chisil or Chesil, a shingly beach, i, 242, 243.

Ciffenes, sieves for meal, from cyve, a sieve, v, 129.

Clive, *sub.*, a cliff, v, 101.

Clyve, *verb*, to rise or climb, clyvid, iii, 14; clyving, iv, 136.

Clyving, *sub.*, seems to mean a cleft in this case, iv, 133.

Choclea, a spiral staircase, i, 96.

Coferer, cofferer or treasurer, ii, 39, 77.

Cokid=cocked, pryed or looked about, v, 116.

Commote, a territorial division in Wales, two or three of which were contained in a cantred or cantref, iii, pref. viii *n.*, 19, 93.

Comprobation, confirmation, v, 72.

Coningly, cunningly, wisely, skilfully, ii, 87.

Conducte of water, a conduit, i, 220, 278; iv, 25.

Conscend, to ascend or mount (a hill, etc.), i, 133, 148, 174.

Consuete, accustomed, usual, v, 129.

Coppe, the top, i, 151.

Cootes, cotes, *i.e.*, salt-cotes, salt-houses or furnaces, where salt is made, ii, 93; iv, 10, 11.

Couchid, placed, set down, i, 154.

County, Count or Earl, i, 327.

Coyletts, quillets, small (? inferior) plots or strips of land, ii, 62.

Coyte, a quoit, "a coyte- or stone-cast," a measure of distance, iv, 113.

Crayer, a small trading vessel formerly used, iv, 88.

Creek, *verb,* the water "crekith," turns or bends, "creking," i, 198, 204.

Custumer of Hampton, collector of customs or dues, v, 278. *See* Accustumer.

Dedignation, disdain, displeasure, ii, 31.
Deflorichid, despoiled, ravaged, iii, 41.
Degres, degrees, steps (in Canterbury Cathedral), iv, 38.
Departith, departs or separates, i, 13.
Disparkle, *verb,* **disparkelid, disparklid,** scattered or dispersed, i, 82, 124; iv, 76, 77.
Dition, rule, sway, i, 68. *See also* iv, 184, 186, 187.
Dok or **bosom,** a dock; "apparently a creek or haven in which ships may lie on the ooze or ride at anchor, according to the tide," N.E.D., i, 51.
Dole, grief, sorrow, v, 116.
Duello, a duel, iv, 148.
Dukke, a duck, iv, 84.

Egge, edge, i, 23.
Entaylid, intaglio, engraved, v, 53. *See* Intayle.
Ering, ploughing, from ere, a variety of ear, to plough, v, 46.
Escrye, out-cry, battle-cry, iv, 125; scry, iv, 97.

Fauburge, a faubourg or suburb (apparently equivalent to a "borough foreign"), ii, 86.
Fletithe, fleatith, *verb,* to fleet, said of waters, to flow, i, 31; ii, 81.
Flette, floated, v, 116.
Flite shot, a flight-shot, the flight of a shot-arrow, a measure of distance, ii, 66; iv, 50, 98; v, 101; "two flite shots," i, 67, 96.
Force, a fort or strong castle, i, 201.
Forcid, strengthened, fortified, i, 96, 100, 319.
Foster, forester (to Penkridge Chase), v, 22.
Frerenhay, the Friars' enclosure, i, 228.
Frith, frith park, a game preserve or deer park, i, 20, 108; ii, 80 *n.*
Fulled, baptized, or washed, v, 116.

Gabylle, a cable, rope, i, 49.
Gainest way, the straightest, most direct way, i, 51.
Gere, gear, *i.e.,* matter or subject, iv, 64.
Gesse, I guess, *i.e.,* I am pretty sure, I think, i, 98; I judge, 108.
Gill, a stream in a narrow ravine or glen, v, 138.

Hard, *adv.* and *prep.,* hard at, v, 105; harde by, 104; hard on, 106; harde withyn, 106; *i.e.,* just or close at, by, on, within.
Hard, *adj.,* in phrase "to the hard ground," to the very ground, v, 104.
Harte brinynge, heart-burning, v, 155.
Havenet, a small haven, i, 51.
Heend, polite, v, 116.
Hem, them, v, 117, 118.
Her, their, v, 116.

Heyne, a saving, niggardly man, iv, 143.

Hiereward, perhaps an error for hithe-ward, the keeper of the hithe, v, 117.

Hillinge, rising, ascending, v, 71.

Holme, a little isle or islet in a river or lake, or near the mainland, iv, 33, 136.

Hope. Leland says "hopes or becks," i, 77, or "small brooks," v, 139; according to the N.E.D. the hopes are the small valleys running down from the hills and opening into a main vale, in each of which a brook or burn runs. This answers the description in the text.

Howys, howe, a hoe, = mattock or pickaxe, v, 116.

Iled, past part. of verb to isle, "when Thanet was full iled," *i.e.*, was entirely an island, iv, 61.

Indubitately, undoubtedly, v, 81.

Intayle, engraved or carved work?, v, 129. *See* Entaylid. *Cf.* the paragraph on "Woulsingham Market," with the next but one as to the *marmoratum* at Durham.

Isled, said of a church, "very elegant and isled," *i.e.*, aisled, i, 148.

I-wysse, certainly, v, 117.

Keching, kechyn, kitchen, i, 40, 53.

Kenning, a marine measure of about twenty miles, i, 191, 201, 222; iv, 188.

Kefinnithes, Welsh kyffinieu (Dr. J. G. Evans), glossed by Leland *confinia*, confines or boundaries, iii, 15; he [mistakes *kefinnith*, a plural form, for the singular (*cf.* kyffin, a limit), and so uses it several times, iii, 16, 17, 18.

Keyes or **peres**, quays or piers, i, 318, 324.

Knappe, top or summit of a hill, i, 174.

Laving, *verb*, to lave, baling, v, 117.

Laund, an open space among woods, N.E.D., i, 13; as place-name, 21.

Lesys, a form of leasows, leasow, meadow or pasture land, i, 38.

Limes, limit or boundary, i, 13; iv, 32.

Lin, a linn, waterfall or torrent, but Leland here uses it for a small stream in low land, i, 95.

Ling, a kind of heather, iv, 32; v, 66.

Lingy, covered with ling, or heather, i, 80.

Lover, louver, a "lantern" or erection on the roof of a hall, with lateral holes to let out the smoke, N.E.D., i, 139.

Lumbe, lome, a weaver's loom, i, 132.

Marchanties, merchandise, i, 206.

Mareed, error for marred, dirtied, v, 116.

Market-stede, market-place, ii, 69.

Mediamnes, little isles formed in the middle of a river, i, 111, 120; ii, 63.

Merche, march, smallage or wild celery which grows on marshy places, v, 6.
Mole, a mass, great piece (of stone), v, 46.
Mownde, a fence or hedge, v, 117.
Mynion, minion, elegant, fine, iv, 33.

Nelyd, *i.e.*, annealed, glazed or enamelled by fire, iv, 131.
Nesch of sand, neck of sand; perhaps *soft piece* is intended, iv, 59.
Nesse, a headland or cape; also used as a verb, to grow into a ness, iv, 67.
Nex, aphetic form of annex, v, 178.
Next, nearest, i, 50.
Nobilitate, *verb*, to ennoble, nobilitating, iv, 100, 111; notablitatyd, v, 223, probably an error of the scribe.

Of, off, iv, 23, 61, 73 (nyne myles of).
Owre, ore of metal, v, 129; **owrische soyles**, containing ore.

Paradise, "a little studiyng chaumber caullid Paradice," i, 46.
Pecoyse, a peck or pick-axe, v, 117.
Peninsulatid, so surrounded by rivers as to form a peninsula, i, 131.
Picard, picart, a small sailing vessel formerly used for coasting or river traffic, i, 170; ii, 57; iv, 136.
Pies, magpies, i, 123.
Pill, a local name for a tidal creek, or a pool in a creek or at the confluence of a tributary stream, N.E.D.; Cornwall, and the Severn, i, 200, 204, 206, 207.
Pill, a castlet or small building?, v, 134.
Pill, *verb*, to pillage, rob, or strip bare, iv, 121.
Piramis, *i.e.*, pyramid, a spire, pinnacle, obelisk, or gable, i, 81, 131; ii, 96; v, 73, 78.
Pirle of water, a bubbling brook or small stream, i, 175, 301.
Plaschsy, marshy or swampy, i, 116.

Place, commune, common pleas, iv, 75.
Pointel, a style or pointed instrument for writing on tables, i, 132.
Policy, improvements made (as by human skill and labour (as we should now say *civil engineering*); Leland applies it to drainage of land or the diversion or improvement of rivers, i, 30, 147, 206; v, 90.
Porturid, portrayed or pictured, i, 72, 124.
Practized, intrigued, schemed, or plotted, ii, 62.

Quaterfors, a place where four streets meet, *quadrivium* (like "Carfax" in Oxford), ii, 41, 57.
Querry, quarry, v, 116.
Quick, lively, stirring, i, 243; v, 38, 39; "a quyk mownde," a quickset or living hedge, v, 117.

Ragusey, an argosy or great merchant ship, iv, 60.
Redid, *verb*, to reed, to cover a roof with reeds, v, 34.

GLOSSARY

Resort, *verb,* often said of water, or one river running into another, i, 90, 168; or into the sea, 177.

Rhe, a river, overflowing water, v, 36, 76.

Rige, here a man's back, "clothed . . . for bed and for back," v, 118.

Rokkettes, small rocky isles (under water), i, 318.

Ruffelar, a vagabond of the sixteenth century, iv, 80.

Rughe, rough, iii, 13.

Rype, ripe, the bank of a river or brook, i, 184; v, 80, 81.

Saufte, safety, iv, 146.

Scry. *See* Escrye.

Se-coal, sea-coal, coal found open in cliffs of the sea-shore, v, 140. This is one explanation, but it does not agree with many uses of the word.

Sele, *verb,* to ceil, to line roof or walls with wood or plaster, v, 83.

Shippeletts, small vessels, i, 177, 242; iv, 88.

Shoute out gunns, to place guns (on a tower) for shooting, ii, 40.

Shrodly pillid (shrewdly pillaged), maliciously stripped bare, iv, 121.

Sidenham, error for sidenhand, or sidehand; adverbial phrase, a-siden-hand, lying on one side of, i, 9. N.E.D.

Skill, *verb,* to reason, to understand, i, 135.

Skirmouch, skirmish, iv, 124.

Sleve, cleft or parting; "sleve of the ocean," the part of the English Channel between Brest and Cornwall, i, 201.

Slypes, slips, narrow strips of woodland, v, 73.

Smouldcrid, smothered to death in a crowd, i, 5.

Sodde, past tense of verb to seethe, iv, 10.

Sparkelid, scattered or dispersed, iii, 38; iv, 5 *n.,* 136.

Spilled, damaged, destroyed, iii, 110.

Stagne, a pond or lake, i, 75.

Staple, a market, i, 168, 169.

Stiliard, steelyard, merchants of the steelyard, a famous guild of foreign merchants in England, connected with the Hanseatic League, iv, 114.

Strete, street, meaning a village or small place not being a market town; *thorough-fare* is also used in the same sense, ii, 113.

Stripe, a blow, a wound caused by beating, iii, 90; strips, v, 3.

Suoping, swooping, said of a river sweeping along, v, 79.

Suarved, swerved, turned aside, iii, 109. Also *swarve,* to fill up, to choke with sediment, which seems to be the meaning in i, 61.

Tainters, tenters or stretchers used in the making of woollen cloth, i, 82 (*cf.* tenter-hooks).

Thakkid, thatched, iv, 26; v, 34.

There, where, v, 116.

Thrwghe-fayre, through fare, a village, ii, 106, 113. *See* Strete.

Thwartheth, passes athwart or across, v, 51.

Tophe, towfe stone, "full of pores and holes lyke a pummice," a quarry of this stone at Dursley resembling volcanic *tufa,* iv, 130; v, 96.

READING FREE PUBLIC LIBRARY

Tracte, delay; slow, long drawn out, iv, 134.

Translate, to change, to alter, said of houses or buildings, i, 104, 105, 163.

Trowehes of lead, troughs or coffins, i, 50.

Tukkyng miles, *i.e.,* tucking mills, fulling mills used in finishing cloth, v, 96 (tucker, West of England for a fuller).

Upper, *adv.,* higher up, i, 176; ii, 189, 194, 203.

Verry, verrey, vaire, a term in heraldry for a kind of fur, i, 159 (thrice).

Vouess, woues, woves, a vowed nun, i, 109, 112, 124.

Wag mier, wagmore, quagmire, i, 107, 205.

Waged a wed, promised a pledge, v, 117.

Walls, *i.e.,* Wales, v, 178.

Wal yee. This appears to be one of Leland's erroneous attempts at etymology. One end of the great Roman Wall is near Bowness on the Solway Firth, the other at Wallsend on the Tyne; it is possible that, writing from his notes, he confused the names of the two places, v, 51.

Water, often used instead of river or brook, i, 62, 256, 258. This was still done in Ireland fifty years ago. *See* "William Allingham's Diary," 1907, p. 46.

Waye=weigh, a lever, v, 116.

Weges, wedges, v, 116.

Wene, to think, suppose, iv, 25.

Witriding, outriding men, Border marauders or thieves, v, 62 and *n.*

Wose, ooze, wet mud, iv, 61; whosy, oozy, muddy, as in the bed of a river or the sea, iv, 49; v, 91.

Woves. *See* Vouess.

Yerth coal, earth or dug coal in distinction from charcoal, iv, 14.

COUNTIES IN THIS VOLUME

(See p. 1, note *)

STOW, VOL. V, AND THIS EDITION.	LELAND'S MS., VOL. VII.	HEARNE, VOL. VII.	BURTON a.
Fos. 53-56 a; Part v, pp. 33-38	Wanting.	Pp. 3-7.	Wanting.
Fos. 107-110, "John of St. Helens—impensis"; Part ix, pp. 1-5,	—	Pp. 7-11. Note, p. 2.	—
Fo. 111, "Bukingham—Wikam"; ix, p. 7	Fos. 5, 6.	P. 2.	Fol. 224, col. b.
Fos. 111, 112, "Chiltern—Tamise"; ix, p. 7	Fos. 2-4.	Pp. 1, 2.	Fol. 224, col. a.
Fos. 111 vº, 112, Market towns, etc.; ix, pp. 7, 8	Wanting.	Pp. 11-14.	Wanting.
Fos. 112 vº-115, "Market towns—limes upon Staffordshire"; ix, pp. 8-12	Wanting.	Pp. 14-19.	Wanting.
Fos. 115-118, "Market towns—Breui"; Part vi, pp. 9-12, 53-57	Vol. v, fos. 22-30.	Vol. v, pp. 19-28.	Fos. 126-129.
Fos. 119-123, "Markets in Carmardin—from Tunge"; vi, pp. 57-65	Vol. v, fos. 30, 31.	Vol. v, pp. 28, 29.	Fos. 129, 130.
Wanting in Stow; vi, pp. 65-67, "Corbet—Wombridge Unc[le to]"			
Stow, fos. 123-148; ix, pp. 12-68	Vol. vii, fos. 32-73, except fos. 36 and 56, which are found in the mixed vol. viii, fos. 53, 47.	Vol. vii, pp. 19-63.	Fos. 224-232.

THE ITINERARY OF JOHN LELAND.

PART IX.*

Comentaria Anglia.†

JOHN of Seint Helen's, so cawlyd becawse he dwelte in S. Helyn's paroche in Abyndon, was the firste beginner and makar of the great bridge of stone over Isis at Abbindon. Afore his tyme it was a fery.

Stow, v, fo. 107. *Abbyngton.*

The makynge of this bridge was a great hinderaunce to the towne of Walyngforde, whithar the trade was of them that came out of Glocestar-shire: but now they passe by Abingdon.

[* Leland's MS., vol. vii. This volume as we now have it is evidently not in its original state, leaves 7 to 31 inclusive are wanting; it seems to have consisted of quires and loose leaves, which were probably bound together by Burton. Some of these loose leaves were gone before he had the papers, as we may judge by what he copied in 1641 (Burton (*a*), Gough, gen. top. 2, fos. 224-232) compared with Stow's copy of 1576 (Tanner, 464, vol. v, 107-148); and by the same standard we see that he mixed up the early leaves, which contain miscellaneous notes and are not in the original order followed by Stow. Burton bound some of the leaves (fos. 22-31) into vol. v of Leland's MS., apparently because they treat of some Welsh counties (see "Leland in Wales," p. 57); others of the lost leaves also contained notes on Wales, and are only known in Stow's copy; both these groups were copied consecutively by Stow, but one was printed by Hearne in his vol. v, the other left in his vol. vii. In the present edition all the Welsh notes are transferred to our Part VI, pp. 53-66. The first pages of miscellaneous notes above are restored to the order followed by Stow, as that most probably right. The Table on the opposite page shows the relative positions of these passages.

(In his vol. vii, pp. 7-14, for part of these passages Hearne gives side references to fos. 14-27, as though he were printing from Leland's original; but I cannot find that these leaves exist, and therefore give Stow's folios only. In my vol. i, pp. 121, 122, *notes*, fo. 14 is thus an error.)]

[† The following pages, 1-7, are found in Stow only, fos. 107-111 see Table opposite.]

V.   B

This John de Seint Helen lyvyed about the begininge of the reigne of Henry the 6.

This John buildyd the faire hospitall by S. Helens in Abyngdon, and gave L. *li*. lands by yere to the maynteynaunce of it and the bridge.

The bridge of archid stone at Dorchestar is but a new thinge to speke of, and there was a ferrey at highe watars over Tames, and the bridge of Abingdon semithe to have bene the . . .

Bullingbroke.   Gul. de Romara, Erle of Lincolne, was lord and ownar of Bullingbroke Castle in Lincolneshire. Syns it was told me that there were 2. cantuaris in the paroche churche of Bullyngbroke of the Romares fundation latly supressyd.

Newborowe.   There is at Seint Salviors at Newborow in Yorkeshire a great paintynge or table in the prior or abbats chambar yet stondinge of all the whole desente and linage of the Moubrays. Mastar Dr. Bellaziz * may send for a copy of it. Mastar Stapleton of London, brothar in law to Sir Thomas Wharton, tolde me that the comon opinion of the people aboute Perith is that Da Raby Erle of Westmerland made muche of the castle that now standith at Perith.[a]

He tolde me also that Darabies armes were and be in dyvers partes of the doungein in the castelle of Cairlues; where apon he conjectithe that it was reedified by hym.

The castle of Shrobbesbyry is set so that it is in the very place where the towne is not defendid with Severne, els the towne were totally environyd with watar.

Dortington.   Dartyngton, the fayre and goodly lordshipe by Totnes in Devonshire, was the Lorde of Audleys, sens by attayntur the Doke of Excester, namyd Holland, that cawsyd his hole howsholde there to drinke wyne browght out of Fraunce. He was Admirall of England, and Sir Baldwine Fulfirte a Knight of the Sepulchre was his undar admiralle.

Corteney Marquese of Excestar had a late this Dartington.

Horseley.   Est Horseley, a mile from Weste Horseley, in Suthrey,

[* Dr. Anthony Belasyse held many grants of monastery lands among which were those of Newburgh priory.]

---

[a] Penrith.

longyd to the Bysshope of Excester, where is a praty lytle manar place. Lacy, Bysshope of Excestar in Henry the 5. and 6. dayes lay sometyme at this howse. This Lacey was dene of Henry the 5. chapell at the battayle of Agincorte. This Lacey made the haule of Excester Place in London.

Talbot Erle of Shrobbesbyri and his sonne Lord Lisle slayne in Fraunce. This erles bones were browght out of Normandy to Whitchurche in Shrobbeshire.

Talbot next erle to hym slayne at Northampton fild, takynge Kynge Henry the 6. parte.

This erle had 5. sonnes, John (that had to wyfe the dowghtar of the Duke of Bukyngham, slayn at Northampton) dyed Erle of Shrobbesbery passynge in jorney at Coventrie. fo. 108. James that dyed of strips taken at Northampton feelde; but he cam first to Shiffenol ᵃ in Shrobbshire a 2. miles from Tonge, where the erles of Shrobbesbyre had a manar place of tymbar and a parke.

George Erle of Shrobbesbyri was borne at Chifenolle.

Gilbert the 3. sonn Knyght of the Gartar and Depute of Calays in Henry the 7. dayes, and lyeth buried at Whitechurche, and there is a chauntery made by hym. He was embassador to Rome with Abbat Bere of Glesteinbyri for Kynge Henry the 7. This Gilbert was sore woundyd at Bosworthe, takynge Kynge Henry the 7. parte.

Syr Christopher, persone of Whitechurche was the 4.

Syr Humfrey Talbote Knyght was the 5. He usyd Calays.

Anne sistar to the aforesayde 5. britherne by the erle was maried to Ser Henry Verney of Thonge, where she is buried in the coledge with hir husbond.

Margaret dowghtar to the erle, and sistar to the aforesayde 5. brithern was wyfe to Chawort a gentleman of Darbyshire.

John Erle of Shrobbsbyry had 2. sonnes, George and Thomas.

Thomas dyed without ysswe.

George erle had to wyfe the dowghtar of the Lorde Hastings that was behedid in the Towre, and had dyvers men and wymen children.

ᵃ Shifnal.

The late Erle of Comberland maried Margaret Georgys dowghtar.

And an othar was maried to the last Erle of Northumbarland. The Lord Dacres maried an othar.

Fraunces now Erle of Shrobbesbyri.

The old Lorde Hastings that was behedyd in the Towre had a sonne Lorde Hastings, that had to wife the dowghtar and heire of the Lorde Hungreforde.

The old Lord Hastings had also a sunne caulyd Richard, a knight that maried the Lady Savelle.

William also was sonn to the olde Lorde Hastyngs.

The olde Lorde Hastings had also a dowghtar that was wyfe to George Erle of Shrobbesbyri.

Hastings Lorde Hastinges, the old Lord Hastings sonne and heire, had by hir Lord Hastings now Erle of Huntyngdon.

He had also a dowghtar wyfe to the Erle of Darby mothar to the Erle of Darby now lyvynge.

Hastyngs Erle of Huntendune had to wife Anne dowghtar to the Duke of Buckyngham, behedyd at Saresbyri. The othar dowghtar of this Duke of Buckyngham was the first wyfe to the Lord Fitzgwalter.

Hastings sonne and heire to the Erle of Huntingdune maried the late Lorde Mountecutes dowghtar. The Lord Stafford maried the Lorde Mountecuts sistar.

The Duke of Yorke sunne caullyd Edward nevar tooke greatar name at the begininge of his warres agayne Kynge Henry the 6. but the name of the Erle of Marche; untyll that one Parre brought hym a 15. C. men to go with hym to . . . felde, and proclaymed hym as he went for kynge.

fo. 109. Mastar Feelde told me that there rennithe a mighty longe diche from . . . toward Lichet Maletravers [a] in Dorseteshire.

I saw in a roulle of the highe lordshipes of the Duke of Yorke at Mastar Garters thes names folowing: Cunsborow [b] Castelle; Clifford Castle; the lordeshipe of the faire Maide of Kent. Mastar Gartar told me that Quinborow Castell in Kent was of this hold; but he shoid me not how, or who shuld be this faire Maide of Kent.

[a] Lychett Matravers.   [b] Conisbrough.

There is a grete hill, or rigge, that stretchethe in lengthe from Glassenbyry on to within 2. miles of Bridgewatar, and is the very highe way to passe from the one from * the othar of them.

This balke or hille is of breadthe to speke of, and of eche syde of it lyethe low marche ground.

Brent Merche goynge from Glassenbyri lyethe on the right hand, and . . . marchis on the left hand.

The howses of the order cawlyd *Sauiniacensis*, otharwyse *Fratres Grisei*, were aftar reducyd on to the ordre caullyd *Cistertiensis*. Stratforde in Essex was of this ordre by the foundatyon of Montfichet. This howse first sett emonge the low marsches was aftar with sore fludes defacyd, and remevid to a celle, or graunge, longynge to it caullyd Burgestede[a] in Estsex, a mile or more from Billirica.

Thes monks remainid at Burgstede untyll entrete was made that they might have sum helpe otherwyse. Then one of the Richards, Kings of England, toke the ground and abbay of Strateforde in to his protection, and reedifienge it browght the foresayde monks agayne to Stratford, where amonge the marches they reinhabytyd.

One Agatha, dowghtar and heire to the Lorde Tresbur, had 2. husbonds. Gul. de Albeneio was the one. She was buried in the priory of Newstede by Stamford. The Lord Tresbor gave in his armes 3. bolts.

Stoke Dawbeney is in Northamptonshire hard by Rokyngham Forest a 2. miles from Pipwell Abbay.

The northen men brent miche of Staunford towne. It was not synce fully reedified. Lincoln-shire.

Staunford was privilegyd but in Kynge Edward's dayes for a borow, as concerninge a place in the Parliament Howse.

Yet it was a borow towne in Kynge Edgares dayes, and then and syns it hathe all way longyd to the Crowne.

There were 7. principall towers or wards in the waulls of Staunford, to eche of the whiche were certeyne freholders in the towne allottid to wache and warde in tyme of neadde.

* [*Sic*; it should be *to*.]

---

[a] Burstead

Cornwall. Where as I writte in the qwaires of Cornwalle that Fawey was caullyd in the olde Cornische, Cowwath, make it Fawathe.*

Cheshire. The chefe occasion, and the originale by likelihod, of the manifolde poolys and lakes in Chestershire, was by digginge of marle for fattynge the baren grownd there to beare good corne. To the whiche pitts the faulle of the waters thereabout and springs hathe resortyd, and bysyds the grownd there beynge so depely dikid there be many springs risynge naturally in them.

fo. 110. There be tokens in Chestershire of dyverse salt pitts besyde them that be commonly now usyd; as by Cumbermere in a wood, and at the Dyrte Wiche ᵃ a late a new pitte besyde the old decayed, and at Aldresey a poore village of a 6. howses a 4. mile from Malpace in the way almost to Chestar muche by weste hathe bene a salt pit, but now decayed, as almoste in tyme owt of mynde.

Suche firre trees overthrowne and coverid with bogge and merche as be in Chestershire, Lancastershire and Shrobbe shire be found in some places of the Isle of Oxolme.ᵇ

Terre Mone is about a 24. miles in lengthe and 21. in bredthe, yet the comon voice makethe it almoste egale in lengthe and bredthe.

Luggershaull sumtyme a castle in Wileshire 10. miles from Marleborow, and a 4. miles from Andover almoste in the wayc betwixt. The castell stoode in a parke now clene downe.

There is of late tymes a pratie lodge made by the ruines of it, and longgithe to the kyng.

A cardinale (Drapar) † and archepisshope of Cantorbyri gave a 1000. markes or *li.* to the erectynge of London Bridge.

Kynge John gave certeyne vacant places in London to builde on for buildinge and reparation of London Bridge.

A mason beinge master of the bridge howse buildyd *à fundamentis* the chapell on London Bridge *à fundamentis propriis impensis.*‡

* [See vol. i, p. 203.]   [† This word is interlined.]
[‡ A whole page here blank.]

ᵃ Droitwich.   ᵇ Axholme.

PART IX

7

Bukingham.

Bucks.

Ailesbyri 5 miles from Notele[a] is a good market toune
havynge one paroche churche and a howse of gray friars, it
stondithe on a lytle broke, and is a mile from Tame streme.
Wikam.

fo. 111.

Chilterne Hilles.

Leland, vii,
fo. 5.

From Henle in Oxfordshire to Wikam[b] in Bukinghamshire an viii. myles. From Wikam to Dunstaple in Bedfordshire a xviii. miles. Al this way goeth Chilternhilles, wherof
many be welle replenishid with wood, and partely with
corne, al the soile being a chalke clay.

Ryvers in Bokinghamshire.

fo. 6.

Use or Ise.
Another Use, or Ise,[c] as of one principal arme risith abowt
Westewikam owt of one of the Chilterne hilles, and so cummith by Wikam the market towne.
The lesse arme is cawllid Higdenbrooke, and risith also
in one of Chilterne hilles a mile above Wikam.
Bothe these streames meate at the west ende of Wikam,
and thens the hole botom with one water goith to Hedon,
so to Owburne,[d] wher the Bishop of Lincoln hath a fair
howse, and thens a mile and more into the Tamise.

Market Towns in Bedfordshire.

Leland, vii,
fo. 2.
Stow,
fo. 111 b.
Beds.

Bedford.
Bigelswade a 2. miles from Wardon[e] Abbay, a good market
and 2. faires.
Shefforde a 3. miles from Bedforde, and a mile from
Chyksand Priory.
Luton a very good market town for barlye.
Ham(ptel.)[f]
Olneys.[g]
Potton.
Owborne.[h]
Dunstaple.

[a] Notley Abbey.   [b] Wycombe.   [c] Wye r.
[d] Woburn.   [e] Old Warden.   [f] Ampthill.
[g] Olney, now in Buckinghamshire.   [h] Woburn.

Beds.

Leland,
fo. 3.
Stow,
fo. 112.

Castelles yn Bedfordshire.

The castel of Bedford hard by the towne, now clene down. There is a place caullid Falxherbar * agayn the castel.

Betwixt Kinges Crose yn the midle way to Newenham and the castel were founde many bones of men buried.

The castle of Hamtel.[a] The Lorde Fanope, a man of greate fame in owtewarde warres, and very riche, buildid this house.

Odel [b] Castel, now nothing but straunge ruines, longging to the Lord Bray. Odel town ys by the castel, and ys as yt wer an viii. myles from Bedford, and by Harold nunnery about a mile of. This Odel was a barony.

Castel Parke a myle from Laundon [c] Abbay [priory], and Landon is withyn a myle [of] Olney. This parke longgid to the Souches, but now lately sold to the Lord Mordant Peraventure this Launden Castel.

Risingho hard by Castel Mille on Use. It longgid to Wardon Abbay, now to Mr. Gostewik.†

Adingreves wher be tokens of diches, wher sum fortres hath bene by Use Ryver, a mile or 2. from Risingho.

fo. 4.

Isis otherwise Use.[d]

Olneye Water.

Undal Water.[e]

Stow,
fo. 112 b.

Market townes in Wicestershire.

Wicestre on Severn.

Eovesham apon Avon Ryver xii. miles from Wicestre.

Brammisgrove [f] x. miles northe from Wicestar.

Persore [g] apon Avon vi. miles from Wicestar.

Kiddermister apon Stowre River xii. Mils toward north-east from Wicestre.

[* Probably once the dwelling of Falco de Breant, on whom King John bestowed the castle. Lewis's Topography.]

[† This seems to be Sir John Gostwick, Treasurer of First Fruits and Tenths in 1544.]

---

[a] Amphtill. [b] Odell or Woodhill. [c] Lavendon.
[d] Ouse r. [e] ? Ouzel r. [f] Bromsgrove.
[g] Pershore.

Bewdele[a] the Sanctuary towne hath hard by it the Kyngs maner of Tikile[b] stonding on a hill.

Castles in Wicestreshire.

Wicester.

The ruines of Hanle[c] Castle vii. miles from Wiccester lower of the farthar rype of Severne.

Aberle,[d] otherwise Abbatisle, somtyme longinge to the Erle of Warwike.

Hartsbery Castle[e] longinge to the Bysshope of Wicestar, set on a stronge roke vii. miles from Wicester.

fo. 113.

Helmelege,[f] where the college is longinge to the Kynge. There stondithe now but one tower, and that partly broken. As I went by I saw carts carienge stone thens to amend Persore Bridge about a ii. miles of. It is set on the tope of an hill full of wood, and a townelet hard by, and undar the roote of the hille is the Vale of Eovesham.

Rivers in Wicestershire.

Severne risithe in a hill cawlyd Plimlimmon. So to Cair Sews,* famous in name, but in dede a pore thrwghe faire. From Mahenclift to Llanidlas a good village, to Newton, and so rinnith within a mile of Montgomeryke to the Walche Pole, and thens passithe within halfe a mile of Ponsbyri College to Shrobbesbyri, to Wrekcester alias Rokecestar,[g] to Bridgnorthe, to Wicester, to Twekesbyry, to Glocester, etc.

Avon.

Arow.[h]

Dowlesse[i] riveret risith, as I lernyd, in Cle Hill in Shropeshire, and cummithe by Clebiry a poore village, and cummithe not far above Bewdele into Severne.

[* Stow's MS. has *llews* (which Hearne read Clews), with a correction, S being written over the ll. The place is doubtless Caer Sws, an old Roman station.]

---

[a] Bewdley.	[b] Tickenhil or Tickil.	[c] Hanley.
[d] Abberley.	[e] Hartlebury.	[f] Elmley.
[g] Wroxeter.	[h] Arrow r.	[i] Dowles r.

Worcester-
shire.

Forests and Chases in Wecestershire.*

Wire^a Forest, where of summe part is sett in Wicester-shire, but the moste parte in Shropshire, and stretchithe up from Holt† apon Severne onto Bruge Northe.^b Bewdley is set in the marchis of this forest, and stretchithe a 2. miles beyond to a watar cawlyd . . . Wire is more then xx. mills compas.

Fekenham^c Forest totally (as I here say) is set in Wicester-shere, and is of lesse compase than Wire.

The Chase of Malvern is bigger then other Wire or Fekenham, and occupiethe a greate parte of Malverne Hills. Great Malverne and Litle also is set in the Chace of Malverne. Malverne Chase (as I here say) is in lengthe in some place a xx. miles, but Malverne Chace dothe not occupi all Malverne Hills.

Wiche^d is a vi. miles by northe from Wicester. There be iii. salt springs, whereof 2. be nere togethar. the third is a qwartar of a mile of. At these be made the finest salt of England.

Withein a mile of Alcestre is a limes.

The Castell of Dudeley is in Stafordshire, but hard by is Wicestreshire.

fo. 114.

Syr Gilbert Talbot knight hath a goodly howse by Bramsgrove market caullid Grafton. ‡

Pakington hath a veri goodly new howse of brike caullid Hampton Court a vi. [miles] § of from Wicestre somwhat northward.

Market townes in Warwikeshire.

Warwike.
Coventre.
Henle. I have it described.
Monke Kyrkby.^e I know the site of this.
Alcestre.

[* *Sic*.]   [† Stow has "frontholt," a careless reading.]
[‡ Stow has Greston. See Grafton in vol. ii, p. 95.]
[§ Not in MS., but doubtless intended.]

---

^a Wyre.   ^b Bridgenorth.   ^c Feckenham.
          ^d Droitwich.   ^e Monks Kirby.

PART IX

Rugby.
Tameworth apon Anker. I have it describid.
Nunne Eton.[a] I have it described.
Atherstone. I have it described.*
Bremischam[b] in the way to Chestre-ward, a xii. mills from Coventre. I have it described.
Southam a vi. mils from Warwike.

Warwicks.
[Vol. ii, p. 104.]

[Vol. ii, p. 96.]

Castells in Warwikeshire.

Warwike.
Killingworthe.[c]
Braundon,[d] a v. mils be northe from Coventre, now deso-latid; sometyme (as I hard say) longginge to the Lord Mortimer.
Brinkelo, a v. mils by east from Coventre, now desolatyd; longynge somtyme (as men say) to the Mortimers.
Bagginton Castell, now desolatyd. It longgid to the Baggetts, a 2. mils from Coventre.
Ascheley Castle.

Rivers.

Avon.
Anker.
Sow[e] risithe nere Hakesbiri[f] iii. myles from Coventre northeste. *Fluit per Sow pagum*, by White le,[g] *et prope Stonle[h] village in Tamam labitur.*
Leme[i] cumminge out of Northamptonshire. It comithe by Granborow,[k] Lemington, Marton, Offekirke[l] pagos, and at Edmund Coote Bridge into Avon.
Colle[m] flu. oritur in Yardle Woodde prope Kinggs Northton, and aftar that by Colleshil he goithe into Tame.
Blithe risithe in Warwikshire nere Routon by Balshaul,[n] Hampton, Pakington, and the[n] goinge betwixt Coleshill and Makstoke[o] nere † Schustok[p] village into Tame.

Stow, fo. 115.

[* These two descriptions seem to be lost.]
[† MS. has *were.*]

---

a Nuneaton.	b Birmingham.	c Kenilworth.
d Brandon.	e Sowe r.	f Hawkesbury.
g Whitley.	h Stoneleigh.	i Leam r.
k Grandborough.	l Offchurch.	m Cole r.
n Temple Balsall.	o Maxstoke.	p Shustoke.

The lenght of Warwikeshire be estimation from Rollerich Stones by Chipping Northton to Tamwort as to the limites of Oxfordeshir and Stafordshire,—thus the lengthe is about xxxvi. mils.

Watelingstrete toward Rugby is a limes apon Leircester-shire.

A mile above Bremicham is a limes apon Stafordshire.*

Market townes in Shropshire.†

Shrewisbiry.

Bridgenorth a xiiii. miles from Shorbbesbyri.

Welington a vii. miles from Shrobbesbyri toward London way.

Drayton ᵇ apon Terne river a xii. miles from Shrewisbyri.

At Blorehethe, a mile above Drayton by north, was a feelde faught bytwene King Edwardes men and Henry the 6. The Erle of Saresbyri and northen men on King Edwardes parte overcam the Lordes Audeley (slain) and Dudeley (woundid) with Quene Margaret, wife to Henry the 6, and Chestershir men lost the feld. She cam ‡ Eccleshall thither. Hauls § Bisshop of Chester her chapeleyn caussid the queene to ly ther.

Whitechirche a xiiii. or xv. miles from Shrewisbyri.

Newport apon a brooke a xii. or xiiii. miles from Shrewis-byri. With in a mile [of] Newport is a goodly large mere or poole.

Ludlo.

Peter Undergod, [a] gentilman longging [to] an Englisch Prince of Wales, did build St. John's Hospital withowt . . . [g]ate of Ludlo [and af]tar gave landes onto hit.‖

[* Five pages printed by Hearne after "Staffordshire" from Stow, vol. v, fos. 115-118, containing the counties of Brecon, Radnor, Mont-gomery, and Cardigan, are removed to Part VI, pp. 9-12, 53-57, im-mediately preceding the part as to Carmarthenshire from Stow's fos. 119-123, transposed thither by Hearne. See Part VI, p. 9, *note*.]

[† With these following pages on Shropshire read those in " Leland in Wales " (our Part III), pp. 50, 54, 65-67, 73-76.]

[‡ *Sic.* Stow has " She cam Eccleshan."]

[§ John Hales, made bishop the year of the battle, 1459.]

[‖ This paragraph not in Stow.]

ᵃ Rollwright.   ᵇ Market Drayton.

Bisshops Castel a very celebrate market.

Castelles in Shropshire.

Shrewsbiri.

Brigenorth on Severn xiiii. myles from Shreusbiri lower on the river.

Caurse ᵃ Castel on a hil v. myles from Shreusbiri by sowth west longging to the Duke of Bokingham, now to the Lorde Staford.

Montgomeri the Kinges Castel (in the Shire, but not *de,**) xii. myles from [Shrewsbyri.] It was ons a great wallid town caullid Cairovalduine.

Chirburi Hunderid was annexid to Montgomerike as a help to have men out of hit for defence.†

Ludlo xx. myles from Shreusbiri.

Newport apon a brooke, or moore, xiiii. miles by east from Shreusbiri.

Whitchirch apon a broket a xvi. [miles] ‡ by west from Shreusbiry.

Draiton apon Terne river a xiiii. miles from Shreusbiri.

Wigmore Castel a xx. myles from Shreusbiri standing on a brooket sumtime almost dry.

Whittington, a castel of the Lorde Fizwaren's, vi. miles from Shreusbiri upward almost on Severn, and by this goith Offa's diche.

Shrawardine § iiii. miles from Shreusbiry, longging to the Erle of Arundel ii. miles from Whitington, bytwyxt Shreusbiri and hit.

Redde Castel by Whitchirch, [a late the] Lorde Audeles. viii. myles plaine [northe] from Shreusbiri, now al ruinus. It hath bene strong and hath decayid many a day.

Middle Castel longging to the Lord of Darbe iii. miles from Shrewsbyri, veri ruinus.

[* These words not in Stow. See note, p. 14.]
[† *I.e.*, before the act 27 Hen. VIII, c. 26. *Cf.* with " Leland in Wales," p. 54.]
[‡ Stow. Omitted by Leland.]
[§ Leland corrected this name twice, from Shrawle to Shrawarden.]

ᵃ Cause.

Shropshire.   Morton Corbet in a marres, iiii. myles from Shreuisbiri by north, longging to the Corbettes.

Knoking [a] Castel in Shropshire now a ruinus thing longid to the Lorde Lestraunge, and now to the Erle of Darby.

fo. 33.   Chorleton [b] Castel on Terne, longging to the Lord Poys, vi. miles from Shrewisbiri, and a myle from Tern village.

Terne is to say a lake or poole.

Cortham Castel apon Corfe riveret, (*unde et Corvesdale*,) xiiii. myles from Shreusbiri by south.

Acton Burnel was a goodly manor place, or castel, iiii. myles from Shreusbyri, wher a Parliament was kepte in a greate barne. It longgid ons to the Lord Lovel, then to the Duke of Northfolke, and now to Syr John Dudle.

Burnelles doughter was maried to the Lorde Lovel, and thereby the Lovelles landes encresid, and after was made Vicount Lovel. Lovel had Acton Burnel.

Sum of thes castelles though they be yn Shropshire, yet thei be not *de.** For they be privilegid, and use their owne lawes and courtes, except the last statute let them.

Oswestre Castel is now in Shropshire.

Kensham [c] Castel clene doun, it stoode within a ii. milis of Ludlo on a hille toppe.

Holgate [d] Castel (sumtime longing to the Lord Lovel)† stondeth under the Cle hilles harde by Corvesdale a vi. miles from Ludlo. The Duke of Northfolk exchaungid it for other landes with Mr. Dudeley.

[* This curious expression, twice over, may be the shortened use of a Latin legal phrase like *de comitatu*, perhaps currently applied at the time and locally in the Marches of Wales to certain lordships, which, though really situated in a named county and therefore presumably owing suit to the shire town, were privileged to use their own laws and courts. The places were *in* the shire but not *of* it for purposes of public justice, until the Act of Union (27 Hen. VIII, cap. 26, 1535-36) annexed them to definite counties under the laws of England and declared their shire towns, adding that they " shall be in nowise otherwise privileged but as hundreds, lordships, towns, etc., united annexed and knytte " to the county of Salop, or otherwise. It was thus that " the last statute let [or hindered] them," this being the Act referred to by Leland. Montgomery, Whittington, Knockin, Cherbury, and Oswestry are among the places there named, secs. 6, 9. See " Leland in Wales," Pref. p. vii.]

[† Marginal note in Leland.]

---

[a] Knockin.   [b] Charlton.   [c] Caynham.   [d] Holdgate.

Bramscrofte, a very goodly place like a castel, longging to the Erle of Shrewsbiri. It stondeth in Cle Hilles or abowt them a . . . miles from Ludlo.

Stokesay longing sumtime to the Ludlos, now to the Vernuns, buildid like a castel v. miles owt of Ludlo.

Syr Richard Ludlo had ii. doughters. One was maried to Humfrey Vernoun, and the other to Thomas Vernoun, bretherne to the late Syr Henry Vernoun of the Peke. The 3. sun [of Henry maried one of Montgomerye's heyres.]

Shepeton Corbet Castel a vi. or vii. miles from Ludlo almost in the way bytwixt Ludlo and Bisshops Castel.

Hopton Corbet[a] half way bytwixt Bisshops Castel and Wigmoore, and a iii. miles from Shepeton.

Bisshops Castel well maintenid is set on a stronge rokke, but not veri hy.

Abbays and Priories in Shropshire.

The Abbay of Shrobbesbyri.[b]

Album Monasterium by Albertbyri, long syns suppressid.

Ombridge,[c] Blake Chanons, in the way to London, ii. miles beyonde Welington market, and a ii. miles beyond Lincel[d] Abbay.

Lincel, [or Lilleshull.]*

Brerewoodde,[e] a priory of white nunnes lately suppressid, in the very marche of Shropshire toward Darbyshire.

Billevoise.[f] Whit monkes.

Haghmon.[g] Blake Chanons.

Wenloch. Blak monkes.

Tunge,[h] a litle thorough-fare betwixte Ulnorhampton[i] and Newport, 7. mile from Ulnorhampton, 5. from Newporte. It is in Shropshire. There is college and wardon, with an almose house of the auncient foundation of the

[* Two words written on the MS. by Burton.]

---

[a] Hopton Castle.   [b] Shrewsbury.   [c] Wumbridge.
[d] Lilleshall.
[e] Brewood in Staffordshire. Shropshire does not touch Derbyshire.
[f] Buildwas Abbey.   [g] Haughmond.   [h] Tong.
[i] Wolverhampton; Leland distinctly writes *n* for *u* (=*v*) in this name.

Shropshire. Vernouns of Haddon in the Peke. Many, or almost al, ly there that were famous of them sins the fundation.

Ther was an olde castel of stone caullid Tunge Castel. It standith half a mile from the toune on a banke, under the wich rinnith the broke that cum[mith from Weston to Tunge. Weston is 2. miles of, and is in Stafordshire.] Syr Henry Vernoun a late daies made the castel new al of [brike.]

Rivers in Shropshire.

fo. 34.   Severne.

Terne risith nere Mere[a] village in Stafordshire; it goeth by Draiton, Ternehil, Besteford and Slepe villages, and cummith into Severn at Acham village a ii. myles from Shrewsbyri. I hard otherwise that hit cam ynto Severn abowt Ternebridge.

Corfe rising in Corvesdale cummith into Teme at Ludlo.

Corvedale plentiful of corne strecchith from abowt Wenlock to Ludlo.

Ree[b] cummyng by Wenloche.

Roden risith in the lake of Cumbremere.* After hit it runneth by Whitchirch, a good market town, by Lee[c] village, and Shabiry[d] village, and at Walcote into Terne. Ther be very gret bremes and other good fischis in Cumbremere.

Oney[e] cummith into Teme abowt Bromefeld a celle to Glocestre.

Harmer Pole a mile from Shrobbesbyri.

Teme river enterith into the farther [syde of Severne not far from Powik mile,[f] a mile and a half beneth Wicester.]

The site and commodites of the soile of Shropshire.

Ther be founde in morisch and mossy ground a vii. miles from Shrobbesbyri, and yn other places of the Shire, fyrwoodde rootes, and also the hole trees hewen downe in olde time; but of whom, or for what cause, no man there can

[* The Roden seems to rise in Colemere (near Ellesmere), and does not run near Whitchurch; the rest of its course is rightly indicated.]

---

[a] Maer.   [b] Rea r. of Shropshire. It is a long way off Wenlock.
[c] Lee Brockhurst.   [d] Shawbury.   [e] Onny.   [f] Powick mill.

telle. They finde them lying yn the grounde, sumtime a   Shropshire.
foote or ii. depe, sumtime a v. or vi. foote depe. Many of
them be of a greate lengthe, and withowt twysxe. Yn bren-
ning they smel welle.

Mortimers Clebyri ^a in Shropshire, a village and a parke by
Wire forest, yn the way bytuixt Ludlo and Beudeley.

Cle ^b hilles be devided ynto 3. partes.

The hilles next to Wenlok be caullid the Broune Cle, and
ther be dere.

Sainct Margeretes Cle toward Ludlo.

Theterston Cle^c betwixt the forest of Wyre, where is fair
timbre, and Ludlo.

·Ledewik broke^d springith in Cle hilles, and renning a
vii. miles goith into Teme at Burforde, wher is the house of
the barony of Burforde longing to Mr. Cornwale.

Cle hilles begin a iiii. miles from Tembyri, and strech
within a iiii. miles of Wenlok. So that be gesse I cownt them
in lenght an viii. or x. miles.

In these hilles risith Rhc^e rivcr, and at Newton Milles in
Wicestreshire a iii. miles beneth Tembyri cummith into
Tame.*

The limites of Shropshire.

Blakemere, a very large parke nye to White-Chirche, ys
(as I have harde say) yn sum parte a limes betwixte Shropshire and Chestreshire. In the parke is a fair maner place.

Monkbridge, a mile beneth Tembyri, is (as I ther hard
say) a limes to Wicestreshire, Shropshir, and Herfordshire.†

Langfelde Dale.

Strettons Dale.

Syr Richarde Manoring, chefe of that name, dwellith a   fo. 35.
iii. miles be est from Price^f village at a village caullid
Hightfelde,^g having a parke and greate plenty of wood
about hym.

[* Leland has Teme in error. This Rea runs through Worcester and
Warwick shires.]

[† Names of gentlemen in Shropshire are given in vol. iii (Wales),
pp. 64, 67.]

---

^a Cleobury Mortimer.   ^b Clent Hills.   ^c Titerstone Clee.
^d Ledwyche brook.   ^e Rea r.   ^f Prees.
                 ^g Ightfield.

Shropshire. Sandford dwellith at Sanforde, wher is onely his place and a parke, iii. miles be south from Whitechirch.

Newport dwellith at a place caullid Archaule.ᵃ It stondith betwixt Roden and Terne rivers toward their mouthes.

Syr John Talbot dwellith a xvi. miles from Shrewsbyri in the way to London toward Hampton village. His howse stondith in a parke [called Pepper Hill.]*

Appley a Manor Place. The hedde howse of the Chorletons [is now at] Appley, half a mile from Welington market, a mile from the Wreken hilles. Howbeit Chorleton castel semith in time past to have bene the principal. Ther be divers of the Chorletons gentilmen of Shropshire.

Chorleton of Chorletonᵇ Castel maried the heyre of the Lorde Powis, and Gray. Sins Lorde Poys maried Chorleton's heyre.

Arture Newton hath almost made away al his landes.

Yerne is made yn certen places of Shropshire, and especially yn the wooddes betwixte Belvoysᶜ and Wenloke.

Colys be diggid hard by Ombridge, where the priory was.

fo. 36.   Market townes in Staforshir.†

Staford.

There is a fre schole for grammar in Stafford made by Syr Thomas Countre parsone of Ingestre by Heywodde, and Syr Randol a chauntre preste of Stafford.

Lichefeld.

Countre and Randol made S. Cedde steple, a fair square tour, and the belles in Stafford toun.

New Castle undar Lyne. New Castel under Line. The paroche is at Stok on [Trent]‡ a good mile of. The toune usith to cum to a

[* Three words seem to have been written by Burton on Leland's MS.]

[† The leaf 36 was bound into vol. viii of Leland's MS. (where it stands, pp. 53, 54, but is bound in by the wrong margin). The damp marks also show that it belonged to this place in Leland's vol. vii. It contains the portions above printed "Market towns in Stafordshir—Duddely castel . . yn Stafordshir," p. 20.]

[‡ Leland wrote *Terne.* Burton corrects this in the margin.]

ᵃ Ercall.   ᵇ Charlton.   ᶜ Buildwas.

chapel of S. Sonday * by the castel. Al the castel is doune save one great toure. Ther was a house of Blak Freres yn the south side of the toune. *The Chapel of S. Sonday in the midle of the Toun.*

Burton apon Trent hath but one paroch chirch and a chapel at the bridge end. Trent cumpasith a great peace of the towne. Many marbelers working in alabaster. *Burton upon Trent.*

Uttok Cestre^a one paroche chirch. The menne of the towne usith grasing, for there be wonderful pastures apon Dove. It longgith to the erledom of Lancaster. *Utokcester.*

It is in the way to Derby from Stafford: and is 9. mile est north est from Stafforde.

[A fre scole foundid bi a prist, Thomas Allen. He foundyd an othar at Stone in the reigne of Queen Mari.]†

Tutburi a smaul market.

Wulnerhampton‡ a very good market town. In it is a fre schole made by Syr Stephane Jenning Maire of London.

Tamworth.

The college of Windesore give the prebendes of Wulnerhampton, and the dean of Wyndesor is [deane there] . . .

Tetenhaul a village and a college about a myle from Wulnerhampton.

Castelles in Staffordshire.

Stafforde not far from Staford town on the river of Sow.

The castel or preaty pile of Careswel § iiii. myles by north fro Stone a late a priori of chanons sumtyme belonging to the Montgomerikes, now to the Giffard.

Lichefeld in old tyme had a castel.

Ther is a causey thorough the pole to the castel, and dyvers brid[g]es yn the causey: a water issuith by them through the causey. This castel standith yn low ground. And it standith as a *mediamnis* yn the poole, the water wherof is yn sum part a quarter of mile brode yn sum place, and yn sum lesse.

[* Leland first wrote Salviour, then corrected as above.]
[† Added by Stow, but not in Leland's MS.]
[‡ Leland first wrote Uller, then corrected to Wulnerhampton.]
[§ Leland first wrote Cawsewel. Now Caverswall.]

---

^a Uttoxeter.

New Castel under Line, so cawllid of a brooke renning therby, or of an hille or wodd therby, so cawllid. There cummith a broke owt of the pole aboute the castel. It longgid to the Duke of Lancaster. Brok renning oute of . . . poole cummith by the toun*

Hely ᵃ a castel of the Lord Audeleys, and a 2. miles of is Audeley village, wherby sum think that it is cawllid Hely Castel for Audeley Castel. The tenauntes of Audeley cum to this castel.

Tutbiri Castel longging to the King now by the Duke of Lancastre. It was afore Ferrares Castel Erle of Darby.

Eccleshaul Castel longging to the Bisshop of Chester.

There be a v. greate poolys. a broke cummith thorough them, and thens issuing oute.

Sturseley, or Stourton, Castel withoute fayle is in Stafordshir, and I hard that there was a Lorde Storton a baron of this Storton. It is the Kinges. Pole lay at it by licens; [and there Cardinal Pole was borne.]†

Tamworth Castel apon Anker river longging to one of the Ferrars. Parte of Tamworth toune stondith in Stafordshir, part ſyn Warwike. But the castel hole withowt fayle yn Warwikeshire.

Not veri far from Stone priori appereth the place wher King Woulphers castel or manor place was. This Byri hille‡ stode on a rok by a broke side. Ther appere great dikes and squarid stones. It is a mile from Stone toward the more lande.

Duddeley Castel hard on the borders of Wyrcestreshire, but the castelle self standith yn Stafordshir.

Rivers in Stafordshire.

Sow§ . . . and rennith by Staford, *per coenobium S. Thomae* a good mile of, by Shutborow,ᵇ and at Heywood bridge into Trent.

[* Note in margin.]   [† These words perhaps added by Burton.]
[‡ Stone is in the hundred of Pirehill.]
[§ Leland left a blank after each name of a river on this folio; some he filled in, others still remain blank; *a* and *b* are marginal remarks.]

ᵃ Heyley Castle.   ᵇ Shugborough.

Trent.

a. I have the cours of Treant to Newarke.

Dove.

Pen fluviolus per Penchrike, & prope Staford in Sow de-
labitur.

Churnet.

b. I have perfectly the course of Churnet.

Blith *flu.* springith at Whetle moore. It rennith by Drai-
cote village, Teyne[a] village, and about Vttokcester goith into
Dove.*

Tame risith . . . *per pontem Tamensem, Hamesworth* [b]
pagum, Aschton, Birmicham, per Crudworth[c] *Bridge, Kinis-*
byri, [*Faresle*][d] *pagum, Tamesworth, et apud Wiknor* [*Bridge*
in Trentam.]

Kinisbyri is a fair manor place and a lordship of [140. *li.*
One Brasebridge is lord of it. It is in Warwikshir.]

Abbaies and prioris in Stafordshir.

Ther wer dyverse tumbes of the lordes of Stafford in
Stone priory made of alabaster. The images that lay on
them were after the suppression of the house caryed to the
Freers Augustines in Forde bridg,[e] alias Stafford Grene, *cis*
flumen. And yn this freres hong a petigre of the Staffordes.

S. Johns a fre chapelle on the grene at Staford hard by
Sow ryver.†

The Gray Freres were at the other ende of the toun, *ultra*
flumen.

Mr. Stretey of Lichefeld told me that one Langton
Bisshop of Lichefeld made the fair palace at Lichefeld, and
the close waulle, and that he made Eccleshaul castel,[f] Shoc-
borow[g] maner place, and the palace by Stroude. This Langton was tresorer to Edward the firste.‡

Ther is a chace grounde[h] yn Stafordeshir having deere

[* It is the river Tean which runs into the Dove.]
[† In the margin of the original.]
[‡ Walter Langton, bishop of Lichfield, a rich man, died 1321.]

---

[a] Tean. [b] Handsworth. [c] Curdworth.
[d] Kingsbury, Fazeley. [e] At Stafford. [f] Eccleshall.
[g] Shugborough. [h] Cannock Chace.

**Stafford-
shire.**

Teddeslechase.

fo. 38.

caullid the vii. Hayes, lying betwixt Lichefeld and Wulnor-
hampton.
    There is a praty chace by Pencriche[a] of [the Kinges,]
where [Littleton of Pillenhaul is foster by inheritaunce.]*

Forestes, parkes and chasis in Staford[shire.]

    The forest of Neede Wodde[b] by Tuttebryi, and betwixt
Tuttebyri and Lichefelde; but the nerest part of it is a v.
miles from Lichefeld. There long to Tutbyri Honor 4.
parkes. The Castel Hay, Hanbyri, Barton, and the New
Park. This forest is mervelusly plenishid with dere.
    Cank[c] Foreste a great thing, merely longging to the
Bisshoprik of Lichefeld. Ther is Bewdesert his place and
parke (Bewdesert in Langedon paroch; and yn this paroch
is a great peace of Cank Forest.) and Shucborough[d] his
place (were is a park now of red dere) is yn the side of
Cank Woode. Shukborow was ons Suchborows with the
long berd, and he, as sum say, gave it to the mitre of Lichefeld. I know no certente of this gifte.
    Sum caulle Shokesborow Heywood by cause it standith
by it.
    Ther is a fair poole betwixt Cank Wood and Shukes-
borow.
    Ther ly a v. fayre pooles by the castel of Eccleshaul, and
the park of Blore a 2. miles of in the same lordship is a v.
or vi. miles abowte, and is the bisshops, and is ful of wonderful fair wood. The chase of Sutton v. miles owte of
Lichefeld, wherof parte was yn Staford, and parte in War-
wikeshir. It is now clene put downe. And this is the place
wher Veysi† Bisshop of Excestre hath plantid housis of stone
and bryk, and many good dwellers yn them.
    One Mountford a knight, atteyntid in Henry the vii.

[* These two paragraphs are on the bottom of fo. 37. Stow copied
them as though written on the bottom of the next page, omitting the
paragraph "one Mountford" that really stands there. Both leaves have
lost the lower edge.]

[† John Harman or Voysey became bishop of Exeter in 1519.]

---

[a] Penkridge, Teddesley Chace.   [b] Needwood.
[c] Cannock.   [d] Shugborough.

tymes, had a manor place here caullid Sutton by Sutton **Stafford-**
toun. This Mountford had a house in Warwikshire caullid **shire.**
Colleshil Haul, and a park [that was given to Syr Simon
Dygby, Leutenaunt of the Toure of London.]

The limites of Stafordshire.*

The site of the shire and commodites of the soile. fo. 39.

Se coles at Weddesbyri[a] a village a 5. miles from Lichefelde by west south west.

Waulleshal[b] a litle market toune in Stafordshir a mile by
north from Weddesbyri. Ther be many smithes and bytte-
makers yn the towne. It longgith now to the King, and
there is a parke of that name scant half a mile from the
towne yn the way to Woluerhampton.

At Walleshaul be pittes of se coles, pittes of lyme that
serve also South Toun[c] 4. miles of. There is also yren owre.

Market townes in Chestershire.† **Cheshire.**
fo. 40.

Chestre apon Dee.

Nantwich apon Wiver,[d] xiiii. miles be west from Chester.
The paroche chirch is impropriatid to Cumbremer.[e] Sum
say that Acton is the mother chirch. It is no market.

Northwich apon Wyver, xii. myles from Chestre. It hath
but a chapel. The paroch chirch is a mile of at Budworth
impropriatid to Norton.

Maxwelle[f] hard on the egge under Maxwel forest, and yet
oute of the foreste: xxiiii. myles northwest‡ from Chestre
toward Darbishire.

Congleton apon Dane a xx. myles from Chester; plaine
easte oute of Chester, and vi. miles owte of Northwike.

[* A blank follows this heading.]
[† See more notes on Cheshire in vol. iii, pp. 91, 92, and the short
narrative, vol. iv, pp. 2-5.]
[‡ Leland's error; it is East.]

---

[a] Wednesbury.	[b] Walsall.	[c] Sutton Coldfield.
[d] Weaver.	[e] Combermere.	[f] Macclesfield.

Cheshire.

Knottesforde ^a market xviii. miles by north est. It hath but a chapel. The paroch chirch is a[t]* Aspebyri † a mile of.

Stoppord ^b apon Mersey a vi. miles from Manchestre. The paroch chirch is yn the toune.

Mr. Warine is caullid there Baron of Stoppord. For one of the Warines of Chestershire maried one Stoppord baron of Stopporde doughter and heyre aboute Henry the 4. dayes. The auncienter house longging to Warines was Poynton, wher he lyith now, for Stoppord maner place is dekayid. At Poynton is a parke. Pointon ys yn the mydle way betuixt Stoppord an[d]‡ Maxwel toune, 4. mile from eche. It is in Prestebyri paroch, yn the wich paroche be divers places of auncient gentilmen.

Castelles in Chestershire.

Chester.

Biston ^c Castel buildid or reædifiyd by Ranulf Erle of Chestre.

Haulton ^d Castel buildid by Randol Erle of Chestre. It standeth abowt the side of Mersey, within a myle of his banke, and within a mile of Runcorn, now a poore townlet by a salt creke.

Shotte Wike ^e yn Wyral.

Looke whither Charteley Castel, buildid by Ranulph Erle of Chestre, be in Chestershire.§

Stafford-shire.

Charteley is yn Stafordeshire an viii. miles from Deuleucrese ^f Abbay, and a v. myles from Uttokcestre Market. Ther is a mighty large parke. The olde castel is now yn ruine; but olde Yerle Randol, as sum say, lay in it, when he buildid Deuleucres Abbay. This Castel stondith a good flite shot from the building and goodly manor place that

[* Omitted by Stow. Letter *t* supplied by L. T. S.]
[† There seems to be some error here. I cannot identify Aspebury.]
[‡ Leland wrote *an*. Stow omits this paragraph, from "The auncienter."]
[§ This is Leland's first note, afterwards filled in by the following lines.]

---

^a Knutsford.   ^b Stockport.   ^c Beeston.
^d Halton.   ^e Shotwick.   ^f Dieulacresse Abbey.

now is ther, as the principal house of the Ferrars, and cam to them be similitude by maryage.

There was a place of the Lorde Audeleys in Chestreshire betuixt Cumbremere and Nantwiche caullid Newhaule Tower. It is now doune. There be motes and fair water. **Cheshire.**

Rivers in Chestreshire.   fo. 41.

Deva.[a] I have his course.*
Wyver.[b] I have his course.

Above Frodesham, Wyver by himself goith to the se.

Daven, alias Dane,[c] risith in the hundered of Maxfeld wher the forest ys. The hedde off Dane is in the very bordre of Darbyshire and Maxwel Forest. And as yt is saide, abowt the hedde of this River be the limites of Chestreshire, Stafordshir and Darbishir.

After that Dane cummith a 3. miles beneth the hedde, if rayne cum fast it ragith on stones, thoug after it cummith from Congleton it runnith on ground sumwhat morisch.

Abbais and prioris in Chestreshire.

Right agayne Lyrpoole [d] ii. miles over Mersey was a priory of canons cawllid Northtton,[e] now suppressid.†

Forests and chacys and parkes in Chestershire.   fo. 42.

The faire and large forest of Delamare, beside the wich I remember none, and there is plenty of redde deere and falow.

The hole Foreste of Maxwel except it be a smaul spek is yn Chestre.

‡ Notable places of Gentilmen in Chestershir.

[* See vol. iii, pp. 67, 68. The blanks after each name still remain.]
[† This paragraph heads a blank page.]
[‡ Stow omits the following notes on "places of Gentilmen in Chestershir" on fos. 42, 43 of the MS., except that he oddly copies a marginal note on Bostok, fo. 43, and another on Randol Manoring, once at the lower edge of the same folio, but now cut off. Stow omits several other short passages in his copy of this Part.]

---

[a] The Dee r.   [b] Weaver r.   [c] Dane r.
[d] Liverpool.   [e] Norton Priory.

Cheshire.   In the southe side of the Forest of Delamere.

Syr John Downe, alias Dane, dwellith at Utkenton [a] within iii. miles of Gunbyri, a mile from Torperle,[b] a long pavid village, or thoroug fare, and iiii. miles from Vale Royal.

The firste house of the Egertons is at Egerton in Malpas paroche. He hath also the Manor of Oldeton.

The auncientis of the Egertons dwellith now at Oldeton,[c] and Egerton buildeth ther now.

The second of the howse of the Starkeis is at Darle[d] abowte a v. miles from Northwiche, a scant mile from Oldeton, and a 3. miles from Vale Royal.

The frutefulnesse of the soile of Chestreshire.

Bunbyri a gentilman not in, but hard by, Wyraul.

Iriene Breton maried William Hanford of Handforde,[e] heyre. But she had a sun afore by Syr John Standely, bastard to Standely, Bisshop of Helye.

Syr Richard Brereton, a younger sun to Syr Randol of Brereton, maried the onle doughter of Wylken Standeley, and heyre to Syr Geffrey Massey of Tatton Manor and Parke.

Mere of the Mere 2. mile from Knotesford, a man of a C. marke land.

Le of Hyle,[f] the auncientest of the Lees of this contery, a mile from Knotesford.

Le of Bouth[g] half a mile from Knotesford, and hath a park.

Le of Adelington a mile from Prestby, a man of 3. C. mark lande.

Leyrcester of Tabeley betwixt Northwich and Knottesford a 3. miles from eche.

Leyrcester of * . . . yonger brother of . . . Toste his manor place, a man of a C. marke lande.

[* No blanks indicated, yet two words are wanting. This note is written on the margin, like many others on these three folios 42-44.]

---

[a] Utkinton.   [b] Tarporley.   [c] Oulton.   [d] Darley.
[e] Handforth.   [f] High Leigh.   [g] Booth.

Daniel of Table,[a] a mile from Leyrcestre.*

Bouth of Dunham dwellith at Dunham a 3. miles from Knottesford. It hath a fair parke, and is a myle from Altringham a pore thing, wher is a mayre.

Bouth of Barton in Lancastreshire is the auncienteste.

Bouth Bisshop of Hereforde was of † yonger brother of Bouth of Barton in Lancastreshire.

Davenport of Bromehaule[b] 2 miles from Stopporde by West dwellith at Bromehaule. He hath a 2. markes landes.

Davenport of Woodeforde a 2. myles from Bromhaule.

The best and firste house of the Davenportes is at Davenport a great old house coverid with leade on the ripe of Daven, 3. miles above Congleton.

Davenport of Henbyri cummith oute of this house.

Henbyri[c] place is a 2. miles playne north from Maxfeld. At Henbyri is a greate poole. This Davenport hath a peace of Bechetons landes. Fitton of Goseworth had a nother peace. Fitton dwellith at Goseworth[d] now, but ‡ not part of Becheton landes.

Fitton.

Syr Perce of Dutton chefest howse is in Dutton a viii. miles from Chestre.

fo. 43.

Hatton a fair place longging to Syr Perse of Dutton, abowte a 4. litle miles from Chestre.

Bostok of Bostok in Henry the 7. tyme had a doughter and heyre maryed to Syr John Salvage. Bostok was of a very auncientnes yn Chestershire, and yn Daneham paroche; and both Bulkles of this paroche, and Lestwike also.

The last Bulkle of Eton[e] was nepos. Venables doughter was his wife, yet alive.

Bulcle of Whatcroft a 2. mile from the Northwich now dwelling yn Wales. William of Bulkle,[f] chefe Justice of Chester, was setter up of Eiton. Bulkle of Eyton had sum land afore he was Justice. These 2. Bulkles contend either

[* *I.e.*, the family Leicester of Tabley.]
[† *Sic.* Perhaps error for *a*.]
[‡ No blank, but *hath* seems to be omitted.]

---

[a] Tabley.   [b] Bramhall.   [c] Henbury Hall (due west).
[d] ? Gawsworth.   [e] Eaton.   [f] Bulkeley.

Cheshire. to be the elder house of that name. The name rose by a lawyer. Bulkle of Wales ys a man of far greater land then the other. Bulkle of Eiton's stok cam to a doughter, and Lestewich had her; but Syr Gul. of Breton bought Eyton.

Ægerton, one of the yongger brethern of Egerton of Egerton, dwellith at Ridle within a halfe mile of Bukle Hille wher

Ridle Poole. the hedde of Wyver river is, and neere is a poole of a mile and more in lenghthe, and owte of [it] issuith an arme, that sone after goith into Wyver, and straite moche encresith hit. This Ridle Hawlle[a] made of a poore hold place the fairest gentleman's howse of al Chestreshire by Syr William Stondeley, helper to King Henry the vii., and he was atteinted, and Ridle was given to Rafe Egerton. There is a very large p . . .

Ridle longid to Danyel, that was servant to Syr W . . . Standle. and few men know what becam of this D . . .

Spurstow hath a place[b] a mile of * . . . and a poole by hit cawllid Newpoole.

Bunbyri College half a mile of. Syr Hugh Calv[eley] made the college of Bunbyri about Henry the 5. dayes.

Syr Hugh Calveley and Syr Robert Knolles were companions and great menne of warre.

Biston dwellith at Biston half a mile from Biston Castel.

Davenport dwellith a iii. dim. [miles] † from Bis[ton] by easte at a place cawllid Calve[ley], havyng certen very hy trees abowte his house that men may se very far of. This Davenport is of lesse landes then the residew.

Prestland dwellith at Wordele[c] in Bunbery paroche. It

Bar flu. is a mile from Calveley. A mile and a half thens is Barbridge and ther rennith Bar riveret, after cumming into Wyver.

Syr Randol Manoring dwellith at Bad[ele][d] a 3. miles

[* The upper part of the letter *R* (as it seems) is extant in the original. perhaps it should be *Ridle.*—*Hearne.* Most of the right edge of fo. 43 is torn, causing loss of a word at end of each line.—L. T. S.]
[† Omitted in MS.]

---

a Ridley Hall.   b Spurstow Hall.
c Wardle.   d Baddiley.

from Nant Wiche by south west, [and hath a parke] and a   **Cheshire.**
mere caulyd Badlemere.*

Starkey the auncients of that stokke dwellith at Wenbyri^a fo. 43 b.
a mile and a half from Cumbremere. There is a parke ful
of mervelus faire wood, but no dere. Abowte these ii. places
is plenty of woodde.

Nedam a knight dwellith at Shenton a iiii. miles from
Cumbremere by est. He hath buildid a faire house. It is
motid. Shenton ys yn Shropshire, and Syr John Nedam
was chefe Justice of Chestre, much set up this name.

Cranage manor and place yn Chestershir 3. miles from
Midlewich longith to Nedam of Shenton. The manors of
Badington, Bromold and Austason cam to Syr Robert
Nedam that now livith by his mother, one of 3. heyres of
Syr John Braundeley. The 2^d. doughter was maried to
Geralde of Brin in Lancastershire, and he had Braundele^b
the hedde house, and Wynnington, both in Staffordshir,
and other lordshipes beside. Harper of Ruschaule^c had the
3. and with her the lordship of Cholmeston^d 2. miles from
Nantwich.

Braundeley † the hedde house of Braundeley † the knight
in Stafordshir in the greate large paroch of Eccleshaul, wher
the Bisshop of Chester castel is.

Syr John Oldford of Oldford a mile from the Northwich.

Fowleciste a iiii. [miles] ‡ from Nantwiche sowth est
hath a faire place, and a man of fair landes. He is a
knight.

John Ascheley of Ascheley 2. myle out of Knotesford.

Syr Henry Delves dwellith a iii. miles est from Nantwiche,
and hath a fayr house.

Richard Letewich of Letewich^e . . . mile from Northwiche . . . on Dane . . . ik a mile . . . then Northwice.

[* Fo. 43, like fos. 37, 38, has the lower edge cut off since Hearne's
day. This paragraph is copied by Stow.]
[† Burton has corrected these words to Bromley, on the MS.]
[‡ Hearne's addition.]

---

^a Wrenbury.   ^b Bromley, Staff.   ^c Rushall.
  ^d Cholmondeston.   ^e Leftwich.

Cheshire.   Malpas.

. . . arbyri of . . . rbyri, wher . . . great Poole . . . e from . . . Northwik.

. . . rse Wer . . . hath is . . . cient house . . . Werbreton . . . Mersey and dwellith . . . reley. He . . . the Winington . . . Winningtons [Lands] 2. C. markes . . . ere. In al he hath 5. C. markes by yere.

Calveley dwellith at a maner place cawllid Le,[a] v. miles from Biston [b] by south west.

The seconde howse of the Breertons wher Syr Randol a late dwellid, ys at Malpas, a litle Sonday market * having iii. streates al pavid. His fair place is at the very ende of the south streate. Syr Randol erected a gramer schole ther, and an hospital.

Cholmeley dwellith at Cholmeley Haul, a fair howse, having a litle mere by hit, a fair woode, and a mosse of fyrwod. It is yn the middes of the way betwixt Malpas and Bunbyri iii. miles from eche.

The eldest howse of the Breertons is Bruerton hawle [c] by the Middle Wiche, possessid now of Syr Wylliam Breerton.

Mynshul dwellith at Mynshul † a v. miles west from the Midle Wiche.

Venables borne ‡ of Kindreton dwellith at Kindreton by the Midle Wiche. Venables be auncient gentilmen.

In Wyrale.

Standeley a knight.

Pole a knighte.

. . . hunter
. . . enour.   [Massey at Puddington.

. . . ravenor . . . dwellith clene . . . §]

[* "A—market." A faint line is crossed through these words, as though they were erroneous.]

[† Minshull. Leland corrected west to north; both are wrong—it should be south-west.]   [‡ The MS. has *barne*.]

[§ This edge was evidently torn in Hearne's day; it is now cut, and the fragments he saw are gone.—L. T. S. ". . *ravenor* . ." Forsan *Gravenor*, corruptly for *Grosvenor*, a known family in *Cheshire*. This conjecture is owing to Mr. THOMAS RAWLINSON, who confirms it from the word . . . *hunter* in the margin, *Grosvenor* being nothing but *a great Hunter.*—*Hearne*.]

---

[a] Leigh.   [b] Beeston, Cheshire.   [c] Brereton Hall.

Market townes in Darbyshire.*

Darby.†
Oresworth.[a]
Bakewelle.
Ascheburn in the Peke.
Chestrefeld in the Peke.
Maunsefeld.

Castelles in Darbishire.

Duffeld had a Castel.
Horeston.
Codnore, sumtyme longging to the Lorde Greys, v. mylis
bi east from Horeston. It is now al ruinose.
Castel of the hy Peke longging to the King.

Rivers in Derbishire.

Darwent risith plaine west a litle above Blakwel[b] a
market town. To Darle in the Peke, to Wennesle[c] village,
to Mattelok village, to Crumford village, and thorough
Crumford bridge, to Watstonde Wel[d] Bridge, to . . . Darle,
Darby, Sawla[e] feri, v. miles be land from Darby, wher it
goith into Trente.
Trent.
Manifold.
Ambre[f] risith east of Chestrefeld, and leveth ii. myles on
the lift hand onto us, to Winfeld[g] village an viii. myles, to
Ambrebridge ii. myles, to Chriche[h] Chase a wood, fast by
wher hit runneth into Darwent.
Wye river good for troutes risith in Darbishire nere S.
Anne of Bukstanes[i] Welle, so to Bakewel a market town, to
Haddon, and therabowt Wye cummith into Darwent.
Æglesburn[k] risith in a roche in the paroche of Oreworthe,[l]

[* Leland's few other notes on Derbyshire are in vol. i, pp. 21, 96.]
[† A space is left after each name on this and the next folio, but
few were filled in.]

---

[a] Probably Wirksworth.
[b] Leland confuses this place with Bakewell on the Wye.
[c] Wensley.   [d] Whatstandwell.   [e] Sawley.
[f] Amber r.   [g] Wingfield.   [h] Crich.
[i] Buxton.   [k] Ecclesbourn r.   [l] Wirksworth.

Derbyshire. thens to Iderse ᵃ a iii. myles, to Dofeld ᵇ chirch a iii. myles. A litle beyond Dovefeld ᵇ chirch at a* place Eglesburn muthe goith ynto Darwent.

Abbais and Priories in Darbishire.†

fo. 46.   The Limites of Darby.

The Frutefulnes of the Shire.

Forestes and Chasis in the Shire.

Notable Places of Gentilmen.

fo. 47.   The Limites of Lincolnshire.

Market Townes in Kesten.ᶜ

Staneforde.
Bourne.
Deping Market chirche is dedicate to S. Gude[lake.]
The chyrch of the other Deping is dedicate to S. Ja[mes.]
A mile from Deping Market is the ruine of a c[astel], caullid Maxeye, wherof sum parte stondith [yet.] It was be al likelyhod the Lorde Wakes house. Of late dayes it apparteynid to the Countes of Richemont, King Henry the 7. mother by the right of the. . . .‡

Lincoln-shire. Sleforde toune nor market is of no price. The orna-mentes of it is the Bisshop of Lincoln's castel, and the late
fo. 48. Lorde Husey's house.

Kyme the goodly house and parke is a 3. miles from Sleford.

Grantham.

[* So both in the orig. and Stowe.—*Hearne.*]
[† These headings, as well as many of the names following, have large spaces left, which have never been filled.]
[‡ The lower edge of fo. 47 is torn. In the margin part of a note can be seen, as follows:—Holand Lord of Maxey. Depyng market *ad differ. alter. op. ejusd. nominis . . . ncti.*]

ᵃ Idridgehay.   ᵇ Duffield.   ᶜ Kesteven.

From Stanford to Granteham al yn Kesten, and by meatly good plenty of woode, xviii. myles. **Lincoln-shire.**

From Stanforde, to Bechefeld,[a] a meane thorough fare, xii. mile, much playne grounde, savinge in the partes aboute Bichefeld self.

From Bichefeld to Ankester, a poore thorough fare, al by playne and much hethy grounde.

From Ankestre to Lincolne xvi. miles, al by like playne grounde in Kestene.

Here marke that al this hethe or playne from Bichefeld to Lincolne berith the name of Ankester.

From Burne in Kesten to go thorough hy Holland to Boston xx. miles al by low grounde and much marsch, and no woode in maner.*

Low Holande. fo. 49.

Croylande.
Quappelode, *vulgo* Hoplode.[b]

Hye Holand.

Boptolpstoune[c] stondith harde on the river of Lindis. The greate and chifiest parte of the toune is on the este side of the ryver, where is a faire market place and a crosse with a square toure. The chife paroche chirche was at S. John's, where yet is a chirch for the toune. S. Botolph's was but a chapel to it. But now it is so risen and adournid that it is the chifiest of the toune, and for a paroche chirche the beste and fayrest of al Lincolnshire, and servid so with singging, and that of cunning men, as no paroche is in al England. The society and bretherhodde [longging] to this chirch hath caussid this, [and now] much lande longgith to this society.

The stepil being *quadrata turris*, and a lanterne on it, is both very hy and faire, and a marke bothe by se and lande for all the quarters thereaboute. There is a

[* Hearne saw a few letters on the torn lower edge of fo. 48, since cut off. Stow's last word is "maner," as above.]

---

^a Bitchfield.   ^b Now Whaplode.
^c Boston, on the Witham r.

goodly fonte, wherof part is of white marble, or of stone
very like to it.

[There] be 3. colleges of Freres, Gray, [Blake] and
Augustines. There ys al[so an hos]pital for poore men,
and yn the [towne, or] nere to it the late Lorde Hus[e
had a] place with a stone toure. Al the bu[ilding] of this
side of the toune is fa[yre,] and marchauntes duelle yn
it; and [a staple] of wulle is usid there. There is [a bridg]
of wood to cum over Lindis ynto [this part] of the toune,
and a pile of stone [set yn] the myddle of the ryver. The
streame wherof is sumtymes as suifte as it we[re an arow.]

On the west syde of Lindis is one lon[g strete], and on
the same side is the White [Freres.]

The mayne se ys vi. miles of Bost[on. Dyverse good
shipps and othar vessells ryde there.]

The Lord Wyllougby had a house at Heresby,[a] and a
parke of blak dere a 2. miles from Spilesby, wher, as I
heere say, [he]* entendith to build sumptuusly.

Spilesby, a mene market toune having houses most
parte thakkid, and sum redid. In it is one meately faire
place, longging to one Hastinges, a gentilman which cam
from Southfolk, where he hath lande. This toune is v. miles
est from Horne Castel, and about as much from the se side
as in the midle way: and it standith on the egge of the
midle marsche of Lowe Lyndesey.

Rivulus praeterlabitur, and many springes be about it,
and the soile sandy.

Alford xvi. miles from Boston. Alforde, a meane market
toune in Low Lindesey Marsche a . . . † myle from the
maine se. The toune is al thakkid and redid,‡ and a brooke
cummith by it.

There is goode whete and benes in moste paroches of
the low marsche yn Lindesey, but litle barle as yn stiffe
clay grounde.

No woode yn the low marsche of Lindesey.

[* Omitted in MS. This note (a marginal one) not copied by Stow.]
[† Blank in MS.]
[‡ Covered with reed, "reeded."]

---

a Eresby.

At Hutetost^a Marsch 4. miles of cum shippes yn from
divers places and discharge.

Wayneflete a praty market stonding on a creke nere to the se. To this toune long smaul vessels.

The schole, that Wainflete Bisshop of Winchestre [made ther] and endowid with x. li. lande, is the most notable [thing of that toune.]

Waynflete vii. myle from Alford toward [Boston.]

Louthe.

Raisun market.^b

Castre standith on a clive side half [a] mile of from Ankeholme ryver, [and a] iiii. myles from Langford Bridge, and [toward] a vi. miles est from Spitel. There is a S[atarday] market. The toune almoste al thakkid, and *in hominum memoria* often hurte with fyer. There is speking of a fortres that hath sumtyme bene ther. There cummith springes from the hilles by Castre.

Launford. Forsan Langforde.

Grimesby.

Tatershaule apon Bane^c ryver; and the Aye or [Rhe],^d a greate river, is aboute a mile of. It is preati smaul market. It is a v. miles from Hornecastel, and 3. from Barden[ey.]

Horne Castelle, as far [as I can] lerne, is [now] moste buildid withyn the circuite of an [old waul]lid toune, or sum hughe castel,* as app[erith from] divers ruines of a waulle. It hath one [faire paroche] chirch. *Alluitur Bano et Verino qui paulo infra [op. Banum.]*

Dr. Thybleby of the Quenes College hath [la]ndes about the olde waulles of Horne Castel. Waring risith of divers springis *aliquot passuum millibus ab oppido.*

. . . *petit. Pons ibi est super Verinum flu.*

The market is very good and quik, occupiers in the toun . . . wood hard. . . .

Bullingbroke hath ons a yere a faire, [but it] hath no

[* Stow omits the rest of this paragraph, but the bracketed words now destroyed must have been seen by Hearne.]

---

^a Huttoft.   ^b Market Rasen.   ^c Bain r.
                    ^d Lindis, now Witham r.

Lincoln-
shire.

wekely market. The cast[el is meately] welle mayntaynid, and motid ab[owte, having a draw bridge.]

fo. 51.

Rivers and Brokes yn Lindcolnshire.

At Kellesthorp,[a] or there abowt, as it were a iii. myles west from Louthe, risith a great brooke ther cawlled Bane, so to Baumburge, peraventure for Baneburg,[b] a village a iiii. myles of, thens to Horne Castel a market town iiii. myles of. Al this way yt runneth most by sowth. After to Tatershaul, alias Tateshaul,[c] flat west yt runneth.

Tatershaul ys a market town v. myles of Horn Castel, and so to Dogdyke Fery abowt a myle, where yt renneth ynto the Ree, alias Lindis,[d] the which devideth Lindesey fro Kesteney.[e]

Lindis. It ebbith and flouith withyn a litle of Dogdike Fery.

Lyndesey lieth by est and Kesteney by west.

The bek or brooke that runneth by the north side of the Abbay of Bardeney, and within a half quarter of a myle lower runneth into the great Rhe of Lindis, is cawllid Panton bek. Thys bek riseth yn Hy Lindesey, as Master West thynkketh not very far fro the quarters wher as the Bane doth rise. Then to Hilles, a maner place of Master Hansard, so to Panton, a village a v. myles of; thens to Wragby village abowt a ii. myles, wherof yt is sumtyme cawlled Wragby bekk; so to Bardeney Abbay a iiii. myles, and then ynto the Ree. The monkes hold opinion that the old Abbay of Bardeney was not in the very same place wher the new ys, but at a graunge or day[re] of theyrs a myle of.

Lude ryver. To Ludebroke village, to Lude alias Louth, the fayre market toun, a 4. miles by Lude Parke. Thens to Grymbleby [f] village a mile, and to Salflete [g] Creke a 4. miles of, and so to the see. Salt [Creke is a havenet, and as the shore lyith it is a vi. miles above Huttoste Creke.]

Meately good plenty of wood about [Bardeney] and Barlinges, Reseby,[h] and Kirst[ede Abbays.]

---

[a] Calcethorpe.   [b] Burgh on Bane.   [c] Tattershall.
[d] Witham r.   [e] Kesteven.   [f] Grimoldby.
     [g] Saltfleet.   [h] Risby.

Dymmok dwellith at Sckrellesby ^a 2. miles from Horne Lincoln-shire.
Castel.

S[ir] Christopher Willoughby's sun and heyre dwellith now fo. 52. at Tupholme Priory, and beside enheritith part of the Lorde Wylloughby's landes.

Copledike dwellith at Harington 2. Miles from Spilesby market.

Asschecue dwellith about Thorton Curtois.^b

Wimbische hath Nokton Parke Priory, and ys beside a man of great possessions and auncient. He maried the Lord Taylbois sister.

Litlebyri at Stanesby^c in Haghworthingham.

The Lord Borow dwellith at Gaynesborow.

Gaynesborow ys his, and much lande ys about Sheffeld in Axholme.

Dalisun a litle a this side Axholme.

Henege at Haynton,^d where he is lorde and patrone.

The olde Henege landes passid not a fyvety poundes by the yere. Haynton is withyn a 3. miles of Raysun market, and a vii. miles from Horne Castel.

Syr Thomas Hennage hath doone much cost ther, yu translating and new building with brike and abbay stone.

Sandon dwellith at Ascheby half a mile from Spilesby.

Porter by Grauntham.

Harington beside Ankestre.^e

Billesby dwellith by Billesby,^f withyn a mile of Markeby Priory.

Fitzwilliams a Maplethorp ^g by Sutton on the [se side.

Hastinges . . . Wlkseby a 3. . . . .]*

Langton at Langton a litle from Wlkesby.^h

Asterby in Billesby a man of mene land.

Totheby of Thothebyⁱ by Alford.

Gedeney of Mavis Enderby a mene gentilman.

Quathering by Waynflete.

[* Torn since Hearne's time. He saw fragments of two lines more. Stow omits all this leaf.]

---

^a Scrivelsby. ^b Thornton Curtis. ^c Stainsby.
^d Hainton. ^e Ancaster. ^f Bilsby.
^g Mablethorpe. ^h Wilksby. ⁱ ? Thoresby.

Lincoln-
shire. S. Paulle.

Misselden about Castre.[a]

Luddington.

Turwithe about Barton apon Humbre.

Turner.

Sutton at Lincoln.

Dymmok of Carleton by Lincoln.

Massingberde beside Waynflet.

Haul by Grauntham.

Welleby at Hanstede a lit[le from Stic]keswald Priory, a man of [fair landes.]

Yorkshire.
fo. 53. Dancastre.*

Wakefeld.

Wakefeld apon Calder ys a very quik market toune, and meately large; wel servid of flesch and fische both from the se and by ryvers, wherof dyvers be theraboute at hande. So that al vitaile is very good chepe there. A right honest man shal fare wel for 2. pens a meale. In the toune is but one chefe chirch. There is a chapel beside where was wont to be *Anachoreta in media urbe, unde et aliquando inventa faecunda.* Ther is also a chapel of our Lady on Calder Bridge wont to be celebratid *à peregrinis.* A forow lenght, or more, oute of the toune be seene dikes and bulwarkes, and *monticulus egestae terrae, indicium turris specularis.* Wherby apperith that ther hath bene a castel. The Guarines Erles of Surrey, as I reede, were ons lordes of this toune. It standith now al by clothyng. The Duke of York, father to Edwarde the 4. was slayne by Wakefeld in bataile.

Bradeforde a praty quik market toune, *dimidio, aut eo amplius, minus* Wachefelda. It hath one paroche chirche, and a chapel of S. Sitha. It standith much by clothing, and
Christopolis. is distant vi. miles from Halifax, and 4. miles from Christestal Abbay.[b] Ther is a confluens in this toune of 3. brokes. One risith above Bouline[c] Haul, so that the hed is a mile *dim.* from the toune, and this at the toune hath a bridge of

[* A blank page except for this word.]

---

[a] Caistor.   [b] Kirkstall.   [c] Bowling.

one arche. A nother [risethe] a 2. mile of, having a mille **Yorkshire.**
and a bridge of [. . . The 3. risith 4. miles of havinge. . . .]

Bouline Haul sumtyme the Boulines. Now it longith to
Tempeste. It stondith a mile . . . Bradeforde.

Beverle.   fo. 54.

Beverle is a very larg town; but I cowld not perceyve
that ever hit was waulled, though ther be certen gates of
stone portcolesed for defence. In the town be a iii. paroche
chyrches; the mynstre wher S. John sumtime Bisshop of
York lieth, and one chapel. Ther is also a howse of grey
freres, and an other of blak, and an howse as a com-
mawndery of S. John's. Ther is a great gut cut from the
town to the ripe of Hulle Ryver, wherby preaty vesseles
cum thyther. Ther cummeth owt of the Bisshopes parke,
Westwoode, therby a litle fresch broke to the town.

To this toune long many great and auncient pryvileges as
to a sanctuary.

The towne hath yn theyr commune seale the figure of a
bever.

Bede cawlleth the place where Beverle is now Sylva Deirorum, Anglice Deirewauld.

In steede of the mynstre there was in old tyme an abbay
of munkkes, and nunnes, destroied almost by the Danes.

Brithung, S. John's decon was sumtyme abbate there, and
ys buried ther.

Ther is also buried S. Winwaldus.

Ledis,[a] 2. miles lower then Christal Abbay on Aire Ryver,
is a praty market, having one paroche chirch reasonably
welle buildid, and as large as Bradeford, but not so quik as
it. The toun stondith most by clothing.

Hulle.*   fo. 54 v°.

Pikering.

[* This and the following seven names with wide blanks left for
notes occupy several unnumbered leaves bound in among those numbered.]

---

[a] Leeds.

Yorkshire. Tadcaster.

Borowbridg. Alboro.

York.

Keterik.[a]

Ripon.

Richemont.

fo. 55. **In Darbyshire.***

Lancashire. Bruscow [b] (Briscot) a priory of blake chanons of the fundation of the Erles of Darby a mile from Latham.[c] It standith not very far from Duggils.[d] Many of the line of the Erles of Darby lyith there.

Holand a priory of blake monkes a ii. myles from Wigan. The Wottons were founders there.

Sawley † stondith on Calder Ryver.

fo. 56. Lancastreshire conteinith v. litle shires.‡

Westarbyshire, alias Darbyshire.

Lyrpole, alias Lyverpoole, a pavid towne, hath but a chapel. Walton, a iiii. miles of nat far from the se, is paroche chirch. The King hath a castelet there, and the Erle of Darbe hath a stone howse there. Irisch marchauntes cum

[* "*I.e.* the hundred of Darby. Briscot is certainly misnamed for Burscough, there being such a priory about a mile from Latham."— (Note on a slip of paper pinned in Stow's copy, written by Hearne's friend, Mr. Prescot, of Chester.) Leland corrected Bruscow to Briscot.]

[† Leland corrects to Wawley. He probably means Whalley, on the Lancashire Calder r. See fo. 58.]

[‡ The piece from "Lancastreshire—a iii in bredthe" (p. 43) is printed from a closely written leaf bound in by the reversed edge to Leland's MS., vol. viii, re-numbered by Burton, pp. 47, 48; it was probably fo. 56 of his vol. vii, and Stow copied it with omissions in this place. On the top of p. 47 is a large cross in pencil, put there by Burton evidently as a reference, but I do not find the corresponding mark; two others like it occur on pp. 224, 225 of his MS *a*.]

---

[a] Catterick.   [b] Burscough.   [c] Lathom.   [d] Duggils.

much thither, as to a good haven. After that Mersey Water cumming toward Runcorne in Chesshire lisith * amonge the commune people the name, and to Lyrpole, a v. mile on the other side in Lancastreshire, is [ca]wllid Runco[rn]e Water.

At Lyrpole is smaule custume payid that causith marchantes to resorte. Good marchandis at Lyrpole, and moch Yrisch yarn that Manchester men do by ther.

Warington, apon Mersey in Chestreshire, a pavid town, one chirch, a freres Augustine at the bridge ende. The town is of a prety bygnes, the paroche chirch is at the tayle of al the tounne. It is a better market then Manchestre.

Thelewaul sumtime a havenet and litle cite, as it apperith by the Kinges Recordes. Now fische garthes marre the haven, and the old toune now a poore village. It stondith a ii. myles upward from Warington.

Thelewaulle so caullid bycawse it was wallid abowt with greate . . . lis that is to . . . de Logges or timber postes.

Wigan pavid, as bigge as Warington and better buildid. There is one paroch chirch amidde the towne: summe marchauntes, sum artificers, sum fermers.

Mr. Bradeshau hath a place caullid Hawe a myle from Wigan. He hath founde moche canel like se coole in his grounde very profitable to hym, and Gerade of Ynse ᵃ dwellith in that paroch. Winwike a good benefice a v. mile of and a iii. from Warington.†

Ormekirk a iiii. miles or v. myles from Lyrpole, and about a ii. miles from Latham. A paroch chirche in the towne. No river by yt but mosses of eche side. Latheham ᵇ most parte of stone, the chefest howse of the Erles of Darby, ii. miles from Ormeskirk.

Newton ᶜ on a brooke cawllid Golforden, a litle poore market, wherof Mr. Langton hath the name of his baronry.

[* *I.e.*, leseth or loseth.]
[† A paragraph in the margin here appears to relate to Waveney, but is too much torn to re-construct, and Stow does not give it: . . . ey apon . . . ey Water . . . to Mersey . . . e Name . . . the beste . . . ace of the . . . te L . . . stondith . . . Parke a mile from Warington.]

ᵃ Ince, near Wigan.   ᵇ Lathom.
ᶜ Newton, near Warrington.

Lancashire. Syr Perse Lee of Bradley hath his place at Bradley in a parke a ii. miles from Newton.

Newton is a iiii. miles from Morley Haulle.

Prestcod[a] a litle market having no notable water abowt hit a iiii. mile from Mersey up toward Lyrpole. Mr. Molineux a knight of great landes a ii. myles from Prestcode dwellith at a place caullid Crostoffe.[b] Tokstaffe[c] a parke of the Kinges harde by his howse. Knollesley[d] a parke having a praty house of the Erles of Darby within a mile of Prestcod.

Syr William Norys dwellith at a howse caullid Speyke[e] a ii. or iii. miles from Prestcod and thereabowt from Flor . eskir . . . Thomas Ireland dwellith [at] . . . [Rumcorne on Mersey river.] *

Mr. Leland rekenith Preston in Andernes to be a litle shire, and so ther be vi. shires or hunderes in Lancastreshire.

Lancashire.

Firre Woode in Chateley Mosse.†

Westerbyshire.

Chateley More[f] in Darbyshire is a iii. or iiii. miles in bredthe.

Glasbroke[g] River cummith within lesse then a mile of Morley Hawle.

There be xii. paroche chirchis in Darbyshir, but they be large.

Winwike personage hath a parke, and is a ii. or iii. miles from Werington.

Flete and a nother broke or ii. cummith into Glasbrooke. and Glasebrooke goith into Mers[ey.]

Dugles[h] Ryver cumming by Wigan Market goith into the se by hit self toward Latham.

Chateley More a vi. miles yn lenght sum [way] brast up within a mile of Morley Haul, and [de]stroied much grounde with mosse therabout, and destroid much fresch water fische

[* Words now gone, seen by Hearne; those in italics seen by Burton (*a*).]

[† This is in Burton's hand.]

---

[a] Prescot.	[b] ? Croxeth.	[c] Toxteth.
[d] Knowsley.	[e] Speke Hall.	[f] Chat Moss
	[g] Glazebrook.	[h] Douglas r.

therabowt, first corrupting with stinking water Glasebrooke, **Lancashire.**
and so Glasebrook carr[ied] stinking water and mosse into
Mersey Water, and Marsey corruptid caried the roulling
mosse part to the shores of Wales, part to the Isle of Man,
and sum into Ireland. In the very toppe of Chate moo[re]
where the mosse was hyest and brake, is now a faire plaine
valley, as was in tymes paste, and a rille runnith in hit, and
peaces of smaul trees be founde in the botom.

Canale and cole pittes in divers partes of Darbyshire. The
great myne of canale is at Hawe 2. miles from Wigan. One
Bradshaw dwellith at Hawe.[a]

Martine Meare[b] towarde Latham is the greatest meare
of Lancastreshire, a iiii. miles in lengthe and a iii. in
bredthe.

Saltfordeshire. fo. 57.

Manchestre.†

Byri on Irwel Water, 4. or v. miles from Manchestre, but
a poore market. There is a ruine of a castel by the paroch
chirch yn the towne. It longgid with the towne sumtime
to the Pilkentons, now to the Erles of Darby. Pilkenton
had a place hard by Pilkenton Parke[c] 3. mile from Manchester.

Bolton apon Moore market stondith most by cottons and
cowrse yarne. Divers villages in the mores abowt Bolton
do make cottons. Nother the site nor ground aboute Bolton
is so good as it is aboute Byri. They burne at Bolton sum
canale, but more se cole of the wich the pittes be not far of.
They burne turfe also.

Yerne in tymes paste made at Orwike[d] a . . . miles from
Manchestre.

Yerne sumtime made abowte Byri a market towne on
Irwel.

Now for lakke of woodde the blow-shoppes decay there.

Wild bores, bulles, and falcons bredde in times paste at
Blakele.[e]

[† A blank after this word.]

---

[a] Haigh.   [b] Martin mere.   [c] Pilkinton.
    [d] Horwich.   [e] Blackley.

Lancashire.

fo. 58.

Market tounes in Lelandshire.

Chorle a wonderful poore or rather no market.

Croston a iii. miles from Chorle toward Latham a vi. miles from Chorle, a poore or no market.

There be abowt a vii. or viii. large paroches yn Lelandshire.

Darwent River cummith thorowgh a pece of Lelandshire.

Darwent cummith by Mr. Langton's place Baron of Newton by Warington a mile above Preston.

Loke better. Ribil risith in Ribilsdale above Salley Abbay, and so to Sawlley. A iiii. miles beneth Sawley it reseyvith Calder that cummith by Walley; and after receyvith a nother water cawllid Oder.[a]

Waulley[b] a x. miles from Preston; Sawlley a . . . miles or more.

Blakeburnshire.*

fo. 59.

Owt of a charte of Merton-College.†

The next river by se movith by Cairluel bakward on the same shore. There is a water made cumming from Chiswik[c] to the se.

The next to that cumming to the se is there cawllid Eske.

Next to that Doden,[d] and betwixt them is set Millum.

Next upward into Lancastreshire is set the mowth of the river of Leven.

Then Kent[e] River cumming to the se.

After is sett Ribyl.

And then Mersey Water.

Dorset.

In a nother Carte of Merton-College.

Bridport is set as midde way betwixt Waymouth and Lime.

[* At head of a blank page.]

[† These notes, from a chart or map in Oxford, must have been written later by Leland on the blank leaf; they break in to the account of the shires of Lancashire. Stow omits them.]

---

[a] Hodder r.   [b] Whalley.   [c] Keswick, and the Derwent r.

[d] Dudden r.   [e] Kennet r.

Lelandus.

At Bridporth be made good daggers.

Lancastreshire.

The hedde of Lune River by al æstimation must be yn Coterine Hille, or not far fro the root of it. Owt of this hille risith Ure, Sawle, and Edon.[a]

Howbeit M. Moore of S. Caterines Haul in Cambridge thus enstructed me of Lune Ryver. Yt risith yn a hil cawlled Crosho, the which is yn the Egge of Richemontshire, and issueth owt of iii. or iiii. heddes. He woold it should be first cawlled Lune in Dentdale, though the name of Dent seme to shew otherwise. North fro Dentdale ys Garsedale, and thorough that rynneth a water that after cummeth into Sebbar Vale, and ther is also a water meeting with Garsedale Water, and a lytle lower yn one streame they go ynto Dentdale Water, which he supposeth to be the streame that afterward is cawlled Lune. Beside the waters afore it receyveth at the foote of Sebbar Vale a great brook, the which cummeth owt of the north betwixt Westmereland and Richemundshire.

This ryver runneth a vii. miles or it cum to Dentdale Foote, and hath receyved into his botom the waters aforesaide. Fro Dentdale Foote yt entereth into Landesdale,[b] peraventure so corruptly cawlled for Lunesdale, and runneth yn it a viii. or ix. myles sowthwarde; and yn this dale is Kyrkby,[c] a very great and famose paroch a iiii. myles fro the foote of Dentdale. Fro Lunesdale yn whos foote ys Hornby Castel longing to the Lord Montegle half a myle fro the Lune. Fro thens it runneth to Lancastre, (set on the sowth side of Lune) corruptly spoken for Lunecastre viii. miles of, wither it ebbeth and floueth.

Sum say that the north arme upward is principal streame of Lune, the which is not of estimation til yt cum ynto Lunesdale.

The ruines of old walles about the bridg were onely of the suppressid priory.

---

[a] Swale and Eden rivers.   [b] Lonsdale.   [c] Kirkby Lonsdale.

READING FREE PUBLIC LIBRARY

Borow ª now a vyllage, set in Lunesdale a vi. myles beneth the foote of Dentdale, hath beene by likelyhod sum notable town. The plough menne find there yn eiing *lapides quadratos*, and many other straung thinges: and this place is much spoken of, of the inhabitans there.

In Westermerland is but one good market town cawlled Kendale, otherwise, as I wene, Kirkby Kendale. Yt hath the name of the river cawlled Kent, *unde et* Kendale, *sed Emporium laneis pannis celeberrimum.* In the towne is but one chirch. The circuite of the paroch by the cuntery adjacent hath many chapels, and divers yn the town self. Abowt half a myle of on the east side of the towne is on a hil a parke longging to yowng M. Par, the chyfest of that name, and ther is a place as it were a castel.

Kent ryver is of a good depthe, not wel to be occupied with botes for rowllyng stones and other moles. Yt risith of very many heddes, be lykelyhod springging withyn the same Shire. * (A vii. or viii. myles fro Kentdale, wher is a mere communely caullid Kenmore.ᵇ) A ii. myles abowt Kendale they cum to one good botom, and so to Kentdale towne that standeth on the west side of yt.

* The Hed of Kenne Rever.†

It risethe at Kenmore ᵇ in a poole somwhat large about a myle in compase and muche fishe in it. The place of the heade and all the Baronye of Kendale is in Westmorland, and kepithe Sher Courts at Apleby, and bysyde thethar cummythe all Westmerland.

Kenne nuage ‡ and more is a 8 myles flat nothe from Kendall on the way to Perithe,ᶜ and ther is a chapell longynge as a parte onto Kendale paroche. Kentmore Haul, Gilpins howse. The first parte of the river descendithe in betwyxt 2 hilles. New bridge 2 miles lower of tymber. Then

[* Marginal note in MS.]

[† This passage *—* is only preserved by Stow, being at the end of some notes which continue his copy of Leland's vol. v. See our vol. iv, p. 33 *note*.]

[‡ *Sic.* Stow has probably copied it wrongly.]

ª Burrow on the Lune.   ᵇ Kentmere.   ᶜ Penrith.

to Barley a smaule bridge* of stone in Staueley hamlet, a myle Westmorland.
lower. Thens 2 myles to Bowstone bridge of stone, then to
Burnes syde a myle, wher the Bellenghams dwell and is of
stone. Then to Kendall a myle and halfe lower, and rennythe thrwghe Stramangate bridge of stone havynge 8 or 9
arches, and the paroche churche by est is towchid with this
ryver; and thens a quartar and more of a myle it goythe to
Nether-bridge of stone of 3 or 4 arches standynge playne
este toward Yorke, and then 4 or 5 miles to Leuenbridge[a]
of stone and then to . . . Kendale Gates notable as wayes but
not defensible. Stricland Gate to Stricland village north-ward.
Stramangate named of the bridge. Kyrkegate, the greatyst
stret lyethe northe and southe. Pronte river goithe into
Ken ryver a myle above Stramangate bridge. Ther longithe
about a 30 chapells and hamlets to the hedd chirche of
Kendale. The parsonage was inpropriate to S. Mari of
Yorke. The castle is by est halfe a quarter of a myle from
the towne.*

Appleby is the Shire towne, but now yt is but a poore Leland, vii,
village, having a ruinus castel wherin the prisoners be kept. fo. 62 contd.

Ther is an old castel on the . . . side of Edon Water
cawlled Burgh.[b]

Abowt a dim. fro the castel is a vill[age cawll]ed Burgh[am],[c]
and ther is a great pilgrem[age to owr lady.] †

At Burgham is an old castel that the commune people no fo.
ther sayeth doth synke.

Abowt this Burgham plowghmen fynd in the feldes many
square stones tokens of old buildinges. The castel is set in
a stronge place by reasons of ryvers enclosing the cuntery
thereabowt.

There is a very greate lake, or mere, wherof part is under
the egge of Furnes Felles, cawlled Wynermerewath,[d] wherin a straung fisch cawlled a chare, not sene els there in the
cuntery as they say.

[* Stow has "a smaule of Stone bridge," doubtless an error in
copying.]
[† Hearne supplies these words. Not in Stow.]

---

[a] Levensbridge.   [b] Brough.   [c] Brougham.
                  [d] Windermere.

Westmor-
land.

Abowt the borders of Westmerelandshire and Lancastreshire be many dales. And in [every] one of them a brooke
givyng name to the dale.

Ther is in Westmerland, as it is said, a famose stone as a
limes of old time, inscribed.

Withyn a myle of Perith,[a] but in Westmerland, is a ruine,
as sum suppose, of a castel withyn a flite shotte of Loder[b]
and as much of Emot Water,[c] stonding almost as a *mediamnis*
betwixt them; the ruine is of sum caulled the Round Table,
and of summe Arture's Castel. A myle lower m[etithe] Loder
and Emot at Burgham Castel.

Durham.

Market Townes in Dirhamshire.[*]

fo. 63.

Duneholm.[d]

Akeland.[e]

Wichingam.[f]

The quikke market of Darlington standing betwixt Teese
and Were.[g]

Stoketon apon Tese.

Wulsingam apon Were almost in the midde way betwixt
Stanhop and Akeland.

Hertilpole.[h]

fo. 64.

Castelles in Dirhamshire.

Duneholm.

Akeland.

Prudho apon Tine.

Stoketon apon Tese.

Barnardes Castel.

Lomeley[i] Castel not far from Chestre.[k]

Abbais and Priories in Dirhamshire.

Duneholme apon Were river.

[* All these four lists of Durham names are written as headings, with
blank spaces between.]

---

[a] Penrith.
[b] Lowther r.
[c] Eamont r.
[d] Durham.
[e] Auckland.
[f] Whickham.
[g] Wear r.
[h] Hartlepool.
[i] Lumley.
[k] Chester-le-Street.

Finkelo[a] apon Were, a celle of xiii. monkes longging to Dirham. Durham.

Weremouth.

Garaw.[b]

There was a priori not farre from Darington,[c] as I remember aboute Teis ryver.

The Limites of Dirhamshire.

no fo.*

Tese river.

Tine river on til he receyve Darwent water.

Erle of Northumbr. Lord of the Honors of Cokermuth et Petworth. Lorde Percy, Lucy. Lorde Poyninges, Fizpaine, Brian.

fo. 66.

Cokermuth cam by Lucy. Petworth by gift of a king [Hen. I.]†

Fizpaine and Brian's landes cam to Poyninges, and by Poyning heyre general al iii. to Percy.

The Erle of Northumbr. Castelles and Manors.

Cokermuth in Cumbreland, a 700. *li.* by yere.

Alnewik, Werkworth castel, Langeley and Prudehow in Northumbreland, Rothebyri lordship on Koket a vii. miles above Anewik, wher is such a toun as Corbridge. Corbridg lordship, wher appere greate tokens of buildinges by square stones. Chatton lordship apon Tille a mile from Chillingham.

Northumberland.

In Yorkshire.

Semar,[d] Hundemanby[e] nere Semar. Poklington market a 2. miles from Semar. Lekingfeld[f] ii. miles from Beverle. Wresil[g] Castel ii. miles from Howden market, where the Bisshop of Dirham hath a faire palace. Catton wher is a parke as is almoste of the lordshipes afore rehersid. Spofford[h]

[* Fo. 65 is a blank leaf, bound in between fos. 64 and 66. The unnumbered leaf above is bound in after fo. 66.]

[† Written by Burton on Leland's MS.]

---

[a] Finchale.   [b] Jarrow.   [c] Darlington.
[d] Seamer.   [e] Hunmanby.   [f] Leconfield.
    [g] Wressell Castle.   [h] Spofforth.

a greate village a 2. miles from Oteley apon Eyre[a] river.
Topclif on Suale a goodly maner house yn a parke. Tad-
castre, and Hele, Lyndeley by Spofford wher Syr Thomas
Johnson now is heyre.

He had yn Kent a 500. mark of Poyning[es landes.] *
In Southsax Poyninges lordship. Petw[orth.]

fo. 67.   Torre Brian in Somersetshire that Master Kitson boute.

The Lorde Marquis of Excester had much of hys londes
yn Devonshire.

He had castelles yn Wales, and was there a greate lorde
marcher. Peraventure Paine Castel by Wy was his. For he
bare the name of the Lorde Fizpaine.

He had sum lande yn Southfolke and Cambridgeshire.

He had Taulaughar[b] a castel about the mouth of Teuy
cumming from Cairmerdine.

Cumberland.   From Cairluel to Burge on the sandes vi. myles.
fo. 68.   From Burg to Workington xii. myles.

From Workington to S. Bees xiiii.

From S. Bees to Furnes by the se cost xiiii. myles.

Lancashire.   From Furnes to Lancastre xii. myles.

From Lancastre to Preston xx. miles.

fo. 69.   *Eske flu. limes est Scotiae et Angliae.*
Cumberland.   *Lithel flu. defluit in Eskam. Lither † defluit in Eskam at
Motel Lithel.[c]*

At Motel Lithel was a moted place of a gentilman cawled
Syr Water Seleby, the which was killyd there, and the place
destroyed yn King Edward the thyrde, when the Scottes
whent to Dyrham, and theyr king was take by Copland at
Dyrham on a hil therby wher was many Scottes buried.

Bolnes[d] ys at the poynt or playne of the ryver of Edon,[e]
wher ys a lytle poore steple as a fortelet for a brunt, and yt
ys on the hyther syde of the ryver of Edon, abowt a viii.
myles from Cair Luel.[f] Abowt this Bolnesse ys part of the

[* Hearne saw these. Neither Stow nor Burton copied fos. 66, 67.]
[† Leland wrote *Lither* twice, but corrected it to *Lithel* in the first
word. This seems to be the Lidd r.]

---

[a] Aire r., but Otley is on the Wharfe.
[b] Tal Llacharne, or Laugharne.
[c] Liddel Strength, Cumberland.
[d] Bowness.   [e] Eden r.   [f] Carlisle.

Pict wal evidently remayning, and yt may be supposed that Cumberland.
yt is cawled Bolnes, as who showld say the Wal yee, or I doute yet
poynt, or end. of this.

Burgh yn the sand stondeth a myle of fro the hyther
banke of Edon. Yt is a village by the which remayne the
ruines of a greate place, now clene desolated, wher King
Edward the fyrst dyed. Burgh stondeth from Bolnes iii.
myles, and iiii. myles or v. fro Cair Luel.

Burgh longid sumtime to the Morvilles.

Here was a xv. yeres ago the Lord Maxwel * sore woundid,
many [sl]aine, and [drou]nid in Edon. [Str]ife ther . . .
tuaine. . . . ge . . . Scotland . . . and [took hym]
prisoner.†

At Drumbuygh ᵃ the Lord Dakers father builded apon old
ruines a prety pyle for defens of the contery. Drumbuygh
ys almost yn the mydde way bytwyxt Bolnes and [Burgh].
The stones of the Pict wal wer [pulled d]own to build
Dumbuygh. For the wal [ys very n]ere yt.

Netherby is a vii. myles north fro Cairluel, and Eske
ryver rynneth on the north side of yt. Ther hath bene
mervelus buyldinges, as appere by ruinus walles, and men
alyve have sene rynges and staples yn the walles, as yt had
bene stayes or holdes for shyppes. On the one side of yt is
the Batable ground; so that it is as a limes *Angliae et Scotiae.*
The ruines be now a iii. myles at the lest from the flowyng
water of Sulway sandes. The gresse groweth now on the
ruines of the walles.

Rokclif a preaty pile or castel of the Lord Dakers over
Edon on the farther ripe, about a iiii. mile from Cairluel.

The towne of Cokermuth stondeth on the ryver of Coker, fo. 70.
the which thwartheth over the town, and Coker runneth yn
Darwent hard at the point of the castel of Cokermuth.

[* This was in the year 1524. (An. reg. 16, H. 8.) See Hall's Chron.
in the Life of H. 8. fol. 129. b. and Hollingshead's History of Scotland,
p. 311. So that this was written by Mr. Leland in the year 1539, being
six years after he had receiv'd his Commission to travel from the King.
—*Hearne.*]

[† The bracketed words in this paragraph and the next seen by
Hearne are now gone. Stow omits these paragraphs.]

ᵃ Drumburgh.

Cumberland. The ryver of Dargwent after that he cummeth to a strayte curse, casteth owt an arme of his abundant water that maketh a poole, or lough, cawlled Use, and afterward strayteth, and at the last cummeth ynto Dargwent, and so maketh an isle.

Forestes.

The great forest of Englewood (Engylwood).

The forest of Nicol longing to the Du[ke of] Lancastre.

The forest of Einerdale.

A xxx. yeres ago not far fro the chapel of [the] Moore, the which is in Come Whitton [a] par[och] in Gillesland, and stondeth a vi. myles est from Cairluel, was fownd a grave, and theryn [bon]ys *inusitatae magnitudinis*.

[Wythyn] a quarter of a myle of Cairl[uel a xx. yere]s ago was take up [pypes of an old conduyte, whos hedde by lykelyhod . . . wlled Typping Castel . . .]

This conduct semed to be the conduit of . . . d not . . .*

The cyte of Cairluel is yn cumpace scant a myle, and ys walled with a right fayre and stronge wal *ex lapide quadrato subrufo.*

In the wal be iii. gates, Bocher gate (south), Caldew gate (west), and Richard gate (north).

The castel being withyn the towne is yn sum part as a closer of the walle.

Leyland. The Irisch men cawle bale a town, and so peraventure did the old Scottes. Thus might be said that Lugubalia † soundeth Luele towne.

In the cyte be ii. paroche chyrches, of the which the one is yn the body of the cathedral chyrch, yn the which be Canons Regulars as els be yn no cathedral chyrch of Englande. The other is of S. Cuthebert.

Ther is yn the towne a chapel of S. Albane, and also withyn the walles ii. howses of freres, Blake and Gray.

[* Bracketed words seen by Hearne, now gone. Stow omits these paragraphs. Of the second, which was in the margin, there is now no trace.]

[† Now Carlisle. *Bal,* a Celtic word corresponding to old English *ton.*

---

[a] Cumwhitton.

In diggyng to make new building yn the towne often tymes hath bene, and now a late, fownd diverse fundations of the old cite, as pavimentes of streates, old arches of dores, coyne, stones squared, paynted pottes, mony hid yn pottes so hold and muldid that when yt was stronly towchid yt went almost to mowlder: as yn M . . . glalbys howse yn diggyng for the squaryng [of]* his gardin and orchard the which ston[d]eth much sowth.

[Th]e hole site of the towne is sore chaungid. For wher as the stretes were and great edifices, now be vacant and garden plottes.

The cite of Cairluel stondeth in the forest of Ynglewood.

The body of the cathedral chyrch is of an older building then the quyer. And [yt ys as] a filial deriveid from S. Osw[ald's fast] by Pontfreyt.

[In the] feldes abowt Cairluel yn plowghing hath be [fownd diverse cornelines and other stonys] wel entaylid for [scales, and yn other places of Cumbarland in plowinge hath be found brickes conteyninge the prints of antique workes.]

The lenght of Cumbreland by the shore is from a water fo. 71. cawled Dudden,[a] the which devideth Furnesland[b] fro Cumbreland, onto a lytle water or mere cawlled Polt Rosse,[c] the which devideth the cownte of Northumberland on the est side from Cumbreland.

The bredeth of Cumbreland is from a water cawled Emot[d] that divideth on the sowth side on the one part Cumberland from Westmerland ontyl he enter ynto the ryver of Edon ii. myles fro Pereth[e] by est, and so on the est side of Edon up to a broke cawled † . . . the which divideth lykewise Cumbreland fro Westmerland, onto the ryver of Eske on the north side, the which devideth Cumbreland fro the batable grownd ontil yt cum to the arme of the se, the which divideth England fro Scotland.

[* Supplied by L. T. S.]
[† Blank in original. Cookburn Beck is intended.]

---

[a] Duddon r.
[b] Furness, part of Lancashire.
[c] Tipalt burn.
[d] Eamont r.
[e] Penrith.

Market townes yn the Shyre.

Cairluel.

Pereth a market towne by sowthe, xvi. myles fro Car-
luel, w[here] as a strong castel of the kinges, and [ston]deth
on a lytle water by force cut owt of Petorol.[a] But Pereth
stondeth [not]able dim. a myle fro the river of Emot, [and
a] myle fro the towne or caste[l of B]urgham,[b] that longeth
to the Erle of [Cumb]reland.

In Perith ys one paroche chirch, and a gray freres.

[Coke]rmuth a market towne stondyng on the [west syde]
of Darwent river iiii. or v. [myles fro the se shore, and] xx.
myles fro [Carluel.]

Also on the west syde of Darwent is a pretty creke wher
as shyppes cum to, wher as ys a lytle prety fyssher town
cawled Wyrkenton,[c] and ther is the chefe howse of Sir
Thomas Culwyn.*

On the est side of the ysle, where as the water of Dar-
guent risith, is a lytle poore market town cawled Keswike,
and yt is a myle fro S. Herebertes isle [d] that Bede speketh of.
Divers springes cummeth owt of Borodale, and so make a
great lowgh that we cawle a poole;[e] and ther yn be iii. isles.
Yn the one[f] ys the hedd places of M. Radclyf,[g] an other is
cawled S. Hereberts isle, wher is a chapel, the iii. ys Vycar
isle, ful of trees lyke a wyldernes.

Abbays or priores yn Cumbreland.

The Chanons of Cairluel.

Wetherhaul,[h] a selle of S. Mary Abbay, iii. myles sowth
est above Cairluel apon the ryver of Edon, on the same
side of the ryver of Edon that Cairluel doth.

Lenercost † an abbay of Blake Chanons viii. myles fro
Cairluel, apon the north side of the ryver of Yrthyng.

[* Stow copies *Curwyn*, not observing Leland's correction of *r* to *l*.
There is a Curwen Island in Windamere.]

[† A small *a* is written above the first *e*, but it does not seem to be
in Leland's hand.]

---

[a] Petterill r., see after, p. 56.   [b] Brougham.
[c] Workington.   [d] S. Herbert's I.
[e] Derwentwater.   [f] Lord's Island.
[g] Ratcliffe, Lord Derwentwater.   [h] Wetheral.

[Ho]lme Cultrayne ᵃ Abbay of white monkes.

[S.] |Beges ᵇ yn Caupland hard on the west se, a selle longing to S. Mary Abbay of Yorke, abowt xxvi. myles or more playne west.

Caldher ᶜ Abbay of whyte monkes yn Cape[land] ᵈ not very far from S. Beges, and nere to Egremont Castel.

At Kiley ᵉ *primis annis* Henrici 8ⁱ. not far from Norham yn the lordship of the Bisshop [of Dyrham,] was fownd, bet[wixt ii. stonys,] bokels of an arming girdel, typpes and barres of [the same of pure] gold, a pomel and a crosse [for a sword of golde, bokels and typps of gold for spurres. D. Ruthall * had some of them.]

Egermont . . . myles by sowth from Cokermuth. Yt longith to the Lord Fizgualter. Yt stondeth by the market towne of Egremont.   *fo. 72.*

At Cokermuth, a good market towne, a castel of the Erl of Northumbreland, the wich joyneth hard to the towne.

Bowe Castel longging to the King x. myles est fro Cairluel.   *On Kirkebek.*

Nere abowt Bou Castel alias Belcastel be fownd Briton brikes, with entayled worke and portretures, yn the old fundations.

Fro Bowe Castel to Naward a fair castel ᶠ of the Lord Dacers iiii. myles sowt fro Naward, viii. myles fro Cairluel.

Millum a castel longing to S[er] John Hudelstan standing on the river of Dudden or Dudden Sandes. (Apon a creke by the se side) a XL. yere ago fisch was fownd ther of an infinite greatnes.

Hyghhed Castel a vi. or vii. myles [from] Cairluel by sowth. Yt stondeth on Yve Bek.

Kirke Oswald Castel sowth sowth † est, xii. myles fro Cairluel, and sowth fro Naward. Yt stondeth almost on Edon.

[* Dr. Thomas Ruthall, bp. of Durham, 1509, secretary to Kings Henry VII and VIII. Was lord of Norham Castle.]
[† Over these words Leland wrote two lines, the ends of which are destroyed, viz.: "*cavit aut re . . . proavus hujus Dacori e . . .*"]

ᵃ Holme Cultran.   ᵇ St. Bees.
ᶜ Calder Abbey.   ᵈ Coupland barony.
ᵉ ? Kyloe in Northumberland.   ᶠ Naworth Castle.

Perith [a] a castel of the kinges b[y the] towne of Pereth xvi. myles so[wth] fro Cairluel, and v. myles sowth w[est] from Kirkoswald.

Ther cummeth at [Ing]mer Medow [owt] of Peterel [a g]ut to Penrith, [and at Carlton] half a [myle] of yt runneth ynto Emot, alias Æymont. Strikland Bisshop of Cairluel [b] did the cost to dig [it.]

Graystok Castel [c] of the Lorde Dacors, xiiii. myles fro Cairluel sowth, and iii. myles west fro Perith.

Rose a castel of the Bisshops of Cairluel [vi. myles] fro Cairleul by [sowth west.] Bisshop Kight [d] made hit very [fresh.] *

Ruines of castels desolated and townes.

fo. 72 b. Remember to aske by the Itineray how the old townes stoode.†

In the forest of Ynglewood a vi. myles fro Cairluel appere ruines of a castel cawled Castel Luen.

Leland v, fo. 101.‡ These thinges folowing I lernid of the Vicar or person of Corbridge at Newcastel.

Northum- Corbridg about a xi. miles from Newcastelle: But to go berland. to it the next way from Duresme it is not past a 16. or 18. miles.

Corbridge is on the same ripe of Tine that New Castelle is.

The chirch of Corbridge is dedicate onto S. Andre.

The personage was ons impropriate to the Priory of Tinmouth, sins by exchaunge to Cairluel.

The toune at this tyme is ful meanely buildid.

The names of diverse stretes that hath beene there yet hath names, as old people there testifie, and great tokens

[* This word seen by Hearne, now gone. In this margin appear to have been two short notes, of which only two or three letters are now visible.]

[† Leland's marginal reminder; did he mean Antonine's Itinerary?]

[‡ These fos. 101-106 are transferred from Part VII. See vol. iv, p. 24, note.]

a Penrith.　　　　　b William Strickland, bp. of Carlisle, 1400.
c Greystoke castle.　　d John Kite, bp. of Carlisle, 1513-21.

of old foundations be yet founde there, and also *Numis-* Northum-
mata Ro. berland.

The stone bridge that now is at Corbridge over Tine is
larg, but it is set sumwhat lower apon Tine then the olde
bridg was.

Ther be evident tokens yet seene where the olde bridg
was, and theraboute cummith downe a praty broke on the
same side that that the toun is on, and hard by it, and goit
into Tine. I thing verely that this broke is caullid Corve,
though the name be not welle knowen there, and that the
toune berith the name of it (Colus flu.).*

By this broke as emong the ruines of the olde town is a
place caullid Colecester, wher hath beene a forteres or
castelle. The peple there say that ther dwellid yn it one
Yoton, whom they fable to have beene a gygant.

There is no bridge on Tyne, as I remembre, bytwixt
Newcastelle and Corbridge.

As far as I can perceyve by the boke of the life of S. Oswin
the martyr, Colebrige is alway put ther for Corbridge. *Colebridge.*

There appere ruines of arches of a stone bridge over Tyne fo. 102.
river, at . . . Castelle longging to the Erle of Westmerland
a 3. miles lower on the ryver then Corbridge.

Chipchace bridg of . . . on Tyne.

Mounbowcher was a man of fair landes in Northumbrelande: and Doctor Davelle † told me that the hospitale yn
Newcastel hath yet landes of his gifte.

The Rudhams were men of fair landes in Northumbrelande about Tille ryver, ontyl one of them having to wife
one of the Humframville doughters killid a man of name,
and thereby lost the principale of 600. marke landes by yere.
So that at this tyme Rudham of Northumbreland is but a
man of mene landes.

Hasilrig of Northamptonshir ‡ hath about a 50. li. lande

[* In the margin.]

[† Dr. Davell, probably Robert archdeacon of Northumberland, one
of the signatories for annulling the marriage of Henry with Anne of
Cleves, 9th July, 1540. Several of the family were in Yorkshire; Henry
Davell was the last abbot of Whitby, and gained a pension of 100 marks
in 1539-40.]

[‡ Burton underlined this word, and corrected it on margin of
Leland's MS., " Leicestershire, of Nouseley," now Noseley.]

in Northumbreland and Esselington, wher is a pratie pile is Hasilrigges, and one of the Colinwooddes dwellith now in it, and hath the over site of his landes.

The ryver of Tame[a] risith a 10. miles by south west within the land, and cummith into Tyne aboute a mile above Getished,[b] and not far bynethe Ravensworth Castelle.

Tarset Castelle ruines in Northumbreland hard by north Tyne long now to the Lord Borow.

There was one of the Grays of Northumbrelande a man of greate brute in the tyme of Edwarde the 4., that was suspect with the Quene of Scottes of adulterie. Wherapon he beying accusid of a gentilman of Scotteland cam with a band, as it is saide, of a 1000. men to Edingborow, and there caste down his glove to fight in the listes with his accuser: but he departid withowte fighteting; yet was it supposid, that Gray was not accusid therof withoute a cawse.

The Herbotelles landes in Northumbreland, that was a 300. markes by the yere, cam of late dayes to 2. doughters, wherof the one was maried to Syr Thomas Percy, that was for treason hangid at Tiburne. The other was maried to Fitton of Chestershir. Mr. Doctor Davel told me that the limes of the Bisshoprike of Duresme goith beyond the mouth on Darwent up apon Trente even to the paroch of Rytoun.[c]

A pile or castelet at Bowes on Watheling Streate.

The Davelles cam owte of Normandie, and sins they have be men of greate possessions yn the north partes of England. But they cam in Edwarde the 2. tyme to decay and ruine. For the chief of the Davelles, that was Syr Loson Davelle and Syr Hugh Davelle, both barons (as Mr. Doctor Davelle sayith, but sufficiently to me provid not,) toke Thomas Duke * of Lancaster and the barons part agayne Edwarde the 2. and Peter Gaveston, wherapon Davelles landes were attaintid and sparkelid.

Yet remanid of the name 4. or 5. younger brethern, that after got meane landes: and one of them after in descent

[* Leland wrote *Duke*, but Burton crossed it through and wrote *Earle* above.]

---

[a] Teame.   [b] Gateshead.   [c] Ryton.

consumid a 100. li. landes by the yere in Notinghamshire in mere hauking and hunting.

There yet remayne meene gentilmen of the name.

The principal land and habitation of the Davelles was about Pontefracte in Yorkeshire.

Much of the Gascoynes lande and the landes of True-whit, alias Turwit, of Lincolnshir, longid to the Davelles.

The name of the originale house of the Davelles yet remainith yn Normandie aboute the partes, as I have heard, of Alaunsun.

Roger Thorton* the great riche marchaunte of New-castelle in Edwarde the 4. dayes, by whom the Lomeleys landes were greatly augmentid, as by mariage of his dough-ter and heyre, buildid S. Katerines chapelle, the towne haulle, and a place for pore almose menne by Sand Hille gate a litle lower then Newcastelle bridge on the very ripe of Tyne within the toun of Newcastelle. The isle, and almost al the landes that the Lorde Lomeley hath in York-shir and Northumbreland, was this Thorntons.†

This Roger Thorton was the richest marchaunt that ever was dwelling in Newcastelle.

One John Warde a riche marchant of Newcastelle made a *maisun dieu* for xii. poore men and xii. poore women by the Augustine Freres in Newcastelle.

One Christopher Brigham, a marchant of Newcastelle, made of late a litle hospital by the Gray Freres in New-castelle.

The waulles of Newcastelle were begon, as I have harde, in King Edwarde the firste day, as I harde, by this occa-sion. A great riche man of Newcastelle was taken prisoner by the Scottes owt of the town self as it is reportid. Wher-apon he was raunsomid for a greate sum: and returning home he began to make a waulle on the ripe of Tyne

---

[* In a small blank in Stow's copy preceding this line is written the following in a hand of the seventeenth century: "This Thornton was at the fyrst very poore, and, as the people report, was a pedler, and of hym to this day they reherse this ryme:

𝔍n at t𝔥e 𝔚estgate came Thonton [*r.* Thornton *or* Thorton] in, 𝔚it𝔥 a 𝔥alfpen[y] 𝔥apt in a 𝔎ams 𝔖kynn.]

[† See further as to the Thorntons and the Lumleys, vol. iv, p. 118.]

Northum- ryver from Sandehille to Pandon gate and beyound that to
berland.   the towre agaync the Augustine Freres.

The residew of the marchauntes of the tounc seying this
towardnes of one man, sette to their helping handes, and
continuid ontylle the hole toun was strongely about waullid,
and this worke was finishid in Edwarde the 3. dayes, as I
have harde.

The strenghth and magnificens of the waulling of this
towne far passith al the waulles of the cities of England and
of most of the townes of Europa.*

fo. 106.   Prior Castel of Dyrham, the last save one, buildid the
toure in Farne Isleland for defence owt of the grounde.
Ther was a chapel and a poore house afore.

Ther was a house of chanons at Ovingeham apon Tyne
agayne Prudehow [a] on the other side of Tyne, a master and
3. chanons, celle to Hexham. Humfranville gave the personage of Ovingeham to Hexham that they should find
certen chanons ther.

Morley of Morpath [b] was ons Lord of Wercworth Castel
on Coket [c] mouth.

Dr. Davel told me, that Antony de Bek buildid or renewid
Kensington, as he hath hard, and gave it to king or prince.
. . . He buildid Duresme Place in London.

Leland vii,
fo. 72 contd.,
see p. 56.
† thens yt goith withyn a myle and lesse of Newcastel, and
so croketh upward toward Tincmuth.

Doctor Davel told me that S. Nicolas chirch in Newcastel stondith on the Picth waulle.

Bytwyxt Thyrwal [d] and North Tine yn the wast ground
stondeth yet notable peaces of the wall, the which was made
ex lapide quadrato, as yt there appereth yet. Looke wher as
the grownd ys best enhabited thorowg the walle, so there yt

[* Part of this page is blank. On it, in a hand of late seventeenth or
eighteenth century, is the note: "*Continet hoc volumen 92 pag.*" The
original numbering of the leaf was 90 (afterwards altered to 104), the
next two leaves are blank. Evidently the original volume ended here.]

[† A blank precedes this paragraph, which appears to relate to the
Picts' wall.]

---

[a] Prudhoe.   [b] Morpeth.
[c] Coquet r.   [d] Thirlwall.

lest appereth by reason of buildinges made of the stones of the waule. The walle on the farther side toward the Pictes was strongly dichyd. Beside the stone wall, ther appere yet yn very many places *vestigia muri cespititii*, that was an arow shot a this side the stone wal; but that it was thoroughly made as the stone wal was yt doth not wel appere there. **Northumberland.**

Fro Bolnes[a] to Burgh[b] abowt a iiii. myles, fro thens yt goeth within half a myle of Cairluel,[c] and lesse on the north side, and crosseth over Edon a iii. quarters of a myle benethe Cairluel, and so to Terreby[d] a litel villag a myle fro Cairluel, then thorowgh the barony of Linstok; and thorowgh Gillesland on the north side of the river of Arding[e] a quarter of a myle of the abbay of Lenarcost, and then a iii. myles above Lenarcost yt crosseth over Arding, then over the litle brooke of Polt rosse,[f] the which devideth Gillesland in Cumberland from Sowth Tyndale yn Northumbreland, then to a castel caulled Thirlewal, stondyng on the same, thens directly est thorowgh Sowth Tyndale not far fro the great [rui]nes of the castel of Cairvorein,[g] the [which] be nere Thyrlewal, and so over North [Tyne, then] directly [est thorowgh the hedd of] Northumbreland. **Cumberland.** **Northumberland.**

There is a fame that Oswald wan the batelle at Halydene[h] a 2. myles est from S. Oswaldes Asche.[i] And that Haliden is it that Bede caullith Hevenfeld. And men there aboute yet * finde smaule wod crossis in the grounde.† **fo. 73.**

‡ Northomberland.

In Sowthe Tynedale, as in that is be syd Hexhamshire except and yet as a parte of Sowthe or Sowthest Tyndale, is but one paroche churche, and that is caullyd Haultewesel.[k] **Stow, vol. v, fo. 143.**

[* Leland interlined *they* over *yet*.]
[† Here ends Leland's vol. vii.]
[‡ From this point to the end of the Part Hearne supplied from Stow, the original leaves being lost. But he does not explain how he guessed his figuring of the folios, which is not in Stow.]

---

[a] Bowness.	[b] Burgh by Sands.	[c] Carlisle.
[d] Tarraby.	[e] Irthing r.	[f] Tipalt burn.
[g] Carvoran.	[h] Hazeldean.	[i] ? St. Oswald's chapel.
	[k] Haltwhistle.	

There be bisyde *aliquot sacella*, where of one is not far from
Willington, and it is caulyd White Chapell. There lyethe
one of the holy Aydans, and othar holy men in the churche
yarde by the chapel.

In Northe Tynedale is but one paroche churche cawlyd
Simons burne.[a] In it is *aliquot sacella*. Sens I hard that
Simons burne is in Sowth Tynedale, and that in North
Tindale is onely Belingeham chaple longinge to Simons
burne.

In Ridesdale be but 3. paroche churchus, the cheffest
is Ellesdene. then Halistene, and Corsansid.[b] To thes
parochis resorte the witriding men othar wyse theues* of
that Englishe marche.

Rede risethe within 3. miles of the Scottyshe marche. It
risethe in the northe, and cummithe sowthwest thrwghe
Ridesdale, and so into North Tyne arme, a litle lowgher
then Belingham, that stondithe somewhat of of † Northe
Tyne, and is a x. mils above Hexam.

North Tyne risithe playne northe, and rennith almoste
playne northe ‡ til he metith with Southe Tyne.

Some hold opinion that at Halistene,[c] or in the river of
Coquet, thereabout wer 3000. christenyd in one day *in primi-
tiva ecclesia* Sax.

Coquet ryver for a certen space of miles devidith Cuque-
dale from Ridesdale.

Coquet cummithe by Herbotell,[d] a goodly castle, and thens
to Linne Briggs, sumtyme of stone, now fallen. Ther about
was great buyldinge, but now desolation.

New Castle a market towne.

Hexham a market towne.

Morpet a market towne is xii. longe miles from New
Castle. Wansbeke a praty ryver rynnithe thrwghe the syde

[* Witriding, *i.e.*, outriding men or thieves. Stow's MS. has
"witeiding," probably mis-read or badly copied. The spelling "wt,"
pron. "ut," for out, is used in old Border writings. The Border
marauders were known as "outriding" men. See New Eng. Dict.,
"outrider," § 3, and "outriding."]

[† Read "standeth off of."]   [‡ Evidently error for *south.*]

---

a Simondburn.   b Corsenside.
c Holystone.   d Harbottle.

of the towne. On the hethar syde of the river is the prin- Northum-
berland.
cipall churche of the towne. On the same syde is the fayre
castle stondinge apon a hill, longinge with the towne to the
Lord Dacres of Gilsland.

The towne is longe and metely well buyldyd with low
howsys, the stretes pavyd. It is far fayrar towne then
Alenwike.[a]

A qwartar of a mile owt of the towne on the hithere syde
of Wanspeke[b] was Newe Minster abbay of White Monks,
plesaunt with watar and very fayre wood about it.

Alnewike market towne.

Banborowgh now no market towne.

Berwike a merket towne.

Castles in Northumbarland.

New Castle.[*]

Chipchace a praty towne and castle, hard on the easte
parte of the arme of Northe Tyne, the whiche devidethe
Tyndale frome Northchumbarland. For Tyndall thowghe it
be as a parte of Northumberland, yet it is as a parte privilegyd within it selfe.

Tynmouth abbay sumtym usyd for a castle.

Dalawele Castle 4. miles from Tynemouthe, and within a
mile of the shore.

Otterburne Castle stondinge on Otter in Ridesdale, the
whiche joynethe hard apon North Tyndall.

There be ruines of a castle longynge to the Lorde Borow
at Mydforde[c] on the sowthe syde of Wansbeke, iiii. miles
above Morpeth. It was beten downe by the Kynge. For
one Ser Gilbert Midleton robbyd a cardinall cominge out
of Scotland, and fled to his castle of Midford.

Morpeth Castle stondythe by Morpith towne. It is set on
a highe hill, and about the hill is moche wood. The towne
and castle belongeth to the Lord Dacors. It is well mayn-
tayned.

Witherington Castle longinge to the Wytheringtons stond-

[* All these four preceding names are left with blank spaces.]

---

[a] Alnwick. [b] Wansbeck r. [c] Mitford.

ethe with in halfe a myle of the shore, somewhat as towchinge agains Coket isleland. By it runnithe a litle broke on
the northe syde, and there is a litle village of the same
name. The broke renneth into the se by it selfe.

Werkworthe Castell stondythe on the southe syde of Coquet watar. It is well maynteyned and is large. It longed
to the Erle of Northomberland. It stondithe on a highe
hille, the whiche for the more parte is includyd with the
ryver, and is about a mile from the se. Ther is a plety *
towne, and at the towne ende is a stone bridge withe a
towre on it. Beyond the bridge is Banborowshire.

Alnewik Castle.

Howwike[a] a litle pile longinge to the . . . a mile from
the shore.

Dunstaneborowgh[b] a 2. miles beyond Howwik harde on
the se shore. It stondethe on a hy stone rok. The castle
is more then halfe a mile in compace, and there hathe bene
great building in it. Therby is a strong . . .

Betwixt Dunstanborow and Banborow is Embleton, a mile
fro the shore, and a mile from Dunstanboro.

Bamborow, sometyme a huge and great castle, one of the
strongest in thos partes.

Agerston[c] a towre apon the south syde of Lindis ryver.

Chillingham Castle longinge to Ser Edward Grey, whos
wyfe was maried to Ser Robert Heldercar.

Foord Castle in Glyndale apon the east syd of Tille.[d] It is
metly stronge, but in decay.

Etel Castel[e] stondinge on playne grownde, hard on the
este syde of Tylle, longynge to the Erle of Rutland.

Eyton Castle longing to Ser Edward Graye 2. miles lower
on Tyle then Etel. It stondithe on the west syd of Tylle.
The Scotts at Floden Fild bet it sore.

Werke Castle[f] on the southe syd of Twede, a praty towne
there.

Norham Castle on the same syde.

Berwike on the northe syd.

[* *Sic* in MS. Read *prety*.]

---

[a] Howick.	[b] Dunstanburgh.	[c] Haggerston.
[d] Till r.	[e] Etal Castle.	[f] Wark Castle.

Howsys of Relygion in Northumbarland.   Northum-
berland.

Bolton * of chanons in Cokedale, whiche they call comonly
Glinedale. The Lord Rose was foundar there.

Halistane nunre in Ridsdale,ª bytwyxt Aidan-bridge and
Hexham.

Hexham.

Lamle ᵇ a nunrye on Sowthe Tyne.

Brinkborne priorye on Coquet. Blake Chanons by moste
likelyhods of the Lisles foundation, or the Feltons before
the Lisles.

Haly Eyland ᶜ monks.

Bambrughe a cell to S. Oswald.

New Minstar.

Farne.

Coquet a cell to Tynemowthe.   fo. 146.

Tinemouth.

Blancheland, Whit Chanons, in Northumbarlandshire. For
it stondithe in the farthar syde of Darwent. From Darwent   Durham.
mouthe to Wyre ᵈ mouthe the low contry betwixt is cawlyd
Wyralshire. Parte, or moste parte of Chester,ᵉ is in Wyrale.ᶠ

Where as the hospital is now of Saynt Edmond at Getes-   Northum-
hed in Wyrale was sometyme a monastary, as I have hard,   berland.
and be lykelyhod the same that Bede spekythe of.

Castles.

Huttun ᵍ a faire castle in the midste of Northombarland,
as in the bredthe of it. It is a iiii. or v. miles northe from
Fenwike pile, and this is the oldist howse of the Swyn-
burnes.

Wallington Castle 2. miles est from Hutten. It is the
chefist howse of the Fenwiks. Ser John Fenwike is now
lorde of it.

Darwent.†

[* On Aln r.]   [† Here begins a list of rivers.]

ª Holystone nunnery in Redesdale.   ᵇ Lambley.
ᶜ Holy Island.   ᵈ Wear r.
ᵉ Chester-le-Street.   ᶠ ? Weardale.
              ᵍ ? Swinburne Castle.

V.   F

**Northum-
berland.**

Thenis[a] a litle river cummithe in to Tyne on the southe syde a mile above New Castle.

Tyne.

Cone ryver[b] comithe by Lanchestre or it come to Chester in the Strete. Lanchester a vi. miles west from Chestre.

Hedle broke metithe at Chestre, or there about, with Cone water.

Pont.

Wansbege.[c]

Coket[d] risethe in Ridesdale in a ground beringe ling, and some what fenny.

Alne.

Rye.[e]

Bremische[f] is the very water of Tille; but at the heade and a certayne cowrse it is caullyd Bremiche, and aftar lesethe the name; and is cawllyd Tylle.

Conke, alias Coquet.

Low.

Glyne[g] risethe in Chivet hills, and so into Glyndale on to Newton village, where is a towr. Ther is a litle broke cawlyd Boubent[h] cumminge owt of Scotland rennithe into Glyn to Langton village 9. miles of, where is a ruine of a towre a myle of. So to Copland[i] village a mile, where the watar brekethe into armes makynge islets; but sone aftar metynge, and so a 2. mills a this syde Forde Castle in to Tylle.

Tyle risethe in the hills of Chivet,[k] and so cummithe into Glindale unto a castle caullyd Chillingham Castle a vi. miles from the Chyvet hylls, so to Forde Castle an viii. miles of, to Ethell[l] Castle on the bridge of stone downe on the est syde a mile, to Hetton[m] Castle on the west syde of the Tylle a 3. miles and halfe of, so to Twislebridge[n] of stone one bow, but greate and stronge, where is a townlet and a towre a 2. miles of; so to Hornecleue a litle village on the east syde not halfe a mile of, and there in to Tweede. Hornecleue[o] is halfe a myle above Norham.

fo. 147.

[a] Team r.	[b] Cong burn.	[c] Wansbeck r.
[d] Coquet r.	[e] Wreigh r.	[f] Breamish r., afterwards Till.
[g] Glen r.	[h] Bowmont Water.	[i] Coupland.
[k] Cheviot.	[l] Etal.	[m] Heaton.
	[n] Twizel.	[o] Horncliffe.

Twede risythe in Twydedale in Scotland at a towne (as I here say) cawllyd Pybbell,[a] and so comithe thrwghe the forest of Eterik in Scotland, and so thorwghe Tynedale in Scotland, the people where of robbe sore and continually in Glyndale and Bamborowshire; and at a litle broke, cawlyd Ryden burne,[*] the whiche partithe England and Scotland by este and west, and comithe in to Twede, the greate streame of Twede towchithe on the Englyshe grownde as a limes betwene Scotland and it. So to Carham a good mile of, a litle village, where is a cell of 2. chanons of Kyrkham[b] in Yorkeshire. At this Carham is a litle towre of defence agayne the Scotts. So to Werke[c] Castle a mile of and more, a meatly stronge fortrese, to Cornehil a litle pile 2. miles of, agaynst the whiche on the farthar rype in Scotland is Cauldstreame[d] a place of nunes. So to Norham Castle where is also a meatly good toune about a 3. miles of. So to Berwike a vi. mils stondinge on the northe syde of Twede a litle. There by at the bridge on the sowthe syde of the watar is Twemowthe[e] as a suburbe to the towne, and thens . . .

In Northumbarland, as I heare say, bo no forests excepte Chivet hills, where is muche brushe wood, and some okke, grownd ovar growne with linge, and some with mosse. I have hard say that Chivet hilles stretchethe xx. miles. There is greate plenty of redd dere and roo bukkes.

The forest of Loughes is in Tindale on the west syde of Northe Tyne, even betwyxt the Tynnes armes.

Betwixt New Castle and Tyne Mouthe litle wood.

Bytwixte New Castle and Morpethe litle wood grownd.

Bytwyxt Morpethe and Alenewik good plenty of wood in certayne places and many parks; xii. miles betwixt New Castle and Morpethe, xii. longe miles betwene Morpethe and Alnwike, xx. to Berwike. So from New Castle to Berwike. Betwixt Alenwike and Berwike litle plenty of wood.

From New Castle to Hexham a xiiii. miles, and that way litle wood excepte at few places.

[* Redden village about two miles west of Carham, the burn falls into the Tweed not far from the present boundary line.]

[a] Peebles.   [b] Stow has Kynkham.   [c] Wark.
[d] Coldstream.   [e] Tweedmouth.

There they reken not Hexham in Tindale, but as a liberty
by it selfe. It is the market of Southe Tindale.

The libertye of Hexham stretchithe a x. miles southe
west one way.

In Bamborowshire, parte of Northumbarland, is litle or
no wood.

In Ridsedale no plenty of wood.

In Glindale here and there wood, and Chiveot servithe
them well; but the great wood of Chiveot is spoylyd now,
and crokyd old trees and schrubs remayne.

From Riddenborn a longe Twed to Barwike almoste no
wood. They burne se cole that be dyggyd at Morton a
litle village in Glyndal a 2. mile from Berwike.

Glindall[a] goethe a longe on Twede fro Rodenburn to
Twede Mouth standinge in Glendale.

Haly Eylandshire[b] conteyneth all alonge the shore from
Agorston[c] to Beele,[d] and so alonge to Bamborow.

[a] Glendale.   [b] Holy Island.
[c] Haggerston.   [d] Beal.

PART X.*

*R*Egnum Northumbrorum ab Humbro flu. antiquitus ad fo. 60 a. fanum S. Joannis in Scotia.

Regnum Northumbrorum divisum in duas partes, id est, in regnum Deirorum et regnum Berniciorum.

Regnum Deirorum ab Humbro ad Thesim Beverle olim dicebatur. 2. Deirewalde, id est, Silva Deirorum.

Nomina regum Deirorum.†

Ella filius Yffi.	Mol, qui et Ethelwoldus.
Ethelricus.	Alcredus.
Ethelfridus.	Ethelredus, qui et Ethebrigh-
Edwinus.	tus dictus.
Osricus.	Alwoldus.
Oswaldus.	Osredus.
Oswius.	Ethelbrightus.‡
Ecfridus.	Osbaldus.
Alfridus.	Eardulphus.
Osredus.	Osbricght et Ella conjuncti.
Chenredus.	Aldene et Eonils juncti.
Osricus.	Ragnaldus.
Ceolwulphus.	Sictricus.
Eadbertus.	Guthefertus§ ult. regum.
Oswulphus.	

[* Hearne's vol. vii, part 2. The original of Leland's MS. for this Part is lost. Hearne printed it from Stow's copy, Tanner MS. 464, vol. iii, fos. 60-81. The first two leaves are headed "comentaria Anglia 3," and evidently were separate from what follows in Stow's time, probably on loose leaves, Stow's fo. 61 v° being chiefly blank. The Itinerary proper begins on fo. 62.]

[† These lists of Northumbrian kings and earls appear to be taken from William of Malmesbury (Rolls series, index, vol. ii, cf. the kings as far as Alwold) and Simeon of Durham (Rolls ser.).]

[‡ Should be Ethelred.]

[§ Guthred; confused with Cuthbert by the old copyist.]

fo. 60 b.

Nomina regum Bernisiorum.

Ida filius Eoppae.
Adda.
Clappa.
Theodulphus.

Fradulphus, alias Frecul-
phus.
Theodericus.
Aethelricus.
Ethelfridus.

Nomina comitum Northumbriae.

Osulphus comes; cui per
Edgarum regem adjunc-
tus * Oslacus.
Vualtheuus.
Wictredus.
Edulphus Cudel.
Aldredus.
Edulphus.
Siwardus.
Tosti.
Morcharus, et postea Osul-
phus adjunctus ei.
Copsius, alias Cospius.

Robertus Comyn.
Cospatritius.
Vualtheuus.
Walcherus episcopus.
Albricus.
Robertus de Mulbreio: quo
capto cessavit comitatus ad-
ministrari à comitibus; et
ex tunc in manu regum,
scil. Gul. Magni, Gulielmi
Junioris, et Henrici man-
sit.†

fo. 61 a.

788.

Elfwaldus rex Northumbrorum occisus à Sigga patritio
apud Scyltecestre juxta murum ‡ anno Domini 788.

Lindisfarne, alias Haly Eland, depopulata à Danis anno
793. Dom. 793.

Haldenus, unus ex principibus Danorum, totam North-
875. umbriam sibi subjugavit anno Domini 875.

941. Anlaphus Danus incendit Tiningham anno Domini 941.

Robertus Curtoys, filius Gulielmi Conquestoris, condidit
1080. Castellum Novum super Tinam anno Domini 1080.

Malcolinus rex Scottorum occisus prope Aile fluvium à
1093. quodam Morello milite anno 1093.

Malcolinus rex sepultus in Monasterio de Tinemuthe.

Rex Joannes fodiendo apud Corbrige thesauros sed frus-
tra quaesivit.

Scotti prioratum Hagustaldensem cum tota villa incendio
1296. destruxerunt anno Domini 1296.

[* Admundus in MS.]   [† Manset in MS.]
[‡ Muru in MS.]

Nomina episcoporum Hagustaldensis ecclesiae.*

Wilfridus.
Eata.
Tunbertus.
Joannes, qui et postea episcopus Ebor. post quem Wilfridus iterum Hagustal. episcopus.
Acca.
Freohebertus.
Alchmundus.
Tilbertus.
Ethelbertus.
Heardredus.
Eanbertus.
Tidferdus, cujus† Danis omnia late depopulantibus, cessavit episcopatus Hagustaldensis.
Thomas archiepiscopus Eboracensis induxit canonicos regulares in ecclesiam‡ Hagustaldensem anno Dom. 1112.   1112.
Henrici regis 13. Aschetillus primus Prior Hagustaldensis ecclesiae, Robertus Pisethe secundus.
Translatae fuerunt relliquiae Accae§ ex coemiterio in   fo. 61 b.
ecclesiam Hagustaldensem post ducentos‖ et quinquaginta annos per Alfredum presbyterum Dunelmensem.
Richardus Macon fuit rector parochialis ecclesiae de Hexam ante inductos canonicos.

Cummynge to Henley I saw in the valley the priorie of   **Oxfordshire.**
Hurley, a celle to Westminster, standinge on the right ripe   fo. 62 a.
of the Thames.

The bridge at Henley is all of tymbre, as moste parte of the bridgs be ther about. It was of stone, as the foundation shewithe at a low watar.

The Hastings, now Erls of Huntendune, chefe lords of Henley. It was the Lorde Molines, then by decent Peverels, Hungerford, and so Hastyngs.

Plenty of wood and corne about Henley. The soyle chalky and hillinge.

[* Bishops of Hexham.]
[† Hearne suggests that instead of *cujus* either *quo mortuo* or *nunc* should be read.]
[‡ *Ecclesia,* MS.]   [§ *Aite* in MS.]
[‖ *Ducenton* in MS.]

Oxfordshire.
*Gray Domi-
nus de Rother-
filde, senes-
challus
Edward 3.*

Rotherfeld about a mile from Henley. There is a parke. It is of moste men caulled Rotherfelde Gray, by cawse that one of the Gray of Ruthyne came to be owner of [it].* Sum put this addition onto it, Gray Murdach, sayynge that this Murdach was a bysshopc, and in comprobation of it there be dyverse myters sene in the haule in Rotherfeld.

There appere enteringe into the maner place on the righte hand 3. or 4. very olde towers of stone, a manifest token that it was sume tyme a castle. Ther is a very large courte buyldyd about with tymbar and spacyd withe brike; but this is of a latter worke. Men of Henley may yet remembar that it was the Lord Lovel's pocession. Sens by attainture it cam by gifte to Knolls.

Stoner[a] is a 3. miles out of Henley. Ther is a fayre parke, and a waren of connes, and fayre woods. The mansion place standithe clyminge on an hille, and hathe 2. courtes buyldyd withe tymbar, brike and flynte. Syr Waltar Stonar now pocessor of it hathe augmentyd and strengthed the howse. The Stoners hathe longe had it in possessyon. Syns one Fortescue invadyd it by mariage of an heire generall of the Stoners, but aftar dispocessyd.

fo. 62 b.

From Oxford to Hinkesey fery a quartar of a myle or more. Ther is a cawsey of stone fro Oseney to the ferie, and in this cawsey be dyvers bridges of plankes. For there the streme of Isis breketh into many armelets. The fery selfe is over the principale arme or streame of Isis.

*Bleselles
Leghe.*

Bleselles Legh[b] a litle village is a 3. mile from Hinkesey fery in the highe way from Oxford to Ferendune, alias Farington.[c] At this Legh be very fayre pastures and woods. The Blesells hathe bene lords of it syns the tyme of Edwarde the First or afore, and there they dyd enhabite. The place is all of stone, and stondithe at the west end of the paroche churche. Blesells were lords also of Rodecote[d] apon the ryver of Isis by Ferendune, wher hathe bene a stronge pile, and now a mansion place. The Blesells cam out of Province in Fraunce, and were men of activitye in

[* Hearne; not in MS.]

feates of armes, as it apperithe in monuments at Legh how **Oxfordshire.**
he fawght in listes with a strange knight that chalengyd hym,
at the whiche deade the Kynge and Quene at that tyme of
England were present. The Blesells were countyd to have
pocessyons of 400. marks by the yere. The last heire male
of them was a-lyve *in hominum memoria*. Legh and Rodecote
cam by mariage of an heire generall of the Blesells onto
Fetiplace.

From Legh I rode halfe a myle and cam to Towkey,[a]
where had ben a village. The churche or chapell yet
remayneth, and ther by in a wood was a manor place now
clene downe. It longethe now as a ferme to Magdalen Colledge in Oxford.

I rode thens a 2. myles and halfe thorowghe fayre champayne ground, frutefull of corne, to Newbridge on Isis.
The ground ther al about lyethe in low medowes often ovar-
flowne by rage of reyne. Ther is a longe cawsye of stone
at eche end of the bridge. The bridge it selfe hathe vi. **fo. 63 a.**
greate arches of stone. Thens I passyd by a fayre mylle a
furow lengthe of, and ther semyd to cum downe a broke
that joynithe with Isis about New Bridge.

Thens 4. myles or more to Whiteney,[b] where is a market
and a fayre churche with a goodly piramis of stone.

Thens a myle to Crauley[c] Bridge of 2. arches of stone
over Winruche[d] ryver that goithe by Whitney. Crauley village is hard by the bridge.

Thens about a myle to Mynster[e] village havynge the
name of Lovell somtyme lorde of it. There is an auncient
place of the Lovels harde by the churche. Mastar Vinton
of Wadeley by Farington hathe it of the Kynge in ferme.

Thens I rode a 3. myles or 4. thrwghe the forest of Wich-
wood longinge to the Kynge, where is plentye of wood and
fallow dere. This forest longed to the Bewchamps Erls of
Warwike, and so dyd Burforde towne.

Then commynge out of the forest I enteryd into a soyle
champayne on every syde, in the whiche, as in slypes, were
some pretty groves and woods.

---

[a] Tubney seems intended.   [b] Witney.
[c] Crawley.   [d] Windrush.
     [e] Minster Lovell.

Oxfordshire. Bekington[a] Maner Place at Bekington with a fayr mille. Bruerne watar renithe by it.

And thus passynge scant 2. mile, I cam to a place caulyd Borow[b] apon the top of a mcane hill, where apperyd a greate ditche to the compace of a quartar of a myle, in the whiche dyd grow very good corne. First I toke it for a campe of men of warre. Aftar I marked in some placis of the toppe of the diche as there had bene a waull set on it. And I marked a place as where a gate had bene in to it toward the este. In dede it was nothinge but a campe of men of warre, and ther is a nothar on the same downes. So halfe a good myle to Cerceden[c] village.

fo. 63 b.
Chirchehille village and lordshipe longginge to Mastar Barentyn is hard be Cerceden. Cerceden was first Golafer's maner, then, as I remembar, Browning's. Horne of late made the faire howse there of sqwarid stone.*

Bruern Abbey a mile of, hard on the right ripe of the river.[d] Good pasture, corne, woodde.

Stow in the Wolde is about a 3. myles of from it.

Burford is a market a 3. myles from Bruerne. Bewchamps Erles of Warwyke were lords of it, and also of the forest of Wichewood. Some say that the Spencers and the Lovels had some dominion in it. Ther is notable quarye of fine stone about Burford.

There was a place in Burford caullyd the Priorie. Horman the Kyng's barbar hathe now the lands of it.

Langley is a myle from Burford. There remayne tokens of an olde maner place in the syde of the forest of Wichewood.

Fro Cerceden to Chepingnorton a 3. good myles. Croftes were the auncient lords of this Norton, syns Rodeney, and then Cometoun that bought it.

Hocnorton[e] a 3. myles all by champaine fro Chepingnorton. There is a fayre parke and an old manar place. It longed to Chaucer; then to the Poles Duks of Southefolke by mariage. Now from Brandon to the Kynge by exchange.

[* As to Sarsden and these families see vol. ii, pp. 2-4.]

---

[a] ? Bledington and the Evenlode. [b] Knoll-bury.
[c] Sarsden.   [d] Evenlode r.   [e] Hook Norton.

Cold norton priory about a myle from Chepingnorton. **Oxfordshire.**
This priory is now impropriate onto Brase-nose College in
Oxford. Aboute a mile beyond the priory is Mastar
Ascheles maner place.

To Tue [a] a 3. myles, where Mastar Reynesford dwellithe.
From Cerceden to Oxford a 15. miles.

From Oxford to Abbandune a 4. myles.* This towne *Abandune.*
stondithe on the right rype of Isis in Barkeshire. The towne **Berkshire.**
of very olde tyme was caullyd Seusham,[b] syns Abendune of
one Aben a monke heremite that began a monasterye in
those quartars, as they imagine right folishely. Tretwthe it
is that one Eanus a noble Saxon began to builde a litle
monasterye by the permissyon of Cissa his master, Kynge of
the Saxons, at a place caullid Chisewel† a 2. myles from
Abbingdon northe northeste in the foote way to Oxford.
The place after not thought convenient, it was translatid on **fo. 64 a.**
to Scusham, wher apon the new monasterye beynge buyldyd,
it was caullyd Abbandune, *i.e., Abbatis oppidum.*

And not longe aftar thys tyme was the nunnery buildyd
at Abbandune on the lifte ripe ot Uche,[c] alias Cooho, ryver,
as at the mowthe of it into Isis the great streme. This place
of nunnes was dedicate unto Saincte Helene, the name wher
of yet remaynithe.

Bothe the abbay and the nunnery were destroyed by the
Danes. Whithar the nunnery were reedified or no I can
not tell. The abbay rose agayne, but it was a pore thinge
ontill suche tyme as Kynge Edgare by the counsel of Ethel-
wolde Byshope of Winchester dyd richely encrese it.

There was one Faritius a straunger and phisician made
Abbate of Abbendune a certeyne tyme after the Conqweste.‡

[* This account of Abingdon should be read with that in vol. i,
pp. 120-122. Leland seems to have found the book "De Gestis Abbatum
de Abbingdune" at the time of this visit, and to have made use of it.
See the short history "De Abbatibus Abbendune," printed in Appendix II to "Chronicon Monasterii de Abingdon," ed. Jos. Stevenson,
vol. ii, Rolls Series, 1858.]
[† See vol. ii, p. 152, Chilswell, the scene of a notable battle in
early times.]
[‡ A.D. 1101.]

[a] Tew. [b] Or Seukesham. [c] Ock.

76 LELAND'S ITINERARY

Berkshire. He remevyd the olde churche that stode then more northerlye where now the orchard is, and made the este parte and transepte of a-new, only adorninge it [with *] diverse smaul marble pillers. Anon aftar cam an abbate, and seynge the howse not sufficiently servcd withe water, devised to turne the streme of Isis, and at the last brought it on to the very abbay syde, and partely thrwghe it. The chefe streme of Isis rane afore betwixt Andersey Isle and Culneham,[a] even where now the southe end is of Culneham.

Oxfordshire. The othar arme that brekethe oute of Isis aboute a quarter of a mile above Culneham, and then cummithe downe Culneham thoroughe Culneham bridge selfe, is now the lesse peace of the hole river. In greate flods and brakkes of water waulls Culneham Water goith partely to the old botom of Isis, and then ther be 3. stremes. There was of olde tyme a fortres or pile lyke a castle in Andersey by south west of Abbandune, sett as almoste in the mydle betwixte the olde and new botom of Isis. The ground that it stoode on is a medow agayne S. Helens of a qwartar of a myle ovar. Sum parte of this fortrese stode aftar the Conqwest, and there were kepte the Kyngs hauks and hownds.

Berkshire. There was an Abbate of Abbandune that perceyvyd welle how it had and shoulde noy the monasterie, and gave the Kinge Suttoun lordeshipe there by for it in exchaunge. It is a myle and halfe lower then Abbandune on the right ripe of Isis in Barkeshire.

There is now an olde barne where the castelet or fortresse *fo. 64 b.* stoode. The place of the common people is yet caullid the Castelle of the Rhae, *à flu. praeterlabente.* The weste parte of the churche of Abbandune monasterie was reedified by one William Asschendune, abbate there. S. Edward the Martir's reliques for the moste parte were kept in Abbing-don, where sum sayethe he was in his tendre age brought up. *Besilles.* Ther were of the Blessells buried there.

All the lands almoste betwene Ainsham[b] and Dorcester

[* *With* not in MS.]

---

[a] Culham.   [b] Eynsham.

longed unto Abbandune. The rents of the abbay were almoste 2000. li. by the yere. Berkshire.

Abbingdoun monasterye upon a ple for fraunchese was spoyled by men of Abbandun, of Newbiry, and of Oxforde; for the whiche great punishement was taken.

Ther was a parke at Radeley longinge onto Abbyndoun, which was disparkid by reason that the scollars of Oxford muche resortyd thethar to hunt.

The chefe paroche churche of Abbyngdon of old tyme was Saint Nicholas by thabbey. The abbat of Abendoun made the hospitall of S. John Baptiste agayne it. This hospitall hathe bene annexid to S. Nicolas. Ther be 12 men in this hospitall.

Seint Helens is now a paroche churche, and to it is the gretyst resorte of all the towne.

At suche tyme as the olde course of the streme of Isis was changyd there were found dyvers straunge thyngs, and amonge them a crosse with an inscription. The nunnrye stode in the very place where now the hospitall is at S. Helincs.

Of auncient tyme there was no bridge to passe over Isis at Abbandune, but a ferie, and then was the way from Glocester to London not thorowgh Abbendune as it is now, and so to Dorchestar, but thorowg the notable towne of Wallingforde. Ther were dyvers mischauncis sene at this passage.

Ex tabula pensili.

Anno 4. Henrici 5, pontes de Bordforde et Culhamforde* prope Abbandune incepti sunt autore rege anno Dom. 1416.†

Dyvers persones drowned at the fery afore the bridge was made. The inhabitaunts of Abbandune askid at the Courte remedie for a bridge and obteyned. *Culneham Hithe fery.*

[* See before, pp. 1, 2.]

[† This date is in another hand than Stow's. At this point Hearne, who doubtless knew Abingdon well, appends a long and quaintly interesting note giving additional particulars of the building of Culham bridge, together with the full text of the Latin and English verses inscribed on the table in the hospital, cited above by Leland, which still existed in 1712. The reader will find this note at length in the Appendix to this Part.]

Pons inchoatus die S. Albani.

Geffray Barbar of Abbandune gave monie chefly toward makynge the bridge and procurynge lands for the mayn teynaunce of it. Ther wrowght that somer 300 men on the bridge.

Hactenus ex tabula.

Sum say at Abbandune that Geffray Barbar was as the greatest foundar of the hospitall of S. Helene. Sum say that one Joannes de S. Helena aboute that tyme had 2 dowghters, and for lakke of issue of them it shoulde go to mayntaynaunce of the hospitall and the bridgs. The land devolvid to that use.

A bridge of stone over the broke of Oche[a] by S. Helene's Hospitale.

A goodly pyramis is the Market Place.

There were, and yet appere, 2. camps of men of warre by Abbandune.

The one is Serpenhil a quartar of a mile by este northe est oute of the toune in a fote way to . . . Here, as it is sayde there comonly, was a battayle betwyxt the Danes and the Saxons. Parte of the trenches of the campe be yet seene.

The other is caullid Barow a litle by weste oute of Abbandune toward Ferendune. Here be also the trenches yet apperinge.

Sum say that thabbate of Abbandune sente a bande of men to one of thes camps, where by the Danes were vanquishid, and lands were gyven to the abbay for the victory.

From Oxforde to Hanney a 8. mils, a 5. mils by hilly ground well wooddid and frutefull of corne, and other 3. mils by low levelle ground in sum partes marschy.

Or ever I cam at Hanney by a mile I passid over a broke, and other this was Ocke Broke that goithe to Abbandune, risinge in the vale of White Horse, or ells it rennithe in to Ocke. It ran from northe west in to the southe.

Thens a 2. myles by low wooddy ground unto Wanetinge,[b] that standithe on the right ripe of a praty broke that goithe

---

[a] Ock r.   [b] Wantage.

downe to Abbandune, distante a 6. or 7. mils from Berkshire.
Wantage.

Ther be 2. churches in this market toune in one chirche
yarde, but the one is but a chapelle. The Lorde Fitzguarine
is one of the chefiste lords of the towne, and of that name
and lyne be 2. sepulchers in the paroche churche.

Thens a 6. myls to Cheping Lanburne [a] a poore Friday
market by hills well cornyd and some wodds; and passinge
the better parte of the way I sawe a greate warren of conies
longginge unto Mastar Estesex, who is lord of the towne
by his mothar the sole dowghtar and heyre of Mastar
Rogers, by whom he hathe bettar then 300. marks of lands
by the yere.

Lamburne water risithe a litle by northe above the towne, fo. 65 b.
levinge it on the righte ripe, and goinge thens a 10. myles
to Dunington,[b] and a litle lower in to Kenet ryver.

From Lameburne on to Ramesbyry [c] towne about a 5. Wiltshire.
mills, firste by champayne grounde fruteful of corne, then
by hills frutefull of woodd and corne. Kenet [d] towchithe the
towne withe his lifte ripe suopinge in a low botom. There
is a fayre and large olde churche in the towne. The Bysshope
of Saresbyri hathe a faire old place halfe a mile upper apon
the lifte ripe of Kenet, that a litle above the place in the
medois makithe out an arme, and a litle benethe the place
resortynge to the hed streme makithe the medois on the
southe syde of the place a *mediamnis* or isle.

There is a right faire and large parke hangynge apon the
clyffe of an highe hille welle woddyd over Kenet, hard on
the southe syde of the place.

Litlecote the Darells chief house is a myle from
Ramesbyri.

From Ramesbyri to Hungerford . . . myls.

From Ramesbyri to Saresbyri good 20. mils.

From Ramesbyri on to Great Bedwine a 3. miles, moste
parte thrwghe the forest of Sauernake.

The towne is prevelegyd with a burges at the Parliament;
yet is it but a poore thinge to syght. There liethe in the
churche in the southe isle one Adam Stoke a famose man,
and a nothar of that lyne by hym under a flatte stone. The

[a] Lambourne.   [b] Donington.   [c] Ramsbury.   [d] Kennet.

Wiltshire. Stokes were lords of Stoke Haule ther by, the lands of whom descendyd on to the Lords Hungarfords; but whereas I harde ons that there was a castelle at Greate Bedwine, I could there heere nothinge of it. Litle Bedwine a myle lower, whither cummith the streame that passinge by Great Bedwine levith it on the right ripe. This watar goithe toward Kenet. And Hungerford is a 3. mils from Greate Bedwine.

From Bedwine a good mile to Chauburne[a] village, the trew name whereof, as I gesse, shuld be Chaulkeburne. For it risithe and rennythe in chalky ground.

fo. 66 a. The howse of the Choks was firste greatly avaunsyd by Choke chefe Juge of England,[*] that attayned lands to the some of 600. marks by the yere, and kept his chefe howse at Longe Ascheton by Bristow, havynge great furniture of sylvar.

There risethe a litle above Chauburne village a broke that gyvethe name unto it, and levithe it on the right rype, and so goinge about a 2. miles lower resortithe to Bedwine watar, or els by it selfe goithe in to Kenet Ryver. Shauburne is a 3. mils from Hungerforde.

From Ramesbiry onto Marlebyri a 3. miles by hilly grounde, frewtfull of corne and wood. Abowt halfe a myle or I cam onto Marlebyri I passyd ovar a broke that cam downe northewcste from the hills, and so ran by sowthe est into the streme of Kenet about halfe a myle bynethe Marlebyri.

The towne of Marlebyri standithe in lengthe from the toppe of an hille flate este to a valley lyenge flat west.

There is a ruine of a great castell harde at the west ende of the towne, where of the doungeon towre partely yet stondithe. There lay Kynge Edward the . . . at a Parliament tyme.

There is a chappell of S. Martyne at the este ende of the towne.

There is a paroche churche of owr Lady in the mydle of

[* Sir Richard Choke, Justice of Common Pleas, 1461.]

---

[a] Shalbourne.

the towne. The body of this churche is an auncient peace **Wiltshire.**
of worke. Sum fable that it was a nunerye.

The chefe paroche churche of the towne standythe at the
very weste end of it bcynge dedicate onto Seint Peter.

There was a priorye of white chanons caullyd S. Margaret's a letle be southe the towne over Kenet,* where now
dwellythe one Mastar Daniell.

Ther was a howse of Friers in the southe syde of the
towne.

Kenet ryver cummethe doune by the weste end of the
towne from the northe, and so by the botom of the towne
and vale lyenge sowthe, levinge it on the lefte rype, and so
renethe thens by flatte este.

Kenet risithe northe northe west at Selberi[a] Hille botom,
where by hathe be camps and sepultures of men of warre,
as at Aibyri[b] a myle of, and in dyvers placis of the playne.
This Selbyri Hille is about a 5. miles from Marlbyri.

From Marlebyri over Kenet, and so into Sauernake (the **fo. 66 b.**
swete Oke) forest, and a 4. myles or more to Peusey[c] a
good village, and there I passed ovar Avon ryver, and so
by playne champine ground, frutfull of grasse and corne,
especially good whete and barley, and so by a village caullyd
Manifordes,[d] by the whiche Avon rennythe; and so to
Newton[e] village 2. myles and more from Peusey, where also
Avon rennythe levynge it on his lefte rype; and thens
2. myles of passyd by Uphavon,[f] a good village 2. myles
lower. There comythe a litle broke into Avon from northe
west at the est ende of Newton churche. The course of it
is latly changyd to the great commoditie of the village lyinge
lowe, and afore sore trowbled with water in wynter.

From Newton to Hilcote an hamlet of the same paroche
halfe a myle.

The[n]† a 7. myles to the Vyes[g] by champayne ground. I *The Vies.*
passyd or I cam nere the Vyes by a broke the whiche goythe
in to Avon ryver by Uphavon vilage.

[* Kevet MS.]   [† MS. has only *The.*]

---

[a] Silbury.   [b] Avebury or Abury.   [c] Pewsey.
[d] Manningford.   [e] North Newnton.   [f] Upavon.
             [g] The Devizes.

Wiltshire.   The towne of Vies standithe on a ground sumwhat clyvinge, and most occupied by clothiars.

The beawty of it is all in one strete.

The market is very celebrate.

Ther is a castell on the southe west syde of the towne
stately avauncyd apon an highe ground, defendyd partly by
nature, and partly withe dykes the yere * where of is cast
up a slope, and that of a greate height to defence of the
waulle.

This castle was made in Henry the first dayes by one
Rogar Bysshope of Salisbyrye,† Chaunselar and Treaswrar to
the Kynge. Suche a pece of castle worke so costly and
strongly was nevar afore nor sence set up by any bysshope
of England. The kepe or dungeon of it set upon an hille
cast by hand is a peace of worke of an incredible coste.
There appere in the gate of it 6. or 7. placis for porte
colacis, and muche goodly buyldyng was in it. It is now in
ruine, and parte of the front of the towres of the gate of the
kepe and the chapell in it were caried full unprofitably onto
the buyldynge of Mastar Bainton's place at Bromeham ᵃ
scant 3. myles of.

fo. 67 a.   There remayne dyvers goodly towres yet in the utter walle
of the castle, but all goynge to ruine.

The principall gate that ledithe in to the towne is yet of
a greate strengthe, and hathe placis for 7. or 8. porte
colices.

Ther is a fayre parke by the castle.

The forest of Blakemore lyethe in a botom toward northe
west, not far from the towne.

I saw as I went out of the towne Bromeham Haul lyenge
in a botom about a 3. myles of.

Steple   From the Vies to Steple Assheton a 6. myles by cham-
Ascheton.   paine, but frutefull grownde and good wood plenty in some
places. It is a praty litle market towne, and hathe praty
buyldinge.

[* *Id est*, eare.—*Hearne.* That is, the earth thrown up by the
digging.—L. T. S.]
[† Roger, bishop, 1107, died 1139.]

ᵃ Bromham. See vol. i, p. 133.

It standithe muche by clothiars.

There is in it a very fayre churche, buyldyd in the mynd of men now lyvynge.

The spired steple of stone is very fayre and highe, and of that it is cawllyd Steple Asscheton. Robart Longe clothyar buyldyd the northe isle, Waltar Lucas clothiar buildyd the sowthe isle of theyr proper costes. The abbey of Ramesey[a] in Hamptonshire had bothe parsonage impropriate, and the hole lordshipe.

Syr Thomas Semar hathe it now of the Kyngs almoste withe the hole hundred of Horwelle, alias Wharwelldoun,[b] with muche fayre woods.

Broke Place.

From Steple Asscheton to Brooke Haule a bout a 2. myle by woody ground. There was of very auncient tyme an olde maner place wher Brooke Hall is now, and parte of it yet appearithe, but the new buyldynge that is there is of the erectynge of the Lorde Steward unto Kynge Henry the vii. The wyndowes be full of rudders, peradventure it was his badge or token of the Amiraltye. There is a fayre parke, but no great large thynge. In it be a great nombar of very fayre and fyne greynyd okes apte to sele howses.

Westbyry Hundrid.

Westbyri a smale market towne is a myle of, and of it the hundred there berithe the name.

Wermister[c] a principall market for corne is 4. myles from Brookehaull, a myle to Westbyry, and so 3. myles forthe.

fo. 67 b.
Bissus flu.

The broke that renithe by Brooke is properly caulyd Bisse, and risethe at a place namyd Bismouth a 2. myles above Brooke village, an hamlet longynge to Westbyry paroche. Thens it cummithe onto Brooke village; and so a myle lower onto Brooke Haule, levinge it hard on the right ripe, and about a 2. miles lower it goith to . . .

Hedington[d] village and priorie a boute a 2. myles from Brooke Haul by . . .

From Brooke Haulle onto Westbyri by low ground havinge wood, pasture and corne a mile and halfe. It is the hedd towne of the hundrede to whome it givethe name. In it is kept ones a weeke a smale market. Ther is a large churche. The towne stondithe moste by clothiers.

[a] Romsey.   [b] Whorwelsdown.
[c] Warminster.   [d] Edington.

Somerset-shire.

Ther risythe 2. springs by Westbyri, one by sowthe, and an othar as by southe west, and sone metinge togethar go abowte Bradley vilage a mile and halfe lower into Bisse Broke that rennithe by Brooke Haule, and so to Troug bridge,[a] and then into Avon.

Bradestoke or Bradeford the praty clothinge towne on Avon is a 2. myles of.

From Trowghbridge onto Bathe by very hilly grownd a 7. miles levinge the wodds and Farley parke and castle on the lyfte hand. And by the way I rode ovar Freshe fore[b] bridge of 2. or 3. faire new arches of stone, and this was a 3. miles from Throughbridge, and a 2. myles beyonde that in the very piche of the botom of a very stepe hill I passyd a wylde brooket rennynge on stones. Thens a myle of in the way was a notable quarey, and thens a playne, and then by a stepe botom onto Bathe about a myle.

From Bathe by champain to Kelston a good village in Wilshire a 3. milles, where Avon goithe somewhat a-lofe on the lifte hand in the botom.

Gloucester-shire.

From Kelston to Biton village in Glocestershire a 2. myles.

A litle above Bitton I passyd over a brooke that at hand semid to come from the northe and to go into Avon by southe.

Ther was a bridge of 3. arches of stone ovar this litle broke.

Thens to Hanham a bout 2. miles.

fo. 68 a.

There be dyvers villages togethar caullyd Hanhams, but withe a difference. At this Hanham dwellythe one Ser John Newton in a fayre olde mannar place of stone caullyd Barrescourte.[c]

Thyngs lernyd of Ser John Newton.

Newton's very propre name is Caradoc.[d] The name of Newton cam by this error and use, by cawse the ground-fathar of Ser John Newton dwellyd, or was borne, at Trene-with in Poise Land.[e]

Somerset.

Gurney was lord of Stoke Hamden, and there he lyethe

---

[a] Trowbridge.   [b] Freshford.   [c] Barr's Court.
[d] Or Cradock.   [e] Powis-land.

buryed in a Colegiate chapell by the ruyns of his castle. *Somerset-*
He was chefe foundar, as some say, of the howse of Gaunts *shire.*
at Bristow. He was foundar of the priorye of nunes in
Somersetshire caullyd Baron Gurney. He was lord of White-
combe, and of Richemonte Castle by Mendepe, 5. miles
from Wells. All the buyldynge of this castle is clene
downe. It cam aftar to Hampton, and then to Caradoc,
alias Newton.

The forest of Kyngs Wodd cummythe just onto Barrescourte, Mastar Newton's howse.

Ther were of ancient tyme 4. comptyd as chefe lords of
Mendepe. First the Kynge, and his parte cam to the bysshope
of Bathe as by a fee ferme. Glastenbyre had a nothar parte.
Bonvill Lord Bonvile, and now Graye Lord Marques of
Dorset was the third owner. The fourthe was Gurney; now
Caradoc, alias Newton.

The lengthe of Mendepe from este to weste by estima- *Mendepe*
tion a 20. myls, and wher it is brodeste a 6. myles, in many *Hills.*
placis lesse.

There is apon the tope of one of Mendipe Hills a place *Dolbyn.*
encampyd caullyd Dolbyn, famous to the people, thus
saynge:

> If Dolbyri dyggyd ware,
> Of golde shuld be the share.

It is 2. mils from Banwelle.

Gurney usyd to ly muche at Richemonte Castle. It
stondithe in the rote of Mendype este from Bristow in the
paroche of Este Harptre by the paroche churche of it. There
standithe yet a pece of the dungeon of it. Syr John Newton
dyggyd up many olde foundations of it toward buyldynge of *fo. 68 b.*
a new howse hard therby caullyd Estewood.

There is a nothar village by Est Harptre caulyd West
Harptre Gurney; and there be the variete of armes that
Gurney gave in the glasse wyndowes, and his cote armure.

At suche tyme as Gurney lyvyd the Lord Fitzwarine was
mastar of Mendepe foreste by inheritaunce, and it was well
furnishid withe dere; but anon aftar for riots and tres-
passys done in huntynge it was deforestyd, and so yet remaynethe.

Gurney's lands cam by this means onto Newton. One

Newton a man of fayre lands inhabitynge at Wyke toward
Banwell had a yongar brothar that maryed one of the
dowghtars and heyres of Hampton, and wyfe afore to one
of the Chokks that dycd without ysswe by hym. This was
the yonggest dowghtar of the 3. that Hampton lette; and
yet she beinge maried onto Newton, fathar to Ser John
Newton, fortunyd to have all the thre partes.

The very lands of Newton of Wyke be discendyd by heires
generals onto Ser Henry Chapell, sonn to Syr Giles that
dwellyd at Wike, and to Mastar Grifithe of Northamptonshire that hathe Braybroke Castle. So that Newton of Bar-
courte hathe no parts of Newton's lands of Wike.

From Barrescourte onto Bristow a 3. myles by hilly and
stony ground withe feren ovar growne in dyvers placis.

The Site of Brightestow.

The castle and moste parte of the towne by northe stondithe apon a grownd metely eminent betwyxt the ryvers of
Avon and Fraw, alias Frome.

There rysethe an hill of an notable highte[a] in respecte of
the plote of the towne selfe from Frome bridge on, so goythe
up alonge onto Seint Austin's, alias the Trinitie, the cathedrall churche, and there endithe.

Gates in the Waulls of Brightstow.

fo. 69 a.
There be in sum partes of the towne doble waulls, a token
that the towne hathe bene augmentyd.

Newgate (as me thinkythe) is in the utar waull by the
castle, and a chapelle over it. It is the prison of the citie.

S. John Gate. A churche of eche syde of it. S. John
Churche. It is hard on the northe syd of it, and there be
cryptae.

S. Gils Gate be southe west of the key where Frome
renithe.

S. Leonard's Gate * and a paroche churche ovar it.

S. Nicholas Gate where is a churche *cum cryptis*.

[* *Gats*, MS.]

---

[a] Brandon Hill.

There be the inner gates of the old towne *cis Sabrinam* as the towne standithe *in dextra ripa defluentis Avonae.* **Gloucester-shire.**

In the utter waullis. Pety Gate. From gate in the uttar waulls. Marsche Gate *è regione Avonae.* The third is callyd . . .

In the waulle *ultra pontem et Avonam* be 2. gates: Radde-clif Gate and Temple Gate; and a greate towre caullyd [T]ower * harrys, at the very ende of the waulle *in ipsa ripa Avonae è regione pontis ad arcem supra Frai brachiolum.*

The Castle of Brightestow.

The ryver of Frome ran sumetyme from the were by the castle, where now is a stone bridge doune by the este syde of it; and so doithe yet a litle armelet of it brekynge out, and almoste the hole streme goithe by the northe syde of the castle, and there goithe by New Gate under an arche.

In the castle be 2. cowrtes. In the utter courte, as in the northe west parte of it, is a greate dungeon tower, made, as it is sayde, of stone browght out of Cane in Normandye by the redde Erle of Glocestar.

A praty churche and muche longging in 2. area. On the southe syde of it a great gate, a stone bridge, and 3. bulle-warks *in laeva ripa ad ostium Frai.*

There be many towres yet standynge in bothe the cowrtes; but all tendithe to ruine.

Paroche Churchis within the Waulls of Brightstowe *cis Avonam.*

S. Nicholas; S. Leonard; S. Lawrence; S. John Bapt.† Christe Churche, alias Trinitie; S. Audoene; S. Werborow; Al Halowes; S. Marie Porte; S. Peters; S. Stephane *intra secunda moenia.*

Ultra Avonam.

S. Thomas *apostolus.*

Templum. Wher as now S. Lawrence Churche it was sumetyme a churche, as it is sayde, S. Sepulchri, where was a nunry. And thereby in the same lane dwellyd the Jewes, **fo. 69 b.**

[* *Ower,* MS.]   [† *Papt.* MS.]

and theyr temple, or sinagoge, is yet sene there, and now is
a ware howse.

Paroche Churches in the Suburbs.

S. Philippus within *cis Avonam* Ford's Gate, now *procul
ab Avona.*
S. Jacobus by Brodemede Strete.
S. Nicholas northe from Frome Gate in *supercilio montis.*
S. Augustines a paroche churche on the grene by the
cathedrale churche.
The paroche churche of Seint Marks in the Gaunts.

Ultra Avonam.

Redcliffe longe pulcherrina omnium ecclesia.

Howsys sumtyme of Religion in Bristow.

*Fanum Augustini, nunc S. Trinitatis. Inscriptio in porta:
Rex Henricus 2. et dominus Robertus filius Hardingi, filii
regis Deciae, hujus Monasterii primi fundatores.*
Barkeley.   Ther be 3. tombes of the Barkleyes in the southe isle
agayne the quiere.

Fanum S. Jacobi.

It standithe by Brode Meade by northe from the castle
on an hilly grownd, and the ruines of it standithe hard but-
tynge to the este ende of the paroche churche.
Robertus consull Cownte of Glocestarshire buryed in the
quiere in the myddle of it, in a sepulchre of gray marble set
up apon 6. pillers of a smaull hethe.* In his tumbe was
found a writynge in parchement concernynge the tyme of
his deathe, and what he was. A brewer in Bristow hathe
this writynge.
This S. James was a celle to Tewkesberye.

Non longe à dextra ripa Frai.

S. Magdalene's a howse of nunes, suppressyd, on the
northe syde of the towne. This howse was suppressyd of
late tymes, when suche as were under 300. marks of rent

[* *I.e.,* "height."]

by the yere were putte downe. Mastar Wiks dwellythe in *Gloucester-shire.*
this howse.

The Gaunts.

One Henry Gawnt a knight sometyme dwellynge not far *Gaunte.*
from Brandon Hill by Brightstow erectyd a college of pristes
withe a mastar on the grene by Seint Augustines. And sone
aftar he chaungyd the first foundation into a certeyne kynde *fo. 70 a.*
of religion, and was governowr of the howse hymselfe, and
lyethe buried in the vesturye undar a flate stone. This had
at the desolucion of the howse 300. marks of land by the
yere. This Henry had a brothar cawlyd Ser Mawryce
Gawnte. He was foundar of the Blake Friers in Brightftow.*

Hospitales in ru.†

Fanum Barptholomaei.
Fanum 3ᵐ. regum juxta Barptolomeanes extra Fromegate.
Aliud non procul in dextra ripa Frai qua itur ad fanum
Jacobi in Lionsmede Strete.ᵃ
One in Temple Strete.
An othar withe out Temple Gate.
An othar by Seint Thomas Strete.
S. John's by Radeclife.
An hospitall S. Trinitatis hard within Lafford's Gate.
The Tukkers Hospitall in Temple.
The Wevers Hospitall in Temple Strete.
Ther was an hospitall of olde tyme where of late a nunrye
was caullyd S. Margarets.
The Grey Friers howse was on the right ripe of From
watar not far from Seint Barptolomes Hospitall.
The Blacke Friers stode a litle highar then the Gray on *Gaunte.*
From in the right ripe of it. Ser Maurice Gaunt, elder
brothar to Ser Henry Gaunt, foundar of the Gaunts, was
foundar of this.
The White Friers stode on the right rype of Frome agayn
the key.

[* See vol. iv, p. 130; and Ricart's Kalendar, Camd. Soc., p. 56.]
[† So without a point in the MS. Perhaps it should read *ruin.*—
Hearne.]

———————

ᵃ Lewin's mead.

The Augustine Friers howse was harde by the Temple
Gate withein it northe weste.

Chapels in and aboute Brightstow *cis Avon.*

Thu Buku Chupell by cawse it stoode by the Bake" by
Avon. It longethe onto Seint Nicholas.

S. Georgis Chapell joyning to the towne howse.

A chapell ovar the new gate.

Owr Lady Chappell on Avon Bridge.

S. Sprites Chapell in Radclef churche yard; this ons a
paroche afore the buyldinge of Radclyfe grete new churche.

S. Brandon's Chapell, now defacyd, on Brandon Hill a
qwartar of a myle by west the Gaunts.

fo. 70 b. Bedemister[b] a mile out of the towne by est southe este is
now mother churche to Radeclife, to S. Thomas within the
towne, and Leighe without the towne.

Bridges in Bristow.

The greate bridge of 4. stone arches ovar Avon.

Were Bridge on From hard by the northe est parte of the
Castle of Bristowe.

There brekythe an arme out of Frome a but shot above
Were Bridge, and renithe thrwghe a stone bridge of one
great arche, and there by at New Gate the othar parte of
From reninge from Were Bridge cummithe undar a nothar
stone, and serving the mille hard without New Gate metithe
with the othar arme.

The Haven of Brightstow.

The Haven by Avon flowithe about a 2. miles above
Brightstowe Bridge.

Seint Anns ferye is a bout a myle and halfe above the
towne of Brightstowe.

Keinesham a 5. miles beyond Bristow *in ripa sinistra
Avonae.*

The shipps of olde tyme cam only up by Avon to a place
caullyd the Bak,[a] where was and is depthe enowghe of watar;
but the botom is very stony and rughe sens by polecye they

---

[a] The Back, a riverside street.   [b] Bedminster.

trenchid somwhat a-lofe by northe west of the old key on
Avon *anno* 1247. and in continuance bringynge the cowrse
of From ryver that way hathe made softe and whosy har-
borow for grete shipps.

Hunge Rode aboute a 3. miles lower in the haven then
Brightstow. At this rode be some howsys *in dextra Avon
ripa.*

About a myle lowere is Kyng's Rode, and there be also
some howses *in dextra ripa Avonae.*

Ther is a place almoste agayne Hung Rode caulyd Port-
chestar, where Hardynge and Robert his sunne had a fayre
howse, and a nothar in Brightstow towne.

Sum thinke that a great pece of the depenes of the haven
from S. Vincents to Hung Rode hathe be made by hand.
Sum say that shipps of very auncient tyme cam up to S.
Stephanes Churche in Brightstow.

A Remembraunce of memorable Acts done in Brightstow,
    out of a litle Boke of the Antiquities of the Howse of
    Calendaries in Brightstow.*

The antiquites of the Calendaries were for the moste parte
brent by chaunce.

The Calendaries, otharwyse cawlyd the Gilde, or Frater-
nite of the Clergie and Comonaltye of Brightstow, and it
was firste kepte in the Churche of the Trinitie, sene at Al
Halows.

The originall of this fraternitie is out of mynd.

Ailarde Mean and Bitrick his sunne Lords of Brightestow
afore the Conqueste.

Haymon Erle of Glocestar aftar the Conquest and Lorde
of Brightstow.

Robertus consul, sunne to Hamon, was Erle of Glocestar,
and Lorde of Brightstow, and foundar of the monasterye of
Tewkesbyry.

Gloucester-
shire.

Barkeley.

fo. 71 a.

[* Though many of the notes on this page and the next were taken
by Leland from "The Maire of Bristowe is Kalendar" by R. Ricart
(*circa* 1480), and one passage is quoted in full, I do not feel sure that
the "litle boke" was Ricart's book itself. Leland must have seen other
records of Bristol, especially of a semi-religious house. Regarding the
Gild of Kalendars see Ricart's Kalendar (Camd. Soc., 1872), pp. v-vii,
73, and Toulmin Smith's "English Gilds," p. 287.

Robertus consull lorde of Brightstow Castle, and foundar of S. James Priorie in the northe suburbe of Brightstow.

Kynge Stephan toke the towne of Brightstow by force from Robert consull.

In the tyme of Kynge Henry the 2. Robert Erle of Glocestar (bastard sunne to Henry the First) and Robert Hardinge translatyd the Fraternitie of the Calendaries from the Trinitie onto the Churche of Al-Hallows. At this tyme were scholes ordeyned in Brightstow by them for the conversion of the Jewes, and put in the ordre of the Calenderis and the Maior.

Hardinge foundyd the monasterye of S. Augustine at Brightstow, and to it was appropriate the churche of Al-Hallows.

Gwalo Cardinale, a Romaine Legate, after the coranation of Henry the third at Glocester cam to Brightstow, and kept a synode there *tempore Henrici Blesensis episcopi Wigorn.*

William Erle of Glocestar, founder of the monasterye of Cainesham, gave the praefecture and mastarshipe of the schole in Brightstow to Cainesham, and tooke it from the Calenderies.

Conducts in Bristow *cis pontem*.

S. John's hard by S. John's Gate.
The Key Pipe, with a very fair castellet.
Al-Halow Pipe hard by the Calendaries without a castelle.
S. Nicolas Pipe withe a castellet.

Ultra pontem.

Redclif Pipe with a castlet hard by Redclife Churche withe out the gate.

An othar pipe withe owte Radclif Gate havinge no castelle.

Another by Porte Waulle withoute the waulle.

Porte Waulle is the fairest parte of the towne waulle.

The sayinge is that * certein bochers made a fair peace of this waull; and it is the highest and strongest peace of all the towne waulls.

[* MS. has *the.*]

"The yere of owr Lorde 1247. was the trenche made and cast of the ryver from the Gybbe Taylor to the Key, by the Comonlty as well of Redclyffe syde, as of the towne of Bristoll; and the same tyme thinhabitants of Redclyffe were combined and incorperatyd to the forsayde towne. And as for the grounde of Saynt Augustins syde of the rivar it was geven and grauntyd to the comonalty of the sayde towne by Ser William Bradstone then beinge abbot of the same monastiry for certeyne money therfore payed to hym by the comonaltye, as it apperithe by writynge therof made betwinge the mayor and comonalty, and the abbot and his bretherne." *   *Gloucestershire.*

This yere came the frere prechers first into England.   1221.

This yere on Saynt Bercheus† Day the Frere Mynors   1225. came first into the realme. Also a man of Adderlay fayned hymselfe Christ, whiche was brought to Oxford, and ther crucified.

This yere beganne firste the Order of the Augustine Friers in England.

The Jewe at Tewxbury.

This yere they made new statuts in this towne, and they   1309. called the senesters ‡ bayliffes of the Kings, and they purchased new ground to the towne, and had new prevylegis gyven them of Kinge Edward.

The almese howse without Temple Yate is called Rogers Magdalens of Nonney whiche was founder of it. And the almese howse by Seynt Thomas Churche is called Burton's Almes Howse. Burton maior of the towne and founder is buried in it.

Another hospitall hard by the greye fryers:

And in Temple Streate.

One Shepward a marchaunt of Bristow made the right highe and costly towre of S. Stephenes in Brightstow.

From Brightstowe to Stoke levinge it on the lifte hand a   fo. 72 a. 3. mils or more by grownd wooddy and forest, as of Kinges-

[* Quoted from Ricart's Kalendar, p. 28, with a slight change in the last few words.]

[† A short form of *Bartholomew's* is meant.]

[‡ In 1311, the two "brother" officers of the Mayor of Bristol, hitherto called "senecalli," or stewards, were styled "ballivi." Ricart's Kalendar, p. 33.]

wod. There is a manor place of the Barkeleys in ruine, and
a parke waulle.* Barkeley of the courte is now owner of it.

From thens by muche forest and parteley bareinge grownd
a 2. mils to Magngots ᵃ Filde village be lyke ground. Here
I saw an olde maner place sumtyme longginge to the Blunts.
Syns Husey had it be bying for his sune the heire generale.
Then it came to the Barkeleys, by purchace or exchaunge.

A mile farther by very champaine, frutefull of corne and
grasse, but somewhat scarce of woode, to Coderington, lev-
inge† it by halfe a mile on the lyfte hand. There dwellyd a
late at Coderington a gentleman of that name.

From Coderington to Derham ᵇ a mile and halfe of, where
Mastar Dionise dwellithe, havinge a faire howse of achelei ‡
stones and a parke.

Thens a 2. mils and a halfe to Dodington, where Mastar
Wykes dwellythe and hathe welle restorid his howse withe
fayre buildings. This maner place and land longyd onto
Barkels. It was purchasyd, and now remaynithe to Wiks.

Mastar Walche dwellithe at Litle Sobbyrye a . . . § mils
from Dodington. Thereby is a faire and large campe with
a doble dyke.

It apperithe by record in Malmesbyri that Malmesbyry
was rewardyd for service done in battayle afore the conquest
at Sodbyry hill.

An othar campe at Horton by lesse.

The third by Derham Mastar Dionise house, and all
towchinge on one hilly creaste.

The 4. at Beketbyri a mile and halfe frome Alderley.

Walche is lord of Litle Sodbyri, and hathe a fayr place
there in the syde of Sodbyry highe hill and a parke.

Olde Sodbyri is a mile from it, and there appere ruines of
an olde maner place longynge as the towne dyd to the Erle
of Warwike, now to the Kynge. To the Erles of Warwike
longgid‖ alias Chepinge Sodbyry, a praty litle market towne

[* *Taulle*, MS.]   [† *Beinge*, MS.]
[‡ *I.e.*, acheler or ashlar stones.]
[§ No blank left, but evidently intended.]
[‖ MS. has *loggid*. There was evidently a blank here in Leland's
original for a name.]

ᵃ Mangot's-field.   ᵇ Dyrham.

and thrwghe fayre to Brightstow. There is a parke of the
Kyngs by this towne, sumtyme the Warwiks. Litle wood in
full light nigh the sowthe partes of the campaine soile aboute
Sodbyry. Ther is great plentye by Southe Sodbyri of wood
in a large valey sumtyme thens clerely to Severn, lyinge in
the forest of Kyngs-Wood. The crests of the hilles that ly
by Sobbyri crokith one way to Glocester.

From Chepinge Sobbyry onto Aldersley a clothing village,
where Mastar John Poynts dwellith, beying lord of it. The
Chanseys were sumtyme lords of it, as in Edward the third
dayes.

Kingeswodd stondithe low a good myle from Aldersley.

The ground betwixt enclosyd and metely welle woddyd.
Some clothyars in it, els a litle and a bare village.

Stones clerly fascioned lyke cokills, and myghty shells of
great oysters turned in to stones founde in parte of the hills
este southe est off of Alderley.

The Course of Acton River.

This brooke of sum is caullid Loden,[a] but communely
Laden, and risith above Dodington, where Mastar Wiks
howse is, and so to Acton[b] Mastar Poyntez house a 4.
myles of, and then toward Brightstow takynge the name of
Frome.

There meate 2. waters halfe a myle by nethe Acton at a
mylle.

Sobbyri water cummithe from the hills therby & re †

The water by Alderley is in evidence caullyd Avon,[c] and
goithe to Barkeley.

From Kyngs Woode to Wotton[d] a praty market towne,
welle ocupyed withe clothiars havynge one faire longe strete
and welle buyldyd in it: and it stondithe clyvinge toward the
rotes of an hill.

There be ruines of an olde maner place at Wotton by the

[* The note written in another hand.]
[† This sentence was probably unfinished in Leland's original.]

---

a Laden r., lower down the Frome.   b Iron Acton.
c Little Avon r.   d Wotton-under-Edge.

Gloucester-
shire.
paroche churche. It longgyd ons to the Berkeleys, and
aftar onto the Lords Lisles. Syns forceable recoveryd of
the Lord Berkeley ther by sleinge the Lorde Lisle.

Thens a 2. myles and more by very hilly and woddy
ground to Doursley,[a] where is a praty clothinge towne stondinge on a pece of the clyvinge of a hill, privilegid a 9. yers
fo. 73 a. sens with a market. There is in the towne selfe a goodly
springe, and is as the principall hedd of the broke servynge
the tukkyng miles about the towne. This watar resortythe
into Severne that is a boute a 4. myles of towchinge by the
way sume other vilagis. This towne had a castle in it sumtyme longinge to the Berkeleys, syns to the Wiks, sens fell
to decay, and is cleane taken downe. It had a metly good
dyche about it, and was for the moste parte made of towfe
stone full of pores and holes lyke a pumice. There is a quary
of this stone about Dursley. Yt will last very longe.

From Doursley to Torteworthe[b] vyllage, wher be some
good clothiars. There rennithe a broke. I take it to be the
brooke that cummythe from Dursley, and that thens it
goithe to Berkley a 3. miles lower. There is by the paroche
churche of Tortworth a maner place, where Mastar Throg-
merton dwellythe.

From Torteworthe to Wike Water[c] a pratye clothinge
tounlet 2. myles. The Lorde Delaware is chefe lorde of it.

Thens moste by champaine ground a 4. myles on
to Sodbery market[d] that longyd withe the village and the
maner place of Olde Sodbyrye onto the Erles of Warwike.

From Sodbery to Tormerton[e] village where Ser Edward
Wadeham dwellythe.

Thens about a 4. myles by playne grownde onto Masche-
feld.[f] This lordshipe longyd to the canons of Cainesham.

Thens a 4. myles farthar I passyd by hilly grownde, and
went ovar a stone bridge, under the whiche ran a broke[g]
that a litle lower went in sight into Avon ryver by the right
ripe of it.

Wiltshire.
Thens by hilly, stony and wooddy ground a 3. miles onto
Bradeford[h] on the right ripe of Avon.

---

[a] Dursley.   [b] Tortworth.   [c] Wickwar
[d] Chipping Sodbury.   [e] Tormarton.   [f] Marshfield
      [g] Box brook.   [h] Bradford-on-Avon

Thens on to Throughbridge[a] a market towne 2. miles.* Wiltshire.
Thens on to Broke by woody grownde 2. myles.

From Brooke onto Frome Celwod[b] in Somersetshire a 4. Somerset-
miles, muche by woody ground and pasture on tyll I cam shire.
within a myle of it where is champaine. *From.*

The towne hathe a metly good market, and is set on the clefe of a stony hille.

There is a goodly large paroche churche in it, and a ryght fayre springe in the churche yarde that by pipes and trenches fo. 73 b.
is conveyde to dyvers partes of the towne.

There be dyvers fayre stone howsys in the towne that standythe moste by clothinge.

In the botom of the towne rennithe From ryver levinge the towne on the lyfte rype, and there is a stone bridge of fyve arches, and a myle by it where by cummythe an armelet thorowghe a bridge of 2. arches. Ther cummithe one arme downe from Mayden Bradley v. myles of, and an othar from Hindon, and mete aboute a myle above the towne of From.

Bruerne[c] 8. myles from Frome.

From Frome onto Nunney Delamare[d] a good village a 2. myles, al by champayne grounde frutefull of corne.

Ther is a praty castle at the weste end of the paroche churche, havynge at eche end by northe and southe 2. praty rownd towres gatheryd by compace to joyne in to one.

The waulls be very stronge and thykke, the stayres narow, the lodginge with in some what darke. It standithe on the lefte ripe of the ryver, devidithe it from the churche yarde. The castell is motyd about, and this mote is servid by watar conveyed into it owte of the ryver. There is a stronge waulle withe owt the mote rounde about, savinge at the est parte of the castell where it is defendyd by the brooke.

Delamare and his wyfe, makers of the castle, ly buryed in the northe syde of the paroche churche at Nunney.

[* For Leland's first visit to Trowbridge and the neighbourhood, see vol. i, pp. 136, 137.]

---

[a] Trowbridge.   [b] Frome.   [c] ? Brewham or Bruton.
    [d] Nunney.

V.   H

Nunney broke cummythe downe, as I markyd, from
southe southe weste, and a 3. miles lower it goithe into
Frome ryver. This castell longed to Delamare, syns to
Powllet Lord S. John.

I rode bake from Nunneye to Frome market.

Thens a bout a 2. myles of I cam to a botome, where an
othar broke[a] ran in to Frome. And in this botome dwell certayne good clothiars havynge fayre howsys and tukkynge
myles.

fo. 74 a. Thens a 2. good myles onto Philipps Northetoune,[b] where
is a meane market kepte in a smaull towne, moste mayn-
teynyd by clothing.

From Northeton to Ferley[c] Castle a 2. myles.

Thens to Bradeforde 2. mils. The lordeshipe was gyven
with the personage by Kynge Æthelred onto the nunry of
Shaftesbyry for a recompence of the mortherynge of S. Edward his brothar. One De la Sale, alias Hawle, a auncient
gentilman syns the tyme of Edwarde the firste, dwellithe at
the . . . ende of Bradeforde.

From Bradeforde to Bathe a 5. myles.

A 2. myles and more by the right ripe of Avon, and
woody and hilly grownde, I passyd firste ovar by Fresche-
forde bridge of stone on Frome.

And a myle and more beyond that at a new stone bridge
I passyd ovar a litle broke that aftar a litle lower goythe in
to Avon *per sinistram ripam.**

A mile a this syde Bathe by southe est I saw 2. parks enclosyd withe a ruinus stone waulle, now withe out dere.
One longyd to the bysshope, an othar to the prior of Bathe.

From Bathe to Tormerton 8. mils all moste all by champain ground.

Tormerton was the De la Rivers lands, sins it descendid
to S. Loes. Olde Wadeham hath it by mariage of one of the
ladyes S. Clo for his lyfe tyme, the whiche was the last De la
Rivers doughtar.

There lyeth buryed in the body of the paroche churche of

[* See similar remarks on Freshford and the brook before, p. 84.]

---

[a] Wheel brook.   [b] Norton St. Philip.   [c] Farleigh.

Thormerton one Petrine De la Ryvers with a Frenche epi- **Gloucester-**
taphie. He was owner of the lordshype of Tormerton. **shire.**

From Thormerton to Sudbyry 2. myles.

Frome thens to Acton 3. myles by woddy grounde.

Dereham village is a 2. mils from Tormerton. There is a fayre maner place longginge to Mastar Dionyse. The lordeshipe of auncient tyme longyd to the Russels. One John Russell and Elizabethe his wyfe lyethe there buryed in the paroche churche; but they had but a meane howse there. From them it cam by heyre generall onto the Dionisies, of whom one Gilbert Dionise was countyd as one of first that there possessyd. Then cam Maurice, and he there buildyd fo. 74 b. a new courte. And Ser Guliam Dionise buildyd a nother courte of late yeres.

The Dionysies hathe here a fayre parke, and also a fayre lordshipe and a praty howse a 2. myles from Dereham at Siseton,[a] and a nothar maner and place cawlyd Aluestone[b] a 2. myles from Thornebyry.

Alverstone at the deforestinge of the old foreste of Kyngeswood was the kyngs.

From Tormerton onto Acton[c] 5. myles, 2. myles by champaine, and 3. by enclosyd ground.

Acton mannor place standithe about a quartar of a myle from the village and paroche churche in a playne grounde on a redde sandy soyle. Ther is a goodly howse and 2. parks by the howse, one of redd dere, an othar of fallow.

The Erles of Heriford were once lords of Acton lordshipe.

From Acton to Thorne a 3. myles or more by enclosyd ground and well wooddyd.

The towne selfe of Thornebyry is set almoste apon an *Thornebery.* eqwalle grounde, beinge large to the proporcion of the letter Y, havinge first one longe strete and two hornes goynge owt of it. The lengthe of the strete lyethe almoste from northe to sowthe. The right horne of it lyethe towards the weste, the othar towarde the southe. There is a market kepte wekely in the towne. And there is a mayre and privileges.

The paroche churche is in the northe end of the towne, a

---

[a] Siston.   [b] Alveston.   [c] Iron Acton.

fayre pece of worke. Whereof the hole savinge the chaun-
sell hathe be buildyd *in hominum memoria.*

There hathe bene good clothing in Thornebyry, but now
idelnes muche reynithe there.

There was of aunciente tyme a maner place, but of no
great estimacion, hard by the northe syde of the paroche
churche.

Edward late Duke of Bukkyngeham likynge the soyle
aboute, and the site of the howse, pullyd downe a greate
parte of the olde howse, and sette up magnificently in good
squared stone the southe syde of it, and accomplishyd the
west parte also withe a right comely gate-howse to the
first soyle; and so it stondithe yet withe a rofe forced for a
tyme.

fo. 75 a.

This inscription on the fronte of the gate-howse: This
gate was begon in the yere of owr Lorde God 1511. the 2.
yere of the reigne of Kynge Henry the viii. by me Edward
Duke of Bukkyngham, Erle of Hereford, Staforde and
Northampton.

The Dukes worde: *Dorenesavant.**

The foundation of a very spacious base courte was there
begon, and certeyne gates, and towres in it castelle lyke.
It is of a iiii. or v. yardes highe, and so remaynithe a token
of a noble peace of worke purposid.

There was a galery of tymbre in the bake syde of the
house joyning to the northe syde of the paroche churche.

Edward Duke of Bukkyngham made a fayre parke hard
by the castle, and tooke muche faire grownd in it very
frutefull of corne, now fayr launds, for coursynge. The in-
habytaunts cursyd the duke for thes lands so inclosyd.

There cummithe an armelet of Severne ebbynge and
flowyng into this parke. Duke Edward had thowght to have
trenchyd there, and to have browght it up to the castle.

There was a parke by the maner of Thornebyry afore, and
yet is caullyd Morlewodde.[a]

There was also afore Duke Edward's tyme a parke at

[* *I.e.,* "From henceforth," or Forward!]

---

[a] Marlewood.

Estewood a myle or more of: but Duke Edward at 2. tymes enlargyd it to the compace of 6. myles, not without many curses of the poore tenaunts.

The Severne Se lyethe a myle and more from Thornebyrie, the marches lyenge betwene.

From Thornebyry to Brightstow a 10. myles.

From Thornebyry to Glocester 18. myles. Sume caull it 20.

From Thornebyry to Berkeley a market towne, havynge *Berkeley.* a maior and privelegis, a 4. myles. A myle or more or I came by the towne I lefte the new parke withe a fayre loge on the hill in it longinge on to Berkeley on the lifte hand. And by a flyte shote or ever I cam on to the very towne, fo. 75 b. standynge on a clive, I passyd over a bridge, and there ran Torteworthe ryver downe on the lifte hond to Severne marches. And at the very enteringe of the towne I passyd over a nothar bridge where ran a broke commynge from the springs of dyvers hills not far of; and this broke in the salte meades a litle benothe the towne meatithe the othar broke of Torteworthe Watar, and goo bothe withe in a myle, or there aboute, by the salte marsche and New Porte havenet in to Severne.

The towne of Berkeley is no great thynge, but it standythe well, and in a very good soyle. It hathe very muche occupied, and yet some what dothe, clothinge.

The churche stondithe as on an hille at the southe ende of the towne.

And the castle stondithe at the southe west end of the churche. It is no great thinge. Dyvers towres be in the compase of it. The warde of the first gate is metely stronge, and a bridge ovar a dyche to it. There is a sqware dongeon towre in the castle, *sed non stat in mole egestae terrae.*

Ther be dyvers lordships there about longynge to Berkley to the some of 1000. marks by the yere, whereof Swynborne is one of the best. There longe to Berkeley 4. parks and 2. chaces.

Okeley Parke hard by.
Whitwike.
New Parke.
Hawlle Parke.
Miche Wood Chace.

Michaelswood Chace.

Gloucester-
shire.

From Berkley to Acton muche by woody ground a 7. milcs.

Litle Sudbury. Thens to Cheping Sodbyri, and a myle from thens to Lytle Sodbyri.

The doble dichyd campe there by on the hill conteynithe a 2. acres. Kynge Edward the Fowrthe's men kepte this campe here goinge to Twekesbyry Filde. Old Sodbyri and Chepinge Sodbyry were the Erles of Glocester's lands, and syns Bewchamps Erles of Warwyke. Gilbert de Clare pocessyd them.

fo. 76 a.

The maner place stode harde by the west end of the churche, now clene downe.

Pulclechurche. From Litle Sodbyri onto Pulklechurche in Glosestarshire a 4. myles; one and a halfe by enclosyd ground, the resydwe by champaine, but frutefull. Here is a parke and a goodly lordshipe longynge unto the Bysshope of Bathe.

Leland, vol.
viii, p. 1.

Edmonde * the Elder King of England was slayn at Pulclechirch, and byried at Glasteinbyri.

Savaricus Bisshop of Bathe, and Abbate of Glasteinbyri, alienatid Pucklechirch from Glesteinbyri to Bathe.

The personage of Pucklechirch impropriate to the cathedrale chirche of Welles.

Somerset-
shire.

From Pucklechirch to Cainesham,[a] sumtyme a good, now a poore, market town, and ruinus, in Somersetshir.

There be 2. bridges of stone at Kainesham, wherof one of 6. greate arches, now al yn ruine, standith holely in Glocestreshir. The other hard therby stondith with 3. great

[* From "Edmonde the Elder" to "[scant a myle]," p. 108, the text is printed from six leaves of Leland's own writing, the only portion of the original of this Part that remains, numbered as pp. 1-12 in vol. viii of his MS. They were placed there by Burton, who seems to have rescued them from decay, but did not know they belonged to a Part (see Introduction, p. xxviii). They come in Stow's copy, vol. iii, fos. 76 a-79 b (old nos.), and in Burton (*a*), pp. 55, 56. Stow omits the two paragraphs, "Savaricus bishop" to "chirche of Welles." At the top of the left-hand margin of fo. 1 Burton wrote, "This is written with John Leyland the antiquary his owne hand, who dyd 18 April 1552, 6 E. 6."]

---

[a] Keynsham.

arches of stone over Avon ryver that ther partith Glocester-shire and Somersetshir. *Somerset-shire.*

There is a park of the Kinges waullid with stone hard withoute Kainesham in Somersetshire.

Stones figurid like serpentes wounde into circles found in the quarreis of stone about Cainsham.

From Cainesham to Pensforde a 3. miles, part by cham-payn, part by enclosure. *Pensford.*

It is a praty market townlet occupied with clothing.

Browne of London yn Limestrete is owner of it. It longid afore onto . . . P. 2.

The towne stondith much by clothinge.

There cummith downe a streame that servith dyvers tukking milles.

From Pensforde to Southetoun[a] village. Here hath Syr John Saincte Lo an olde maner place, 2. long miles by hilly and enclosid grounde, meately wel woddid.

Syr John Saincte Lo descendit of a younger brother of the Lordes Saincte Lo, and hath litle of his landes. For the laste Lorde Saincte Lo lakking heyres male, the landes de-scendid by heyres generale onto the Lorde Hungreforde, and the Lorde Botreaux.

A good peace of Syr John Saincte Lo landes cummith to hym by De la Rivers doughter and heyre, his father's wife or mother.

There is a faire maner place like a castelle building at Newtoun Sainct Lo,[b] 2. miles from Bath by Avon, sumtyme one of the chief houses of the Lordes Sainct Lo. The Lorde Hastinges Erle of Huntingdon hath it now.

From Southetoune onto Chute[c] a mile *dim.* by fayre enclosid ground. It is a praty clothing towne, and hath a faire chirch. P. 3.

And at the southe side of the chirch is a faire manor place of the Bisshop of Bathe.

There be dyvers paroche chirches there aboute that ons a yere do homage onto Chute theyr mother chyrche.

There hath beene good makyng of cloth yn the towne.

Syr John Saincte Lo graundfader lyyth in a goodly tumbe of marble on the northe syde of the chyrch.

---

[a] Sutton.   [b] Newton St. Lo.   [c] Chew Magna.

READING FREE PUBLIC LIBRARY

Hubley [a] is a 3. miles by southe from Southetoun. There is an old meane maner place. The gate house of it is castelle like. There is a parke by it. It longgid to the Lorde Chedder, whos greate landes descendid by heyres generales onto the Lorde Lisle, Dawheney, and Newton.

From Southetoun onto Wike [b] 8. long miles.

There is a large maner place, wherof most parte was buildyd by Newton chief Juge of Englande. This lordship was the Lorde Chedders, and then Newton's, whos ii.

P. 4. doughters were maried the one onto Griffith of Braybroke, the other onto Syr Giles Capel, and so dooth Hubley and Wike and dyverse other lordeshippes remayne in partition onto them.

Banwelle is a 2. or 3. miles from Wike, and there hath the Bisshop of Bathe a goodly lordship.

There was at Banwelle in the tyme of Alfride King of the Westsaxons a notable monasterie of . . .

Banwelle standith not very holsomly, and Wike worse. The fennes be almost at hande. Woode meately good aboute them.

Kenne village is aboute a mile from Wike. There dwellith Mr. Kenne, a man of a 200. markes of lande by the yere.

Wrekeshale [c] is a 3. miles from Wike towarde Brighte-stow. Here hath Syr Wylliam Gorge a meane old maner place in a valley, and on eche side of it on the hilles is a fayre parke.

Barow Gurney a 2. miles from it nerer Brightstow, that is
P. 5. 4. miles distante of Barow. Here was of late a nunnery, now made a fair dwelling place by Drue of Brightestow.

Southetowne is 7. miles from Brightstow.

From Southetowne onto Estewoode 3. miles by hilly grounde. It is yn the rootes of Mendepe Hilles. There was a goodly castelle at this Estwoode caullyd Richemonte,* wher noble Gurney lay much. Yt is now defacid to the hard ground, and Syr John Newton now lorde of it hath made his house harde by it of the ruines thereof yn the

[* See before, p. 85.]

---

[a] Ubley.   [b] ? Wick St. Lawrence.   [c] Wraxall.

very place wher the graunge of Richemont Castelle was yn Somerset-
Gurneys tyme.

From Estewoode onto Welles v. miles.

From Southetoun onto Midsomer Northtoun by sumwhat
hilly and enclosid ground a 5. miles.

I passid over a praty broke a 2. miles or I cam onto
Northeton. It ran downe on the lifte hand as I rode.

From Midsomer Northeton to Philippes Northton a v.
miles.

From Midsomer Norton onto Melles^a by chaumpayne
grounde 5. miles.

Melles stondith sumwhat clyving, and hath bene a praty
townelet of clothing. [It] longgid onto Glessenbyri.

Selwood Abbate of Glessenbyri seing the welthines there P. 6.
of the people had thought to have reedified the townelet
with mene houses of square stones to the figure of an Antonie
Crosse; wherof yn deade he made but one streatelet.

The chirch is faire and buildid yn tyme of mynde *ex lapide
quadrato* by the hole paroche.

One Garlande a draper of London gave frely to the building of the vestiarie, a fine and curiose pece of worke.

One . . . a gentilman dwelling there yn the paroche
made a fair chapelle in the north side of the chirch. There
is a praty maner place of stone harde at the west ende of
the chirche. This be likelihod was paitely buildid by Abbate
Selwodde of Glasteinbyri. Syns it scrvid the fermer of the
lordeship. Now Mr. Horner hath boute the lordship of the
king. There cummith a broke from the cole-pittes in Mendepe, and strikith by south in the botom of Melles, and thens
rennith into Frome ryver, and so to Frome Selwood a market P. 7.
towne, that is 3. miles from Melles.

The foreste of Selwood ys in one parte a 3. miles from
Melles. In this forest is a chapelle, and theryn be buryed
the bones of S. Algar, of late tymes superstitiusly soute of the
folisch commune people.

The foreste of Selwood as it is nowe is a 30. miles yn
cumpace, and streachith one way almoste onto Werminstre,
and a nother way onto the quarters of Shaftesbyri by estimation a 10. miles.

^a Mells.

Somerset-
shire.
From Melles onto Nunney Delamere a 2. miles partely by
hilly and enclosid grounde.

Thens aboute a mile by like soyle onto Tut . . . a longe
village, wher the paroche chirche is onto Nunney Delamere.

Thens half a mile farther, and so into the mayne foreste
of Selwood. And so passing half a mile farther I lefte on the
righte hand Witham [the late Pri]orie of Cartusians not in
[the foreste, but] yoining harde on the [egge of it.

Thens] partely by [forest grounde and partlye by champaine a 4. myles onto Stourton.]

Wiltshire.   The village of Stourtoun stondith yn the botom of an hille
P. 8. *in laeva ripa Sturi.*

The Lorde Stourton's place stondith on a meane hille,
the soyle therof beyng stony. This maner place hathe 2.
courtes; the fronte of the ynner courte is magnificent, and
high embatelid castelle lyke.

There is a parke emonge hilles yoining on the maner place.

The ryver of Stoure risith ther of 6. fountaines or springes,
wherof 3. be on the northe side of the parke harde withyn
the pale. The other 3. be north also, but witheoute the parke.
The Lorde Stourton gyvith these 6. fountaynes yn his armes.

The name of the Stourtons be very aunciente yn those
parties.

There be 4. campes that servid menne of warre aboute
Stourton, one towarde the northe weste parte withyn the
parke doble dichid. I conjecte that heere stode a [ma]ner
place or castelle. My Lorde [Stourton]* sayith nay.

P. 9.   There is a nother campe a mile *dim.* of Stoureton doble
dichid in the toppe of an high hille. This is caullyd communely Whiteshete Hille.

The other 2. campes be a brode yn the lordship.

There is on † an hille a litle withoute Stourton a grove,
and yn it is a very praty place caullyd Bonhomes, buildid of
late by my Lorde Stourton. Bonhome of Wileshire, of the
auncienter house of the Bonehomes there, is lorde of it.

From Stoureton onto . . . a 4. miles muche by woddy
grounde. Heere I passid over Cale water at a great forde,

[* Stow omits this sentence, Hearne must therefore have seen the
word, which is now gone.]
[† MS. *an.*]

and so rydde scant a mile over Moreland, and a mile be- **Wiltshire.**
yonde I lefte . . . Master Carentes house and parke on
the lifte hande; and thens a mile farther I cam onto Staple- **Dorset.**
ford[a] a praty uplandisch toune of one streate meately welle
buildyd, [where at the] northe ende of the town [is a churche]
and there [one Thornehul of Thorn]hulle lyith [buried on
the southe syde of] the qu[ier in a fayre chapele of his owne
buyldynge.]

The lordeship and townelet of Stapleforde in Blakemore **P. 10.**
hath longgid of aunciente tyme onto the abbay of Shirburne.

Cale ryver cummith downe from Morelande onto Stapleforde, leving it on the righte ripe.

Stapleforde is by estimation a 7. miles north from Wike-
hampton,[b] from whens Calebrooke cummith.

From Stapleforde onto Thornehul[c] a mile by good grounde
enclosid. Here dwellith Master Thornehul an auncient
gentilman.

From Thurnehul onto Stourminster a 2. miles by enclosid
and woddy grounde; and yn the mydle way I passid over a
stone bridge of 5. archis under the whiche rennith a brooke
caullyd [*Liddon Bridge*].

[Then I passid over] a wodde bridge [on Stoure a litle]
above the [town.]

The townclet of Stourminstre standith in a valley, and is **P. 11.**
no greate thing, and the building of it is mene. There is a
very good market. It stondith *in ripa sinistra* of Stoure.
There is a very fair bridge of 6. arches at the towne ende
made of later tymes chiefly by the Vicare of Stourminstre
and the persone of Shinington[d] agayne Eyford Bridge *in ripa
dextra Sturi* yn the way to Blanforde. (Eyford Bridge 2.
miles beneth Stourminstre.)

At the . . . ende of the bridge *in ripa dextera Sturi flu.*
is a faire maner place of an hille made stepe rounde by
mannes hand caullid yn olde writinges Newton Castelle.
King . . . gave this Stourminster and Newton onto thabbay
of Glossenbyri. The castelle syns clerely decayed, and the
abbates of Glessenbyri made ther a fair maner place, and
usid to resorte onto yt.

---

[a] Stalbridge. See Part VIII, fo. 52.   [b] Wincanton.
   [c] Thornhill.   [d] ? Shillingstone.

Dorset. The personage of the towne was impropriate onto Glessen-byri, [and the] revennes of the lorde[ship mount] to a 80. *li.* [by the yere.] *

P. 12.   From Stourminster over the bridge, and lesse then a mile †
farther I passid over a bridge of 4. arches that standith, as I
remember, over Devilles broke, and thens aboute a mile
onto Thornehul.

From Thornehul onto Caundel a praty village a mile.
The Lord Stourton hath a fair maner place. It was the
Chidiokes maner. (There be diverse villages caullid
Caundelle.)

From Caundel onto Shirburne 3. miles by enclosid and
sumwhat hilly grounde meately welle woddyd.

The parke of Shirburne excepting a litle aboute the logge
is enclosid with a stone waulle.

From Shirbourne onto Wike,ᵃ now Mr. Horesey house,
a late the Abbate of Shirburne maner place, set on the
righte ripe of Shirburne water, alias Ivel ᵇ ryver, scante 2.
miles.

[Th]ens to Bradeforde ᶜ a pratye [village on the] righte
ripe of [Ivel and thens to] Clifton Mr. Ho[rsey's maner
place scant a myle.] ‡

Stow, fo. 79b.   Bradford Bridge of 2. arches a litle above the toune.

Clifton standithe on the ryght ripe of Ivel in the paroche
of Yatminster,ᵈ where be 3. prebends longinge to Salisbyry.
This lordeshipe longyd to the Mawbanks, whos heires generall were maried onto Horesey, and Ware, and they partyd
the lands. Ormond Erle of Wileshire aboute Kynge Edwarde
the 4. tyme invadid Clifton, and possessyd it by violence
withe a pretencyd tytle, and began a greate foundation there
for stable and howsys of office, and entendyd to have

[* This paragraph is omitted by Stow; the bracketed words are gone
since Hearne saw them.]
[† MS. has *miles.*]
[‡ Burton (*a*), p. 56, adds here to his copy, perhaps from some loose
paper, two notes inserted in Lancashire, Part IX, viz., "Bridport is
sett as middeway betweene Weymouth and Lime. At Bridport be
made good daggers." See before, p. 44.]

ᵃ Wyke Farm.   ᵇ Yeo r.   Bradford Abbas.
                    ᵈ Yetminster.

buyldyd a castle there, but shortly aftar Clifton was restoryd **Dorset.**
to Horsey.

The auncient name and maner place of the Horeseys was
at the end of the greate hylle that goithe from Glessenbyry
almoste to Bridgewatar. It is about a myle from Bridge **fo. 80 a.**
Watar, and Ser John Horsey possessithe yet the lande.

The broke of Sherburne and Myllebroke water metithe togethar a qwartar of a myle or more by nethe Clifton.

From Clifton onto Ivelle[a] a good market towne a myle **Somerset-**
or more. It stondithe plesauntly on a rokky hille, and is **shire.**
meatly welle buildyd. It stondithe in Somersetshire *in laeva
ripa flu. Ively.*[b]

The towne is privilegyd withe greate libertes, and kepithe
courts for decidinge of suts. The paroche chirche is faire
and lyghtesom. In it be 4. or 5. cantuaries endwyd withe
lands.

There is at the weste ende of the churche a greate and
fayre olde chapel, the whiche semithe to be a thinge more
ancient then the paroche. It is usid for a chauntrey.

There is a bridge a litle from the toun of 3. great arches
of stone apon Ivel, and is the highe way from Shireburne
westward. Shireburne is 3. myles or more from Ivele towne.

A litle above Ivel bridge brekethe out an arme of Ivel,
and aboute the bridge the armes mete agayne togithar and
make a fayre medowe as an isle.

The streame goithe from Ivel Bridge onto Ilchester a 3.
myles, and thens rennythe northe to Mychelborow[c] levinge
Athelney somewhat distant on the lyfte ripe, and so onto
Lambourne,[d] and to Bridge Northe[e] that standithe hard on **Lambowrne.**
the lifte ripe of it.*

Lamburne hathe bene a right praty towne, and a good
market. In it were many fayre howses. Now it decayithe.

From Shireburne onto Milburne Porte[f] about a 2. mils. **Mylburne.**
It hathe had a market, and yet retaynithe privileges of a
fraunchisyd borow.

[* There is error here, the river Yeo falls into the Parret at Langport.]

---

[a] Yeovil.   [b] Yeo r.   [c] Muchelney.
[d] Langport.   [e] Bridgewater.   [f] Milborne Port.

Dorset.

There comythe a broket downe by the towne, and resortithe onto Shireburne Watar.[a]

Thens a myle to Tonmer Parke encompasyd with a stone waulle.

fo. 80 b.

The lordeship of Tonmers was one Tonmers whos heire generall was maried onto one of the Carents, and there by was Carents lands moste augmentid.

From Tonmer to Stalbridge a myle. This towne was privilegyd withe a market and a faire by the procurement of an abbat of Shirburne. The market is decayed. The fair remaynithe.

The abbot of Shireburne, lord of the towne, had there a maner place on the southe syd of the churche.

There is a right goodly springe on the southe syde of the churche waullyd about.

Stowre is the next water on it, and that levithe Stalbridge aboute a mile on the right ripe.

Calebridge on Cale ryver is a mile and halfe of.

Marnelle[b] on the . . .* rype of Stowre is a good uplandishe towne, and the lordshipe there longid onto Glessenbyri.

Marnelle is aboute a 6. myles from Shaftesbyry.

From Stalbridge onto the causey that ledithe to Scheftesbyry a myle. Thens to Fyvebridge[c] upon Cale ryvar a bout a 2. myles. There be 5. principall arches, where of it takethe name, but ther joynethe hard onto a longe stone causey, in the whiche be dyverse archelets.

Al the countre aboute Fivebridge is a flate vale of a greate cumpace environid withe high hills.

Passynge a myle farthar I roode over a broke that be lykelihode resortythe to Stowre.

Schaftesberye.

Thens aboute a 3. miles on to Shaftesbyry a great market toune stondinge on an highe hille havinge 4. paroche chirches in it.

The abbay stode by . . .* of the toun.

There was an inscription on the right hond enteringe of

[* Blanks in MS.]

---

[a] Yeo r.   [b] Marnhull.   [c] Five Bridges.

the chapiter howse set up by Alfredus, Kynge of the West- **Dorset.**
Saxons, in knoledge that he repayred Schaftesberye, dystroyed
by the Danes. The inscription of the remaines of the whiche
William of Malmesbyri spekethe stodd in the waulle of
S. Marie's Chapell at the townes end. The chapell is now
pullid downe.

Stowre ryver levithe Schaftesbyri . . .* the lyfte ripe.   fo. 81 a.

From Sheftesbyri towarde Myre ᵃ I passid a 2. mils by
woody grounde, and ther I passyd ovar a broke that ran
downe on the lifte hand toward Stowre, and so goynge
thoruge a peace of Gillingham Forest I passid over a nother
broke.

[* Blank in MS.]

ᵃ Mere.

APPENDIX TO PART X

BURFORD, CULHAM, AND ABINGDON

(Note by Thomas Hearne. See page 77.)

THO' King Henry the Vth. is here said to be the founder not only of Burford, but of Culham, Bridge, yet this is to be understood only by way of complement, and 'tis grounded only upon the liberty given by him for building the bridges, and upon some other small privileges that he allow'd at this time. For 'tis certain that John of St. Helen's was the first beginner of Burford Bridge, to the maintenance of which and of the hospital of St. Helen's that he had founded, he left an estate in land of 50. pounds a year, which estate (I suppose) now belongs (at least it ought to belong) to the present hospital, call'd Christ's Hospital, that was built by K. Edward the Sixth and Sir John Mason. And 'tis withal as certain that Geffry Barbour was the principal founder of Culham * Bridge, towards which, and to the finishing of Burford Bridge, and to the making of the fine causey between both bridges he gave a 1000. marks, which was punctually laid out upon this work. The best artists that could be found were imploy'd, and every man had a penny a day, which was the best wages, and an extraordinary price in those times, when the best wheat was now and then † sold for twelve pence a quarter. 'Twas likewise in

[Burford, Berks.]

[* In Oxfordshire, near Abingdon, which is in Berks.—L. T. S.]
† See pag. 92 of a certain Leiger Book, now lying in the hall of Christ's Hospital at Abbington, intitled A Monument of Christian Munificence, written in the year 1627. by Francis Little, sometime Mayor of Abbington, and one of the Governours of this Hospital. In which book (written with no great judgment) is a short account of the Monastery of Abbington, of the Hospital of the fraternity of the Holy-Cross, and of divers other things relating to this place.

v.   I

those times that in the feasts of the fraternity of the Holy-Cross in Abbington they spent yearly six calfs, which cost two shillings and two pence a piece, sixteen lambs at twelve pence a piece, above four score capons at three pence a piece, above four score geese at two pence half penny a piece, eight hundred eggs at five pence a hundred; besides many marrow bones, much fruit and spice, and a great quantity of milk, cream and flour, all in proportion too to the prices that I have specify'd: and upon these days of rejoycing withal they us'd to have twelve minstrels, viz. six from Coventry and six from Maidenhead, for which and for other uses of the fraternity William Dyar, Vicar of Bray in Berks, gave them five tenements in East St. Helen's Street, three tenements in West St. Helen's Street, and other lands in Abbington. So that considering the cheapness of things in those times, Geffry Barbour's contribution was very great and extraordinary, and 'tis nothing but justice to style him the founder of the bridge, the stones whereof, as well as those of Burford Bridge, were taken out of the quarries of Bessilsleigh and Stanford, and were given them by Sir Peter Bessils, who moreover, besides the money he gave for carrying on the building of the bridges, by his last will and testament, dated Octob. 23. 1424. gave all his lands, tenements and reversions in Abbington towards the perpetual maintenance and repair of them. Besides Geffry Barbour's benefaction to this work, he was likewise so great a benefactor to the hospital of St. Helen, that some look upon him now, as they did even in Mr. Leland's time, to have been the chief founder of it. He was also in other respects a very great friend to this town, and did so much good in the place, that he is always mention'd by the inhabitants with the most profound respect. He was first of all buried in the Abbey Church; but upon the dissolution he was translated from thence in the most solemn manner to St. Helen's Church, where I have seen his grave-stone, and find the following inscription upon it: *Hic jacet Galfridus Barbour, Mercator de Abendon, quondam Balivus Bristoliae, qui obiit vicesimo primo die Aprilis anno Domini 1417. Cujus animae propitietur Deus.* 'Tis this great respect which the inhabitants of the town have for him that hath prevented the destruction of the brass-plate upon which the inscription

.s ingrav'd. Other old monuments have been defac'd and utterly destroy'd by Puritans, Presbyterians, and the rest of the whining crew, purely out of a vain, idle conceit, that the memory of no Roman Catholicks ought to be preserv'd. This town hath been famous for fanaticks, and 'tis no wonder that there is so little of such kind of antiquities remaining amongst them; and yet these principles have not prevail'd so far upon them as to erase out of their minds the honour that is due to Geffry Barbour; which, perhaps, may be owing, in some measure, to this, that they do not believe him to have been a rigorous Roman Catholick, but rather an enemy to the Pope. We cannot conceive what rejoycing there was upon the finishing of Culham Bridge, not only because a stop was put by this means to the mischiefs which us'd to happen in ferrying over the water, but also because it conduc'd very much to the inriching of the town by influencing travellers in their way from Gloucester to London to pass through it, and not through Walingford as they had been accustom'd to do. And 'tis to be noted that 'twas nothing else but a sense of the many benefits that accru'd from hence to this place that occasion'd Mr. Richard Fannand, iron-monger, in the year 1457 (being the 36. year of the reign of K. Hen. VI.) to put up a table in the hall of St. Helen's Hospital in memory of Geffry Barbour, etc. in which we have an exact, tho' rude and barbarous, description of the proceedings in building of Culham Bridge, together with some Latin verses at the beginning (in which K. Henry the V. is mention'd as the founder of both bridges) and the rebus of Abbington at the end, (which differs somewhat from that in Dr. Plot's letter.)* 'Tis this table that is here cited by Mr. Leland, and 'tis now hanging in the hall of the present hospital, but being like to come to decay in some time, I shall here beg leave to transcribe and publish it, that posterity may know to whom it is that they

[* Dr. Robert Plot, antiquary (1640-96), in a letter to Dr. John Fell of Oxford (printed by Hearne at the end of vol. ii of Leland's "Itinerary," second edition, p. 136), in which he plans out a philosophical journey through England and Wales, cites the rebus thus:

"The first letter of our fore-fadyr, a worker of wax, an I and an N, The colour of an ass, and what have you then?"—L. T. S.]

are chiefly indebted for the benefits that follow'd from the foundation of Culham Bridge.

Henrici quinti regis quarto revoluto
Anno, rex idem pontem fundavit utrumque,
Supra locum binum Borford dictumque Culhamford.
Inter eos namque via regia tendit alta.
Annis adjunctis dat inter gradientibus amplum;
Principium cujus Abendoniae situatur.
Annis tunc donum* M. quater C. numeratis,
Ex sexto deno cum fecit opus pietatis.
Vos qui transitis hujus memores bene sitis,
Et vestris precibus fundator sit relevatus.

Off alle Werkys in this Worlde that ever were wrought
Holy chirche is chefe, there children been chersid.†
For be baptim these Barnes to blisse been i brought,
Thorough the grace of god, and fayre refresshed.
Another blissed besines is brigges to make,
There that the pepul may not passe after greet showres.
Dole it is to drawe a deed body oute of a lake,
That was fulled in a fount stoon, and a felow of oures.
Kyng Herry the fifte in his fourthe Yere,
He hathe i founde for his folke a brige in Berke schure.
For cartis with cariage may goo and come clere,
That many Wynters afore were mareed in the myre.
And som oute of her sadels flette to the grounde
Went forthe in the Water wist no man whare.
Fyve Wekys after or they were i founde,
Her kyn and her knowlech caught hem uppe with care.
Then the commons of Abendoñ cryed on the Kynge,
Upoñ Dukes and Lordes that were in this londe.
The Kynge bad hem begynne apoñ goddes blissinge,
And make it also stronge as they couthe with stone, lyme or sonde.
Apon the day of seynt Alboñ they began this game,
And John Huchyns layde the firste stoon in the Kynges name.
Sir Peris Besillis knyght curteys and heend,
For his fadir soule and his frendes he dyd as he scholde.
He gaf hem stonys i nowhe into the werkys ende,
Also mony as they nedid feche hem if they wolde.
Than crafti men for the querry made crowes of yre,
Weges, and wayes, and mony harde howys.
Jeffray Barbour bad pay hem her hyre.
Then must they have mooldes to make on the bowys.
They cokid for cartes, and cast for her clusyng,‡

[* Hearne gives *demum* as a possible reading.—L. T. S.]
[† ? Chershid, *i.e.*, cherished.—L. T. S.]
[‡ Hearne suggests *chisyng* for clusyng, *i.e.*, chysyng or selecting.— *Cokid, i.e.*, pryed about (like a cock).—L. T. S.]

They founde oute the fundement and layde in large stones.
They reysid up the archeys be geometre in rysyng,
With xi. laborers lavyng at onys.
Ther was mater i nowhe, stone, lyme and gravel,
Werkemen als wise as they coulde fynde any.
And ever bad the Barbour pay for her travel,
Til a M. Marke be spende eche a peny.
Then the strenghe of the streme astoned hem stronge,
In labor and lavyng moche money was lore.
Ther loved hem a ladde was a water man longe,
He helpe stop the streme til the werke were a fore.
It was a solace to see in a somer sesoñ,
CCC. I wysse workynge at onys.
iiii. and iiii. reulyd be resoñ,
To wete who wrought best were set for the nonce.
The peple preved her power with the pecoyse, *
The mattok was mañ handeled right wele a whyle,
With spades and schovelis they made suche a noyse,
That men myght here hem thens a myle.
Wyves went oute to wite how they wrought :
V. score in a flok it was a fayre syght.
In bord clothes bright white brede they brought,
Chees and chekenes clerelych A dyght.
These weren the dyches i diged in ful harde grounde,
And i cast up to arere with the wey,
Sethen they were i set with a quyk mownde
To holde in the bunkes for ever and ay.
The gode Lorde of Abendoñ of his londe,
xx

For the breed of the brige iiii. fote large.
It was a greet socour of erthe and of sonde,
And yt he abated the rent of the barge.
An C. pownde, and xvˡⁱ. was truly payed
Be the hondes of John Huchyns and Banbery also,
For the waye and the barge thus it must be sayed.
Therto witnesse al Abendoñ, and many oon moo.
For now is Culham hithe i com to an ende,
An al the contre the better and no man the worse.
Few folke there were coude that wey wende,
But they waged a wed or payed of her purse.
And if it were a begger had breed in his bagge,
He schulde be ryght soone i bid for to goo aboute,
And of the pore penyles the hiereward wold habbe
A hood or a girdel, and let hem goo withoute.
Many moo myscheves there weren I say.
Culham hithe hath causid many a curse.
I blyssed be our helpers we have a better waye,
Withoute any peny for cart and for horse.

[* Peck or pick-axe.—L. T. S.]

Thus acordid the kynge and the covent,
And the commones of Abendon as the Abbot wolde.
Thus they were cesed and set al in oon assent,
That al the brekynges of the brigo the towne bere schulde.
This was preved acte also in Perlement,
In perpetual pees to have and to holde.
This tale is i tolde in noon other entent
But for myrthe and in memory to yonge and to olde.
Now every good body that gothe on this brige,
Bid for the Barbor jentil Jeffray,
That clothed many a pore man to bed and to rige,
And hathe holpe to rentis to holde up this waye.
The wiche rentes right trewe men have i take on honde,
And graciously governed hem now a good while.
Who so have hem hereafter withe trewthe but he stonde,
It schal be knowen openly he dothe hymselfe begyle.
I councel every creature to kepe hym from the curse.
For of this tretis wil I no more telle.
And be not to covetous to youre owne purse,
For peril of the peynes in the pit of Helle.
Now god geve us grace to folowe treuthe even,
That we may have a place in the blysse of Heven. AMEN.

* r. A.B.I.N.D.O.N. R.F.I.

Take the first letter of youre foure fader with A, the worker of wex, and I and N, the colore of an asse; set them togeder, and tel me yf you can what it is than. Richard Fannande Irenmonger hathe made this tabul, and set it here in the yere of Kyng Herry the sexte xxxvi^{te}.

* This Letter stands for *rebus*, unless I am mistaken. [See note, p. 115.—L. T. S.]

PART XI.*

Nomina episcoporum Dorcacestrensium.†   Oxon.

*B*IRINUS *obiit* 3. *Call. Decembar anno dom.* 650.‡   fo. 48 a.
   Agelbertus.
Elutherius.
Jaromanus.
Atithla.
Sexulphus.
Eadtheaad.
Athelwinus.
Eadgarus.
Bertinus tempore regis Offae.
Kinebright.§

[* Leland's original of this Part is lost; printed from Stow's copy
(MS. Tanner 464, vol. ii, fos 48-116) where it is headed, "Comentaria
Angliæ"; a late hand has added figure 2 in the left-hand corner. The
text runs on to fo. 71, then comes a blank leaf, the text beginning
again on fo. 73 a, with figure 3 in the left-hand corner, and the heading
"in navi ecclesii Warwike." See after, p. 150. Hearne (vol. viii, Part
II) prints this as a continuation of fo. 71, and we follow the same
order.]
   [† *Dorcacestrenses*, MS. This list appears to have been compiled by
Leland chiefly from Bede and the Anglo-Saxon Chronicle for the names
from Birinus to Edhed (Eadtheaad), and from William of Malmesbury,
Gesta Pontificorum, for the rest. He introduces, however, two bishops
of Lichfield, Jaroman and Sexwulf, among the early names, also Bertin
a doubtful name in this connection; could he possibly have had some
local register before him now destroyed or lost? It seems unlikely, as
Dorchester and Leicester were joined to Lichfield 705-737, according to
Stubbs, and the seat of the bishopric was removed to Lincoln in 1070,
Remigius being the first bishop there. Some of the spellings may be
due to errors made by Stow in copying Leland.]
   [‡ In Part II of the Itinerary (vol. i, pp. 117, 118) is Leland's narra-
tive of what he saw in Dorchester, where he notes the burial of bishops
Birinus and Æschwin.]
   [§ Cyneberht.]

119

Eadbaldus.
Alewy.
Ealdwulphus.
Ceofwulphus.
Eadwulph.
Brithredus.
Leofwinus qui conjunxit duos episcopatus, scilicet Dorcaster et Leircester.
Alnoth.
*Ascleninus.**
Alphelmus.
Eadnothus.
Eatherinus.†
Eadnothus.
Wulpfe.
‡ Wuwine tempore Wilhelmi Bastardi.

Nomina episcoporum Lincoln. à conquestu.

Remigius.
Robertus Bloeth: deceased anno 1123.§
1123.   *Alexandar.*
Robertus de Elienneto:|| *deceased anno* 11 . . .
Galfridus qui translatus fuit à Lincoln. Ebor.
Gualterus de Constantia.
S. Hugo.
Gul. de Montibus.¶
Hugo Wells.
fo. 48 b.   *Robert Grosteste: deceased anno* 1253.
Henricus Lexington: coram cap. S. Mar. in or.
Richard Gravesend.
Oliverus Sutton.
Johannes Dalderby.
Henricus Burwasche.

[* Æscwyn.]   [† Ætheric.]
[‡ *Wuwinæ,* MS. It should be Wulfwig, his predecessor being Ulf.]
[§ The dates and words "deceased anno" in this page were added later, perhaps by Stow himself.]
[|| Querceto, *alias* de Katineto (Dugdale) or Chesney, de Chennehai, etc. (Le Neve).]
[¶ William de Bleys or Blois (Dugdale and Le Neve).]

*Thomas Weke.**   **Lincoln.**
Joannes Gynwelle, sepul. in occident. par. eccles.
Joannes Bukingham.
Henricus Beaufort, translatus ad Winton. et postea card.
S. Eusebii.
Philippus de Ripington.
Richardus Fleminge.
Gul. Gray.
Gul. Alnewik, sepultus occidentali. par. ecclesiae.
Marmaducus Lomeley.
Joan. Chedworth, sepul. boreali parte prope Sutton.
Thomas Rotheram translatus ad Ebor.
Joann. Russelle.
Gul. Smith, sepult. occiden. parte ecclesiae.
Thomas Wolsey translatus ad Ebor.
Gul. Awater, sepul. occid. part. eccles.
Johannes Longeland erexit sacellum cum sepulchro simillimo † sepulchro Russelli.
Frater Adam scripsit vitam S. Hugonis episcopi Lincoln. et librum ‡ dedit R. Priori et monachis Withamensibus.
S. Hugo natus in territorio Gratianopolitano.
Petrus monachus Cisterc. postea archiepiscopus Tarentasiensis, praeceptor Hugonis.
Hugo praenotatus per Henri. 2ᵐ. venit ad Witham in Anglia, ubi paulo ante . . . Henr. monaster. Cartusianorum instituerat.

Sepultures in Lyncolne.   fo. 49 a.

Henry Burwasch Bisshop of Lincoln buried in the est ende of the churche toward the northe.

There is also buried at his fete Robart his brothar, a knighte of greate fame in the warrs.

And there also is buried Barptoleme sunn to Robert Burwasche, and they foundyd 5. prists, and 5. pore scollars at gramar schole in Lyncolne.

In owr Lady chappell, at the est ende of the northe syde of the churche, is buried the bowells of Quene Elianor. The armes of Castle be on the syde of the tombe.

[* Thomas Bek or Beake (Le Neve and Stubbs).]
[† *Simillimum*, MS.]   [‡ *Libre*, MS.]

Lincoln. In the southe est chapell next to it is buried one of the Lorde Nicholas Cantilupes.

This Cantilupe foundyd a mastar and 2. or 3. cantuaris, aftar augmentyd to vii. Now the colledge is corruptely cauled Negem College.

And thereby at his hed lyethe one of the Wymbisches,* a residensary of Lincolne in a fayre highe tombe.

In S. Nicholas Chapell is a merveylows fair and large Psaltar, full in the margin of goodly armes of many noble men.

S. Hughe liethe in the body of the est parte of the chirche above the highe altare.

Bysshope Fleminge liethe in an highe tumbe in the northe isle of the upper parte of the chirche in the walle; and thereby undar flate stones ly Oliver Sutton, and John Chadworthe byshope.

Bysshope Russell and Longland,† now bisshop, tumbes be in to chapells cast out of the uppar parte of the southe wall of the churche.

Agayne this chapell is Fitz William knight buried.

In the southe parte of the presbytery lyithe in 2. severalle highe marble tumbes in a chapell Catarine Swineforde, the 3. wife to John of Gaunt Duke of Lancaster, and Jane her dougtar Countes of Westmerland.

Byshope Thomas lyethe in the highest cross northe isle.

Robert Grosted lyethe in the hygheste southe isle with a goodly tumbe of marble and an image of brasse over it.

Bysshope Repington lyethe under a flate stone thereby.

In the lower northe crosse isle lyethe Bysshope Thomas Weke.

fo. 49 b. In the lower southe crosse isle laye Bysshope Dalberby; but his tumbe was taken away *nomine superstitionis.*

John Multon knyght lyethe in the body of the chirche.

Bysshope Gwyney‡ lyethe in the body of the churche, and buyldyd a greate chapell of Seint Magdalene without the very northe waull, but joyninge on the north syde of the cathedrall churche, and foundyd a 5. cantuaries. and this

[* Wimbush family.]
[† John Longlands, bp. 1521-38.]
[‡ John Gynwell, bp. 1347, seems intended.]

churche was aftar translatyd into the northe syde of the **Lincoln.**
eskeker by the peace of west area of the churche yarde.

Where the Deane of Lyncolnes howse is in the minstar
close of Lyncolne and there about was a monasterye of
nunes afore the tyme that Remigius began the new mynstar
of Lyncolne: and of this howse yet remayne certayne tokens
of it.

The body of the churche of Lyncolne to the first crosse
isle hathe viii. arches pilloryd with marble on eche syde.

The first crosse isle is greatar and more in lengthe then
the second crosse isle is.

The quiere betwixt the 2. crosse isles hathe on eche syde
4. arches and pillor of marble.

The est ende of the chirche hathe 5. arches on eche syde
withe pillors of marble.

At the northe ende of the upper crosse isle is the cloystre,
and in the este ende of it is the chapitre house, the este
ende whereof is very fayre *opere circulari*, and the *fornix* is
susteinid with a pillor of marble.

There is a very fayre dore in the upper part of the churche
southeward to go into the close, and agayne this lyithe the
bisshops palace hangginge *in declivio*.

Al the hole close is environid withe an highe stronge
wawle havynge dyvers gats in it, whereof the principall is
the Escheker Gate.

The paroche churche of Scint Margarete is within the
close by of est southe est.

In paroch. eccle. de Gainesburge.

Dominus Thomas Burgh miles ordinis garterii obiit anno
Dom. 1408. *Sepultus est in australi parte supremi altaris*   1408.
cum Margareta domina de Boterax[a] *ejus consorte.*

Dominus Edmund Cor[n]ewaille dominus de Thonak jacet
boreali parte ecclesi. et instituit ibidem tres cantuarias; obiit
anno Do. 1322. 16. *die Decembris.**   1322.

[* *Decembar*, MS.]

---

[a] Botreaux,

Qwatermayne foundyd an hospitall at Tame in Oxfordshire.

One of the Qwatermains is buried in Tame Churche.

The Qwatermaynes were men of faire lands in the quarters of Oxford, Bukynghame and Barkshire.

The last of the Qwatermains left moste of his lands to
one Fowlar, whose sune was after chauncelar of the Duchye
of Lancastar, and this chaunselars sonne sold away all.

Ricote was one of Quatermains manor places.

Yonge Chambarlayne of Oxfordshire tolde me that the
lordshipe of Cotes about Northampton was the auncients
manor of the Chamberleins. He tolde me all * that they had
also the lands of a knight caulyd Helke by heires generalle.

*Gul. de Perci in tempore Gul. com. dedit s. feodos militum
collegio de Beverley, totidem S. Wilfrido de Ripon, totidem
hospitalariis, totidem templariis, totidem S. Hildi de Whitby.*

Ther was in the olde rowle set the name of Agelnoun with
one of the first Percys.†

*Hic Gul. fundator fuit de Whitby. Alanus ejus filius con-
firmator.*

Emma de Port nupsit Gul. Percy.

*Gysbritus Tisonn fundator monasteriorum de Malton et
Watton fuit dominus de Alnewik et Malton.* This Tisonn
gave the lordeshipe of Watton to a nece of his.

*Gul. filius Gisbrighti interfectus in bello inter Haroldum
et Guli. reges.*

Surely, as far as I can perceyve, the Vescys heires to
Tison were foundars of Watton and Malton, and not Tisonn
himselfe.‡

*Guil. Tisonn reliquit etiam unicam filiam, quae nupsit
Yvoni de Vescy op. Normanniae.*

*Gisbrightus habuit etiam juniorem filium Richardum, cui
multas ter. dedit.*

And Richard's heires males in tyme decayng cam by a
doughtar Bona Tisonn to Gul. Hilton. Gul. Percy 3. *fundator de* Hanke.

Ther was notyd in the old rolle apon the name of Joce-

[* *Sic.*]   [† This paragraph is written in the margin.]
[‡ The charters given by Dugdale show that Leland was right.
"Mon. Ang.," vi, 970, 971.]

linus de Lovain, sonne to the Duke of Brabant, how that at
suche tyme as he shuld mary the heyre of the Percy, that fo. 50 b.
he shuld othar take the name of Percy, or els Percys armes
witheout addition of the armes of Brabant; whereapon he
toke the name of Percy, and kept in his armes the blew
lyon the armes of Brabant.

Percy cam by the Lucys land by meane of an heire generall of the Lucis that he maried, and she havynge no children by hym, and dyenge afore hym made hym hir sole heire
by dede of mere gifte.

Ex tabula pencilibus Dunelmensis.*   Durham.

Anno Domini 1346. *vigilia S. Lucae hora* 9. *bellum inter* 1346.
Scottos et Anglos in loco dicto Nevill's Crosse.

Rex David cepit Lidel.

Rex David venit ad Bewrepark, ubi fixit tentoria.

Hoc tempore exercitus Anglorum erat apud Akeland.

*Barthram Copland mane irruebat cum parte exercitus in
Scottos.*

*Menille et Henri. Percy postea fortiter cum Scottis dimica-
bant.*

*Gul. de la Zuche archiepiscopus Ebor. et Mowbray ejus dia-
conus, ac Robertus Ogle ejus subdiaconus fortiter pugnabant.*

*Thomas Carre vexillarius dixit Joanni Copland, cape Da-
videm regem.*

Mundingden locus prope Norham caede Scotorum insignis.

Jacobus occisus apud Brankston.

Intelligit Gul. de la Souch archiepiscopum Ebor.

Sit pater invicte, sicco de stipite dicte,
Grande tuum nomen, tibi conditor attulit omen.
Sit laus armorum comiti valls calamorion.†

*Berdwith miles comitis Tosti violans pacem S. Cuthberti
periit.*

A stronge wardyd gate at Geteshed.   fo. 51 a.

[* Hearne suggests *pensili Dunelmensi* in emendation of Stow's error,
or *tabulis p. Dunelmensis.*]
[† *Sic* in MS., *vallis calamorum.*—Hearne.]

Tyne bridge hathe 10. arches and a stronge warde and towre on it.

A gate at the bridge ende.

Then turninge on the right honde to the key a chapell of the towne withe a *Maesun Diew.*

Then a certen houses with a watar gate and a sqware haull place for the towne, and a chapelle there, as I remembar.

Then a mayne stronge waull on the haven side to Sandgate to Tinmouthe way.

Then 5. towers to Pandon gate.

There harde by dothe . . . Deene watar dryve a mille, and passithe thrwghe the * . . . on this watar there by is a litle archid bridge.

And about this quartar stoode the howse of the Friers *ordinis S. Trinitatis.*

From Pandon gate to Pilgrime gate 15. towres.

Thens to Newgate 8.

The Observant Frires Howse stode by Pandon gate. It was a very fayre thinge.

And lower in the same strete, but on the contrary syde a litle with a lane, was the house of the Augustine Freires.

From Newgate to Westgate a mightye stronge thinge of 4. wardes, and an yron gate 13. towres.

The faire place of Blake Freres stode bytwixt Newgate and Westgate.

The Nunnes Dene havinge 2. bridges resortithe towards Pilgrime gate, and so downe ward to Tine.

The watar of boothe the Denes cummithe from the cole pitts at Cowhil or Cowmore halfe a mile owt of New Castelle.

Ther is a parke waullid and a lodge witheout the Blak Freres and the towne waulle.

From Westgate to Tine side 16. parte almoste round, parte sqware. There I saw the hospitall of S. . . . and then the White Freres, whos garth cam almoste to Tine syde.

Ther be 5. hedds of conduiths for fresch watar to the toun.

[* *Sic.*]

Sepulchra episcoporum Dunelmen. in capitulo.   fo. 51 b.
                                                          Durham.

Robertus de Insula* in vario marmore.
Turgotus episcopus, Aldunus, et Walkerus † in uno tumulo.
Edmundus et Edredus in uno tumulo.
Guil. de Capilepho.‡
De Groystane natus jacet hic Robertus humatus.§
Nicolaus Ferneham episcopus.
Philippus episcopus. Richardus de Marisco.
Ranulphus,‖ as some say, buyldyd Norham Castle.
Walkerus † that was slayne at Gatshed was first byried at
Jarway.
Alterum sepulchrum sine inscriptione.
Ranulphus episcopus, Galfridus episcopus, Gulielmus 2.,
Walterus.

In Choro.

Skirlaw ad boream sub arcu.
Hatfeld ad austrum sub arcu.
Ludovicus Bellemont coram mag. altari sub plano marmore.

In orientali transepto ecclesiae.

Antonius¶ de Becco sub plano lapide** ad borealem partem.
Richardus de Byri ad austrum.

In Galilea.

Thomas Langeley cancellar. Angl. tempore 3ᵘᵐ. regum
sepultus in Galilea.
Est autem Galilea eccl. adjecta occident. parti mag. eccl.
Habet†† in latitudine 5. partes distinctas, et unaquaeque pars
arcus 4.
Langeley made the songe and the gramer schols at Dirham.
Robert Neville Bisshope of Durham lyithe in a highe

[* Robert of Holy Island (Lindisfarne).]
[† Walcher, first buried at Jarrow.]
[‡ Error for *Carileph.*]
[§ Robert of Graystanes, sub-prior and historian of Durham.]
[‖ Ralph Flambard.]   [¶ MS. *Antornius.*]
[** MS. repeats "*ad Becco sub plano lapide*" between "*lapide*" and
ad."]
[†† *Habit,* MS.]

Durham. playne marble tumbe in the Galile. As some say this Nevill made the *Feretrum S. Cuthæberti* as it is now.

There liethe at the hedde of this Neville Richard de Castro Barnardi undar a flat stone. There liethe at his hed one of the Nevilles. There is also a tumbe of Dede the noble monke.

Two of the Lomeleys ly at the northe syde of the churche in the churche garthe *in vario marmore.*

fo. 52 a.   Things that I lernyd of Mastar Hinmar Chauncellar of Durham.

A bysshop of Durham gave, as it apperithe by writinge, the lordeshipe of Ravensworthe apon Tine to a nephew of his. Sins it was one Humfrevills, then Lomeley, and now Gascoynes.

Bointon was owner of this castle no very longe tyme sens.

The lands wher now Greatham Hospitale is by Hertelpole was longinge to Peter Mountefort of the Erldome of Leyrcestar, and beinge attaynted the kynge enteryd on the lande. Then the Bysshope of Duresme made sute to the kynge, sayenge that attayntyd land in the byshopriche shuld be his, and provynge that to be trew, he had the land, and made there an hospitall, and induyd it withe the same.

Henricus de Puteaco brothar to Hugh Puteacus * was foundar of Finkeshal Priorye on Were 2. mils benethe Duresme, and there is he buried; and also S. Goodelak the Heremite.

There is a place in the very hedde of Weredale caullid the Bysshop Stones, and there is the limes of the Bisshoprike.

There be 8. prebends or portions at Northton apon Tese a bout a mile above Stokton.

Yarham Bridge is 2. mils above it. Waltar Skirlaw Bysshope of Durehame made Yareham Bridge. He made also the Gate Howse at Akeland, and also Finkley [a] Bridge on Were of 2. arches, or rathar one arche withe a pillor in the midle of it, was made by Skyrlaw. It was throwne

[* *Puteaus*, MS.]

---

[a] Finchale.

downe 2. or 3. yeres agoo for lake of reparations in tyme. Durham.
It stode a mile above Duresme.

This Skirlaw made all, or a peace of the lanterns at Yorke
Minster, cast out of the vaults of the isles of eche syde of
the highe altar. For there be his armes sette.

Skirlaw made at Swine in Holdernesse, where he was
borne, a fayre chapelle, and there indued to cantuaries.
His fathar, as some say, was a makar of ciffenes * for mcale.

There is bothe yren and lede owre, and also cols in
Werdale.

The water of Were is alway of a trobelyd color, as cumminge thoroughe morishe and owrische soyles.

Litle or no fishe is taken but eles in the upper parte of
Were. For fishe can not ther well lyve in it.

Woulsingham Market in Weredale is cleane decayed. For
none repayre thither with ware or intayle on the consuete
day.

As far as Stanhope men of knowledge say that there nevar fo. 52 b.
was market.

Mastar Chauncelar of Duresme holdithe opinion that the
marmoruarium † that is at Duresme in divers parte of the
churche was taken nother out of Tese nor Were but at a
meaner broke by Woulsingham.

There is a very good quarre of gray marble at Angleston.

Hugo de Puteaco, as the Dene of Duresme tolde me,
made the howse that the Byshops of Duresme have at
Darlengton.

Ex antiquo Codice Dunelmensi.

Tempore Berthrami Prioris vaccaria quaedam prope Beaurepaire.
*Dunelmum mutata est in locum solatii et aedificiis ornata; à
quo tempore dicta est Beaurepair, id est, bellus reditus.*

*Omnes episcopi Lindisfarnenses et Conicastrenses ab Aidano
ad Walkerum* ‡ *Normannum fuerunt monachi.*

*Crux lapidea in coemiterio Dunelmensi delata erat à Lin-
disfarn cum corpore S. Cutheberti, in quo sculptum* § *erat
nomen episcopi facientis illam, s. Ethelwaldi. Prius erat*

[* Cyve, a sieve.]   [† Read *marmoratum.—Hearne.*]
[‡ Walcher the Norman.]
[§ *Seluptio erat*, MS.—*Hearne's correction.*]
V.   K

Durham. *fracta à paganis; sed postea plumbo artificiose partes erant reunitae.*

Insula Lindisfernensis continet 8. milliaria.

Ecclesia et villa de Norham per Ecgredum episcopum aedificatae et S. Cuthberto datae.

Corpus S. Cuthberti delatum Cregam,[a] ibi requievit 4. mensibus, et postea delatum est Cestram.

Hardeknute contulit S. Cuthberto totam terram inter Tese et Tine. Scotti in Mundingham prope Norham viri absorpti * propter terras S. Cuthberti ab eis spoliatas.

Corpus S. Cuthberti requievit in Cestra annis 113. et postea apud Ripon 3. mensibus.

Darlington. *Stire nobilis vir dedit S. Cuthberto Darington cum perti-*
Lumlea villa. *nentiis, et duas carucatas in Lumlea.*

Swaculf filius Kikelli dedit S. Cuthberto Bradebyri, Mordun, Sockburn, Griseby cum saca et socna.

Walkerus contulit Yarow cum pertinentiis.

Waldeophus comes Northumbr. dedit monachis de Yarow Tinmouthe. Gul. Rufus rex dedit Alverton[b] S. Cuthberto.

fo. 53 a. *Hugo de Ponteaco[c] episcopus Dunelmen. fecit murum castelli in porta aquilonari usque partem australem. Hugo etiam fecit pontem de Elvet, turrim de Norham.*

Hugo fecit op[p]idum apud Alverton. Hugo Sadbrigiam[d] eruit à Richardo rege.

Waltherus episcopus Dunelmen. interfectus anno Dom.
1080. *1080. et ejus episcopatus anno 9. sub quo monachi introducti erant in Dunelmum anno Dom. 1083. 7°. Cal. Jun. feria 6. annis 89. ex quo corpus S. Cuthberti illuc delatum.*

Gul. Conquestor fecit Novum Castrum super Tinam.

Leiland. *Hoc opus Roberto Gul. Bastardi filio ascribitur.*

Canutus rex dedit S. Cutheberto Stanthorpe et Raby cum aliis terris.

Epitaphium Matildae imperatricis.

Ortu magna, viro major, sed maxima partu,
Hic jacet Henrici filia, sponsa, parens.

[* *Absorti*, MS.]

---

[a] Craike.   [b] Allerton.
[c] Hugh de Puiset or Puisac, otherwise Pudsey.   [d] Sadbergh.

Filia Henrici 1^{mii}* *regis Angl. uxor. Henrici imperatoris,* Durham.
mater Henrici 2. regis Angliae.

Tilleredus abbas Heffereham dedit Yoden australe S. Cuth-
berto.

Gutheardus dictus episcopus praestitit plures villas cuidam
Alfredo filio Birutuswici exulis.

Elstanus rex Wermuth australem cum suis appendiciis re-
stituit S. Cuthberto.

Chronica feretri S. Cuthberti.

Robertus Courthose condidit Novum Castrum super Tinam.

Sedes Ebor. post mortem S. Wilfridi primi vacavit annis
30. quo tempore Lindisfarnenses episcopi Colmannus, Aidanus
et Finnanus dioecesim illam regebant.

Aecfridus rex dedit Crege S. Cuthberto.

Ethelstanus rex multa ornamenta ecclesiastica dedit mini-
stris S. Cuthberti.

Aethelstanus rex restituit S. Cutheberto australem Were-
mouth cum undecim villis.

Episcopi Dunelmenses à tempore Ludovici Bellemont.

Richardus Byri consecratus 14. Call. Januarii anno Dom.
1333. *obiit 8. Cal. Maii anno Dom.* 1345.   1333.

Thomas Hatfeld consecratus est 11. Jul. videlicet 6. Idus fo. 53 b.
Julii anno Dom. 1345., *obiit 1. Non. Maii anno Dom.* 1381. 1345.

Johannes Fordeham consecra. Nonis Januar. anno Dom.
1381. *et translatus est ad Eliensem 3. Non. Apr. anno* 1389.

Walterus Skirlaw consecra. 3. die Apri. anno Dom. 1389.
obiit 8. Cal. Apr. anno Dom. 1406.

Thomas Langele consecratus 7. die Maii anno Dom. 1406.
obiit 28. d. Novembris anno Domini 1437.

Robertus Neville translatus à sede Sarum consecra. 27. die
Januarii anno Dom. 1437. *Alii scribunt consecr. esse 8. die*
Apr. anno Dom. 1438. *obiit 9. die Jul. anno Dom.* 1457.

Lawrentius Bouth consecra. 25. die Septembris apud Shir-
burn in Elvet anno Dom. 1457. *translatus fuit ad sedem*
Ebor. die S. Firmini episcopi.

Provocatus est rex Edwardus contra Antonium de Bek
episcopum Dunelmensem, eo quod †*pacem inter ipsum et*

[* MS. has *in.*]
[† *Pace inter ipsum et Priore m. rege in intam non,* MS.]

Durham. *Priorem mediante rege initam non observasset, et ex aliis caussis cum hac castrum Bernardi cum pertinentiis ab eo abstulit, et comiti de Warwik contulit, Hert et Hertnesse Roberto de Clifford, Kevreston,*[a] *Galfrido de Hertilpole, quae episcopus habuit ex forisfactura Jounnis de Balliolo, Roberti de Bruse, et Christophori de Seton. In charta tamen dicti regis addebatur istud verbum, salvo jure ecclesiae Dunelmensis.*

Thomas Melsanbe Prior Dunel. fabricavit eccl. Dunelmen. de novo adjuvante Nicolao Fernham episcopo Dunelmen. prius reginae medico.[*]

1264. *Anno Domini 1264. Hugo de Derlington Prior Dunelmen. fecit mag. campanile, parcos de Beaurepair et Muggeleswik, stagnum de Fery Pitington, Benliffe, Mukelinge. Ille fecit manerium de Ketton, capellam,*[†] *aulam et cameras de eodem, cameras de Pitington, West-Stow et Wardlaw, postea à Scottis*
Brown: flu. *destructas. Fecit insuper cameram de Mugleswik, aquam de*
Divernesse. *Devernensset et de Brown.*

1408. *Ab anno Dom. 1408. usque ad annum Dom. 1498. expendebantur ad aedificationem claustri Dunelmen. 838. li. 17. sol. et ob. ex quibus Walterus Skirlaw dedit 600. libras; ex quibus episcopus vivens 200. eo mortuo executores 400.*

fo. 54 a. *Skyrlaw dedit etiam ad constructionem dormitorii 350. marcas. Aquae ductus in cellarium derivatus anno Dom. 1433. Blakeburne descendit*[‡] *in Horselehopbourne,*[b] *inde Horselehopbourne descendit in Derwent in orientali parte, sicut Hawkesburn*[§] *descendit in Roneleshopbourne, et inde sicut Roneleshopbourn descendit de Derwent.*

Owt of a Table in the Chapell of S . . .
withe in Barnard's Castell.

Yorkshire. *Cest memoratum avint le an del incarnation mil e deus*
1233. *cenz e trentre troys al entre del an el secunde moys tut droyt le quart jor de Fefrer. dunc trepassa le franc gerrer Alen le seignur de Galweyth. Pries ad dieu ke sa alme lui playse. Amen.*

[** Medici, MS.*]   [† *Capella, aulē,* MS.]
[‡ *Descen,* MS.]   [§ *Hawkesbarn,* MS.]

---

[a] Keverston.   [b] The burne of Horsley-hope.

Things lernyd out of a Petigre of the L. Scrope.

Walter le Scrop the first that was memorable of that name. The fifthe in descent aftar Water was Philipe, and he lefte 2. dowghtars that were maried, and died witheout issue.

Simon was brother to the aforesayde Philip, and was heire, and had isswe male. Philip and Simon ly buried in the southe porche sydes of Wencelaw paroche on Ure a mile or more above Midleham.

Henry le Scrop was in the beginning of the reigne of Edward the 3. a Baron of the Eskeker and * made a lord of the Parliament, and dyenge was buried in the beginning of Edward the 3. dayes at S. Agathas by Richmont, where dyvers othar of that name were beried.

The Chanons of Seint Agathas tooke one Roaldus for theyr originall foundar. Som thinke that † he was of the Scropes, some thinke rather nay.

Henry Lorde Scrope had a brother caulled Geffray, partaininge to the law, and he was made Lorde Scrope of Massham.

Richard Lorde Scrope was Chauncelar of England in *Scrope Chanselar.* Richard the 2. dayes. This Richard made out of the grownd the castle of Bolton of 4. greate stronge towres and of good lodgyngs. It was a makynge xviii. yeres, and the chargys of the buyldinge cam by yere to 1000. marks.

One Blaunche dowghtar to Michael de la Pole was maried *fo. 54 b.* to this Richard. This Richard had a sonne caullyd Gulielme, whom Kynge Richard the 2. made Earle of Willeshere. He was aftar behedyd, and had no isswe. Yet Richard lyved, and thowghe he wer not restoryd to his office of Chaunselar, yet was he made Threasorer to the Kynge, and dyed *Scrope Treasurar.* in honor.

Some of the Scropes wer buryed at S. Agathas by Richemount, and moaste of late dayes at Bolton.

There were of the Scrops of the Plessyes, and of the Frankes buried in the Grey Friers at Richemount.

One Robert Tipetote died in Edward the 3. days, and he had 3. dowghtars and heires, whereof one was maried to

[* The MS. has "Edw. 2," and a meaningless figure 3 after "and."]
[† The, MS.]

Le Scrop,* and by this Tipetote Le Scrope had the castell of Langham in Notinghamshire, where was a principall howse of the Tipetots.

William Scrope and heire of the Scropes † afore they were lords, and the Lord Neville were founders of the . . .

One *Robertus de veteri ponte* was Lorde of Appleby in Kynge John's tyme, and so was one of them in the first yeres of Edward the 1.

Radulphus filius Ranulphi was Lorde of Midleham, and lefte 2. dowghtars. Mari the elder was maried to Nevile, Johan to Tateshall, and he dyenge witheowt isswe the hole cam to Nevile.

Snape lordshipe, where now the Lord Latimer dwellithe, was Fitz Randols.

The innar parte of the castle of Midleham was buildyd or ever it came to the Neviles hands.

Mounteacute Erle of Saresbyry was Lorde of Perithe Castle.

Yorkshire.

Richard Lord Scrope that buildid Bolton Castle boute the heire generall of S. Quintine that was ownar of Hornby Castle in Richemountshire.

This Richard was content that one Coniers a sarvant of his shuld have the preferment of this warde; and so he had Horneby Castle.

fo. 56 a, error for fo. 55.

Gul. Coniers the first lorde of that name, grauntfathar to hym that is now, dyd great coste on Horneby Castle. It was before but a meane thinge.

There standithe the ruine of a castlet, or pill, in the toppe of an hill, and is callid Penhil. It standythe a 2. mills from Midleham. It longed to Rafe Fitz Randol, as Midleham dyd.

The fayre bridge of 3. or 4. arches that is on Ure at Wencelaw, a mile, or more, above Midleham, was made 200. yer ago and more by one caullyd Alwine, parson of Wencelaw.

Sepul. archiepiscoporum in orient. parte ecclesiae.

1277.   *Walterus Giffart obiit* 7. *Cal. Maii anno Dom.* 1277.
1153.   *Henry Murdak obiit anno Dom.* 1153.

[* Lelcrop, MS.]
[† See continuation of notes from the Scrope pedigree on p. 137.]

Gerardus obiit 12. *Cal. Jun. anno Dom.* 1108.   Yorkshire.
Defuit inscriptio.   1108.
Joannes de Thoresby, quondam Menevensis, postea Wigorn.
et Ebor. archiepiscopus, qui fabricam . . . *obiit* 6. *die Nov-*
embris anno Dom. 1373.   1373.
   Thomas junior obiit anno Dom. 1113. 5. *Idus Mart.*   1113.
   Johan. Romanus obiit anno Dom. 1295.   1295.

In bore. lat. Capel. S. Mar.

   Rotheram archiepiscopus fuit cancellarius Angliae et
Franciae. Obiit 29. *die Maii anno Dom.* 1500.   1500.
   Georgius Nevile archiepiscopus obiit apud Blitheborow
redeundo ad ecclesiam suam anno Dom. 1476.   1476.

In Sacello S . . .

   Thomas de Masham dominus de Scrope, vir nobilis, obiit
. . . *Fecit in sacello S* . . . *duas cantuarias.*
   Henricus primogenitus Joannis Domini Le Scrope obiit
infans.
   Philippa, uxor Henrici Domini Le Scrope et de Mashum,
filia Guidonis domini de Brieu, obiit 19. *die Novembris anno*
1406.
   Dominus Joannes le Scrope de Upsaule[a] *obiit anno Dom.*
1455.
   Stephanus Le Scrop, archidiaconus Richemond, obiit anno
Domini 1418.
   Jacent et alii 2. *ejusdem nominis extra sacellum, sed ante*
fores ejusdem.
   Salvage archiepiscopus Ebor. sepultus in choro in boreali   fo. 56 b.
*parte super altari.**
   In australi ex traverso ecclesiae. Gualterus Grey.
   Wilhelmus de la Souche. Obiit anno Dom. 1352.   1352.
✕ *Rogerus de Asc*[b] *fundavit monasterium monialium S. An-*
dreae † *de Marig*[c] *in fundo sui patrimonii assensu domini sui*   Marrig.
Warnerii filii Gummari, et concessione Conari comitis de
Richemonte. ✕

   [* *Altaris*, MS.]   [† *Andre*, MS.]

---

[a] Upsall.   [b] Aske.   [c] Marrik.

Yorkshire.

Ex libr. de archiepiscopis Ebor. eccles. usque ad mortem Thurstini, incerto autore.

Paulinus 1ᵐᵘˢ. archiepiscopus Ebor. tempore Sax.

Edwinus rex Northumbr. fundator Eboracensis eccle.

Paulinus fundator* eccl. Lincoln.

Honorius consecratus in archiepiscopum Cantuar. à Paulino in eccl. Lincoln.

Paulinus fugiens è Northumbr. barbarorum propter persecutionem factus episcopus Rofensis, ibique mortuus est.

Cedda 2. arch. Ebor. factus cum sedes vacasset proprio carens episcopo 30. annis. Hic Cedda ante fuerat abbas de Lestingei.ᵃ Usus est episcopatu 3. annis, et postea amore quietis vitae honori cessit. Postea ab Wulphero Merc. rege factus est episcopus Lichefeldensis in ecclesia S. Mariae; sed post constructa ibidem ecclesia S. Petri ossa ejus eo translata.

S. Wilfridus 3. arch. Ebor. Primo factus fuit ab Alchfrido, rege Berniciorum, episcopus Haugustaldensis, postea ab Oswio factus archiepiscopus Ebor.

Wilfridus exulabat inperio Ecfridi regis.

Wilfridus factus episcopus Selesiensis.ᵇ

Wilfridus rursus factus episcopus Hagustaldensis,ᶜ vixit in episcop. annis 45.

Bosa 4. episcopus Ebor. rexit episcopatum 10. annis, et principio regni defunctus Ebor. sepultus est.

S. Joannes quintus de gente Anglorum natalibus nobilis.

Joannes bonis artibus instructus in monaster. de Streneshaul.ᵈ

Postea Joan. heremiticam vitam duxit in loco super ripam.

fo. 65 a.†   Isabell Percy weddyd to Gilbert de Acton.

[* *Fundatus*, MS.]

[† Here Stow's own numbering of leaves makes a jump from 56 to 65, and continues on to the end. Hearne, after thinking so much was lost, "changed his mind." But there is no doubt that the eight leaves are gone, the proof being that an index to the volume in Stow's own hand—or one contemporary—makes reference to the missing folios. The subject-matter of fo. 56 b concerns the Archbishops of York, being extracted from a book of York; fo. 65 begins in the midst of a genealogy of the Percys, probably a "petigre." The quire must have been dropped out before the volume was bound.]

ᵃ Lastingham.   ᵇ Selsey, Sussex.   ᶜ Hexham.   ᵈ Strensall.

Henry the 6. had 2. wives, Mary dowghtar to therle of Lancastar. The 2. was the Lady Lucy. She dyed witheowt ysswe.

Mary had Henry the 7. Thomas Percy and Rafe.

Henry the 7. dyed at the Batell of Shrewsbyry before his father. He was the 14. lorde.

Henry the 7. had to wife Elisabethe, dowghtar to the Erle of Marche.

They had Henry the 8. and Elisabethe weddyd to the Lorde Clifford.

Henry the 8. the 2. Erle of Northumbarland maried Elianor dowghtar to the Erle of Westmerland.

They had Henry the ix. the 3. Erle. Thomas Percy Lord Egremount.

Gul. Percy Bysshope of Carlile. Ser Richard Percy. George Percy. Katerin Percy that maried Edmund Lord Gray of Ruthen. Ser Rafe Percy Knight. John Percy buried at Whitby. John Percy dycd yonge. Anne Percy. Henry Percy died yong. Ser John Percy Knight.

Out of a Petigre of the Lord Scrop.

Lord Richard Scrope, builder of Bolton Castell, was sett with the Lord Spensar's doughtar his wyfe.

Guliam sunn to Richard and Erle of Wilshire that was behedid by Henry the 4. was set withc his wyfe, Lady of the Isle of Man.

Rogcrus Scrop was set next with his wife dowghter to the Lord Tipetote.

The Lord Tipetot that was in Edwarde the 4. dayes had suche lands as were left only to the heire mals of the auncienter Lorde Tipetote, that was in Edward the therd's dayes and Richard the second.

Then was set Richard Scrope 2. and his wife, dowghtar to the Erle of Westmerland.

Then was Henricus 2. set with his wife, dowghtar to the Lorde Scrope of Massham.

Then was set John Scrope, Knight of the Gartar, and his wyfe, dowghtar to the Lord Fitzhughe. fo. 65 b.

Then was set Henry Scrope the 3. and his wiffe, dowghtar to the Erle of Northumbarland.

Yorkshire.   Then was set Henry Scrope the 4. and his wyffe, dowghtar to the Lord Scrope of Upshall, and his second wyfe, dowghtar to the Lorde of Dacre and Graystoke. This Henry had no ysswe by his first wyfe; but he had the Lord Scrope that is now by his second wyfe.

And this Scrope hathe som by the Erle of Corberland's * dowghtar.

The trewthe is that Richard Lord Scrope bowght of the kynge the 3. dowghtars and heyres of the Lorde Tiptote, whereof the eldest was maried to Roger his 2. sonne. The 2. dowghtar was maried to William his eldist sonn, aftar Erle of Wilschere, by whom she had no ysswe, and aftar was maried to Wentworthe, by whome she had issue, and that parte of land the Lord Wentworthe hathe now. Stephan the 3. sonn of Richard Scrope maried the yongest dowghtar, and the isswe of this Scrope remaynethe yet.

Come Castell in the diecese of Wiceter.

Richemount-shire.   Ther be 5. wapentaks in Richemontshire, and the hole contery of Richemont in discribinge of Yorkeshire is countid in the Northe-Rydynge.

Bysshops-Dale lyethe joyninge to the quarters of Craven.

Ure cummith thrughe Wencedale adjoininge to Bisshops-Dale.

The hed of Ure in a mosse about a myle above Coteren Hill is about a 14. miles above Midleham muche westward.

The uppar parte of Wencedale is forest of redd dere, longgynge to the kynge.

fo. 66 a.   All the toppe of Coterne Hille, and somewhat farthar is in Richemondshire. And at the utter parte of the hill, or thereabout, is a bek cawlled Hell-Gille, because it rennithe in suche a deadely place. This gill commithe to Ure, and is divider of Richemont and Westmerland-Shires.

There is no very notable bridge on Ure above Wencelaw [a] Bridge, a mile above Midleham and more.

Bainbridge is above Wencelaw Bridge, Aiskar [b] Bridge above it, where Ure ryver faullethe very depe betwixt 2. scarry rokks.

[* *Sic, i.e.,* Henry Clifford, Earl of Cumberland, *temp.* Henry VIII.]

---

[a] Wensley.   [b] Aysgarth.

There be a greate numbar of hopes, or small broks, that Yorkshire. cum into eche syde of Ure out of the rokky mountayns or evar it cum to Midleham.

The bridge over Ure by Midleham is but of tymbar.

About a mile benethe Gervalx ᵃ Abbay is a great old bridge of stone on Ure, caullyd Kilgram Bridge. Then almoste 4. miles to Mascham ᵇ Bridge of tymbar a litle by-nethe Masseham, and vi. miles lower Northbridge at the hether end of Ripon, it is of vii. arches of stone. And a qwartar ot a myle, or lesse, lower, Huwike Bridge ᶜ of 3. arches. Skelle cummithe in betwixt thes 2. bridges.

Swadale ᵈ lyithe by yond Wencedale, and out of the hills rokks on eche syde cum many broks into Swale ryver.

There is a fair bridge on Swale at Gronton ᵉ a 5. miles above Richemount; then Richemount bridge, and 3. miles lower Keterike ᶠ bridge of 4. arches of stone; then 5. mile to Morton bridge of wood; then 5. miles to Skiton ᵍ bridge of wod; then 3. miles to Topclif bridge of wood, and a 3. mils to Thorton ʰ bridg of stone, and . . . miles to Miton,ⁱ whereabout it goithe into Ure.

There be 4. or 5. parks about Midleham, and longing to it, whereof som be reasonably wooddyd.

There is meatly good wood about Ure Vaulx Abbay.

Bolton Village and castell is 4. miles from Midleham. The castell standithe on a roke syde; and all the sub-staunce of the lodgyngs [in] * it be includyd in 4. principall towres. Yt was an 18. yeres in buildynge, and the expencis of every yere came to 1000. marks. It was finichid or Kynge Richard the 2. dyed.

One thinge I muche notyd in the haulle of Bolton, how fo. 66 b. chimeneys were conveyed by tunnells made on the syds of the wauls bytwixt the lights in the haull; and by this meanes, and by no lovers, is the smoke of the harthe in the hawle wonder strangly convayed.

Moste parte of the tymber that was occupied in buyld-

[* Added by Hearne.]

ᵃ Jervaulx.   ᵇ Masham.   ᶜ Bridge Hewick.
ᵈ Swaledale.   ᵉ Grinton.   ᶠ Catterick.
ᵍ Skipton-upon-Swale. ʰ Thornton.   ⁱ Myton-upon-Swale.

Yorkshire. ynge of this castell was fett out of the forest of Engleby in Cumberland, and Richard Lord Scrope for conveyaunce of it had layde by the way dyvers drawghts of oxen to cary it from place to place till it cam to Bolton.

There is a very fayre cloke at Bolton *cum motu solis et Lunae,* and othar conclusyons.

Ther is a parke waullyd withe stone at Bolton.

Ther is a hille withe a leade mine 2. miles beyond Bolton.

Ther be some vaynes of coles found in the upper parte of the west montaines of Richemontshire, but they be not usyd for incomoditie of cariage to the lower parte.

Moste of the coale that be occupied about the quartars of Richemount toune be fetched from Rayle Pitts toward the quartars of Akeland.

The vaynes of the se coles ly sometyme open apon clives of the se, as round about Coket Island and othar shores; and they, as some will, be properly caullyd se coale; but they be not so good as the coles that are diggyd in the inner parte of the lande.

The vayne of coales somtyme lyethe as a yarde depe of the substaunce of the coale. Sometyme the vayne it selfe is an ele in depthe, somtyme the hole heithe of a man, and that is a principall vayne.

The crafte is to cum to it with leste paine in depe digginge. Some vaynes of coales ly under rokks and heades of stones: as some suppose that coales ly undar the very rokks that the minstar close of Duresme standithe on.

I redde in a booke at my Lord Scrops that Lucy, Fitz-Gualtar, Haverington and Multon were heires to the Lord Egremont's lands.

fo. 67 a. And I red in the same booke the claymes of rights of privilegis that Joannes de Britannia Earle of Richemont required bothe for his shire and towne of Richemount, as in makynge of writts at his courts, and liberties of his burge withe 2. faires in the yere at it, and gayle by hymselfe for his shire. And besyde fre warren in his grounds and forest ground in Wencedale with dyvers othar.

I rede in the same boke that Joannes de Britan: Erle of Richemont withe Beatrix his wife dyd compact withe the Prior of Egleston that vi. chanons shuld synge and be perpetually resydent in the castle of Richemount.

PART XI 141

Baronia de Gaunt partita inter Rogerum de Kerdeston, et Julianam* de Gaunt, et Petrum de Manley, heredes Gilberti de Gaunt. Patet recorda de anno 19. Edwardi 1.

Anastasia † uxor Radulphi Fitzrandol. Robertus Tateshal Dominus Baroniae de Tateshal in Lincolnshire.

Part of the lands of Great Badelesmer of Kent cam to the Lord Scrope by mariage.

Genealogia comitum Richemont.

Yorkshire.
Richmont Erles.

Eudo, comes Britanniae ante conquestum, filius Galfridi ducis, genuit 3. filios successive post eum praesidentes Britan. Alanum, dictum Rufum vel Fregaunt, qui venit in Angliam cum Gul. Bastard.

Gul. Bastard auxilio Matildis reginae suae dedit Alano honorem et comitatum ‡ comitis Edwini in Eborashiria, qui inde § vocatus Richemont.

Hic Alanus incepit facere castrum et munitionem juxta manerium suum de Gillinge pro tuitione suorum contra Anglos exheredatos et Danos; et nominavit dictum castrum patria ‖ lingua Richemount, i.e. montem divitem. Hic obiit sine exitu corporis sui, et sepultus est apud S. Edmundum.

Alanus niger ejus frater successit ei in honorem Richemont, cujus gubernat. an. 16. quidam miles Acharias, filius Bardolfi, fundavit monaster. apud Fors in Wendeslay Dale, quod postea translatum est ad Witton per Stephanum comitem, et vocabatur ¶ Jorvalis. Hic Alanus niger obiit sine liberis. Stephanus ejus frater successit ei. Stephene genuit filium nomine Alanum, et obiit anno Dom. 1164. Sepultus fuit apud fo. 67 b. *Beger.** Cor ejus sepultum est in monaster. S. Mariae juxta Ebor. quod ipse prius construxerat et ampliss. possess. donaverat †† anno Dom. 1088.*

Alanus filius Stephani obiit in Britann. 3. April. anno Dom. 1166.

Conanus filius Alani comitis Britann. et Richemont comitis successit. Hic accepit in uxorem Margaretam Gul.

[* *Juliana*, MS.]   [† *Annastastia*, MS.]
[‡ *Comitatem*, MS.]   [§ *In*, MS.]
[‖ *Patia*, MS.]   [¶ *Comite, et vocatur*, MS.]
[** Begar, near Richmond, Yorkshire, a cell to Begar in Brittany.
[†† *Donavit*, MS.]

Yorkshire. *regis Scotiae filiam, ex qua genuit Constantiam, quam Galfredus frater Richardi I. regis Angl. accepit in uxorem. Hic Conanus aedificavit turrim magnam in castro Richemont. Obiit in Britann. et sepultus est apud Begar anno Dom. 1170.*

Constantia filia Conani ex Galfredo genuit Arthurum, quem Joannes rex Angl. occidi fecit. Constantia postea nupsit Ranulpho comiti, à quo divortiata est propter adulterium, et postea nupsit Guidoni Tearcho,* et ex eo genuit filiam nomine Adeliciam, quae † post mortem parentum remansit in custodia regis Fraunciae; et postea nupsit Domino. Petro Manclerk militi suo cum ‡ Britannia. Obiit in Britann. sepulta apud Begar anno Dom. 1201.

Adelicia obiit in Britann. et sepulta est apud Plonarmel anno Dom. 1221.

Joannes, filius Adeliciae, obiit in Britan. anno Dom. 1214. Nunquam fuit comes.

Joannes, filius Joannis, comes Richemont desponsavit Beatricem filiam Henrici regis, ex qua genuit Arthurum, Petrum et Joannem. Occisus fuit Lugduni in coronat. Clementis pontif. Ro. anno Dom. 1305. ibidemque sepultus est. Arthurus dux Britan. sed non comes Richemont, filius Beatricis obiit in Britan. et sepultus est apud Plonarmel anno Dom. 1311.

Johannes, frater Arthuri comitis,§ obiit in Britan. sepultus apud Vanes[a] anno Dom. 1330.

Joannes, filius Arthuri comitis, obiit in Britann. sepultus Plonarmel anno Dom. 1341.

Sepulchra nobilium in eccles. de Ripon. In boreali parte insulae transm7.‖

fo. 68 a.   Two tombes withe ymagis of the Markenfelds and theyr wyves. And a tumbe of one of the Malories in the southe

[* *Guy de Toarche,* or Th̄ouars. (Dugdale, Bar., i, 49 a.)]
[† *Adelicia, quem,* MS.]   [‡ *Sic.*]
[§ *Arthurus comes,* MS.]
[‖ Perhaps *transepti,* Hearne; it is not clear.]

---

[a] Vannes.

parte of the crosse in a chapell: and without, as I herd, **Yorkshire.** lyethe dyvers of them undar flate stones.

On the northe syde of the Quiere.

Ranulphus Picot obiit anno Dom. 1503.

S. Wilfridi reliquiae sub arcu prope mag. altare sepultae, nuper sublatae.

There be v. fayre arches in the syde isles of the body of the churche.

The body selfe of the churche is very wyde, and was a late new buildyd, especially by one . . . Prebendary of the same churche. Sence I hard say he was but paymastar of the works.

In the crosse isle on eche part be 2. or 3. arches.

Inscriptio: in novo muro Capellae S. Mariae Ripitoni.

S. Cuthebertus episcopus* Lindifarnensis hîc fuit monachus.

S. Eata archiepiscopus Ebor. hîc fuit monachus.

S. Wilfridus archiepiscopus Ebor. hîc fuit monachus et 1. *abbas.*

S. Willebrordus archiepiscopus Walretensis hîc fuit monachus.

Nid ryver risethe muche by west 5. miles above Pateley *Nid ryver.* bridge of wood, a litle a this syde a chapell caullyd Midlemore, and as I could learne it is in the paroche of Kirkeby Malesart.

From Patley bridge and village, a membar of Ripon paroche, to Newbridge of tymber 3. miles. Thens to Killinghal bridge of one great arche of stone 3. miles, and 3. miles to Gnaresbrughe, where first is the west bridge of 3. arches of stone, and then a litle lower Marche bridge of 3. arches. Bothe thes bridges serve the towne of Knaresborow. Gribololbridge is about a mile benethe Marche bridge, and is of one very greate bridge for one bowe. Then to Washeford [a] bridge a 4. miles, it is of a 4. arches. Then to Catalle [b] bridge of tymebar a 2. miles, to Skipbridge of tymbar and

[* *Episcopis*, MS.]

---

[a] Walshford.   [b] Catal.

Yorkshire. a great caussy. The last and lowest bridge on Nidde is this
Skipbridg.

fo. 68 b.   This cawsey by Skipbridge towards Yorke hathe a 19. small
bridges on it for avoydinge and over passynge carres cumming out of the mores thereby. One Blake[burne],* that was
twys Maior of Yorke, made this cawsey, and a nothar without one of the suburbs of Yorke. This Blakeburne hathe a
solemne *obiit* in the minstar of Yorke, and a cantuari at
Richemond.

This Blakeburne had very onthrifty children; wherefore
he made at Yorke 4. cantuaries at Alhowen in the Northe
Strete, and as many at Alhalow in the Thauimen.†

The hed of Cover is muche by west a 6. miles above
Coverham Priorie, and a very litle above this priorye over
Cover is a bridge, and thens scant 2. miles it goithe som-
what benethe Midleham Bridge into Ure.[a]

Ther is no notable thinge to speke of from the head of
Cover to Coverham Priorie.

Bowrne risethe at a place by west in the west hills caullid
More Heade, and thens goithe into Ure a litle benethe
Massenham bridge and towne on Ure.

Agayne the mouthe of this on the othar syde of Yore
ryver lyethe Aldeburg village.

And a mile farthar by est liethe Thorpe, one of Mastar
Danby's howses. Howbeit he hathe one that he more occupiethe at Farnbey a 2. miles from Leeds.

There be 2. lordshipps lyenge not very far from Ripon,
that is Norton Conyers and Hutton Coniers. Norton hathe
Northeton Coniers, and Malory hathe Hutton Coniers. Thes
lands cam to theyr aunciters by two dowghtars, heirs generall
of that Coniers.

Malory hathe an othar place caullyd Highe Studly a litle
from Fontaines. There be 3. Studeleys togethar: Highe,
Midle and Lowe.

Plomton of Plomton a mile from Gnaresburghe.

[* No blank here, but half the name was omitted.]
[† *Sic*, but should be "Pavement," *i.e.*, the Church of All Saints
on the Pavement.]

---

[a] Ure or Yore r.

This Plomton hathe by the heire generall a good parte of the Babthorps lands: but Babthorpe the lawyer kepithe Babthorpe selfe, that is, as I remembar, in Holdernesse.   Yorkshire.

Markenfilde dwellith at Markenfelde,[a] and his manar place berithe his name.   fo. 69 a.

Wiville dwellithe a litle above Masseham on the farther ripe of Ure.

The Lorde Lovelle had a castelle at Killerby within a quartar of a mile of the Ripe *citerioris* of Swale a myle benethe Keterike Bridge.

There appere gret ruines.

Mastar Metecalfe hierithe the lordeshipe of the Kinge. Som say that ther cam watar by conductus into the topps of som of the towres.

There was a howse at Barwike *ordinis S. Trinitatis;* but Antony Beke, Bysshope of Duresme, destroyid it, and then one William Wakefilde mastar of the howse in Barwike at the defacinge of it cam to New Castelle, and by the aide of Gul. Acton and Laurence Acton bretherne, bothe marchaunts of New Castell, buildid within the towne of New Castell a howse of the religion *S. Trinitatis*, where Wakefeld hymself was first master.   Northumberland.

There cum diverse smaul broks *ripa ulter.* into Weland or evar it rennithe by Rikingham.[b]   Rutland.

Litle Eye cummith into Weland halfe a mile benethe Rokingham Bridg *ripa ulteriori*, and this broke is limes betwixt Leircestershire and Ruthelandshire.

Wrete or Wrek[c] cummithe into Weland halfe a myle benethe Colyweston Bridge *ripa superiori*. There is a bridge archid with stone at Ketton a mile above the place where it enterith into Weland.

Washe cummethe from a litle above Okam[d] in Rutheland, and thens a 8. mile to Byry Casterton,[e] where is a bridge of 3. arches, and then a mile, or more, to Newstede Bridge, and sone after into Weland.

Bridges on Weland ryver bynethe Rokingham Bridge. Coliweston, Stanford, Uffington, Westdepinge, Estdeping, Croiland.

---

[a] Markingfield.   [b] Rockingham.   [c] Wreak r.
    [d] Oakham.   [e] Great Casterton.

V.   L

Westmor-
land.

Thyngs learnyd of a man of Westmerland.

There is a greate broke caulled Owse Water,[a] in Westmerland. The hede of this watar lyethe about a myle by west
from the hedde of Loder, that cummethe by Shap Priorye.
The place where it risethe is caullyd Mardale. First it ren-
fo. 69 b.   nith aboute halfe a mile in a narow botom, and then *stagnescit*,
makinge a poole [b] of a 2. mils in lenght, and then it cummithe again *in alveum*, and so renninge halfe a mile, it goithe
by Bampton village strait into Loder.[c]

Bampton is 3. mils lower then Shap.

The poole cummith agayne to a narow botom, and betwixt the lower end of the poole and the mouthe of Ose
into Loder is a bridge of stone.

On Loder be no more bridges of stone but Shap Bridge
a this syde Browgham.

Ther be about halfe a mile lower then Brougham on the
west ripe of Aymote [d] ryver, hard by the ripe, certeyne caves
withe in a rokke, as haul chaumbers and othar necesary
romes.

The castell of Pendragon is by the farther ripe of Suale,
and ther the ryver is a marche betwixt Richemontshire and
Westmarland.

Pendragon is not far distaunt from the very hed of Swale.
Ther standithe yet muche of this castell.

Gentlemen of name in Westmerland.

Loder.
Mosgrave.
Thwarton.
Sandeford.
Sawkille.

Yorkshire.   The way on Watlyngestrete from Borow Bridge to Carlil.

Wattelyngestrete lyethe about a myle of from Gillinge and
3. miles from Richemount.

From Borow Bridg to Caterike 16. miles, xii. to Lemig,[e]

[a] Hawes Waterbeck.   [b] Hawes Water.   [c] Lowther r.
        [d] Eamont r.   [e] Leming.

a pore village, and vi. to Caterike. Thens x. good miles to **Westmor-**
Gretey,[a] then v. miles to Bowes, a very excedinge poore **land.**
thorowghe fayre, and viii. myle to Burgh [b] on Stane More,
and * v. so to Appleby about a 4. miles, and v. to Browham [c]
where the strete cummithe thrughe Whinfelle Parke, and
ovar the bridgs on Eimote and Loder, and levinge Perithe [d] a
quartar of a mile or more on the west syde of it goithe to
Cairluell xvii. miles from Brougham.

The toune of Brougham is now very bare, and very ill fo. 70 a.
buyldyd. Yt hathe bene some very notable thinge.

Eydon [e] ryver rennythe within a quartar of a myle of
Broughe.

Mayden Castell, where now is nothinge but an hille diked,
is harde on the est syde of Wathelynge Strete, v. miles a this
syde Browgh.

Robert Englyshe and Thomas Thirland, Maiors of Noting- **Notts.**
ham, and riche marchaunts, buryed in S. Marie's Churche.

There were vi. or vii. gates in the towne waulle, now all *Notyngham.*
be downe save 3.

S. John Hospitall almoste downe without the towne.

The Gray and White Friers.

As far as I can lerne the chefest howse of the Chaundose *Chaundoz.*
that they had in England was at Cowberley in Wileshire. *Cowberkeley.*

Syns I red that the name was Cow, and of Berkeley Cow-
berkley.

Chandois had fayre pocessions in Gascoyne, and of them
he had paiment owt of the Kyng's Eskeker.

Ther were dyvars knyghts of fame of the Chaundos afore
the tyme of hym that was in Edward the 3. dayes a noble
warriour. This Chandois dyed witheout ysswe, and left his
two systars heires, whereof one was maried to Bridgs, and
the othar to Pole.

Bridges had Cowberle and othar lands to the some of
300. marks by the yere.

Poole had Rodburne [f] withein 4. myles of Darby, and
othar 300. marks of land by yere.

[* *Sic.*]

Greta.	[b] Brough.	[c] Brougham.
[d] Penrith.	[e] Eden r.	[f] Radbourne.

Chaundois in his old writyngs namithe hymselfe *vice-comitem S. Salvatoris.*

Chaundois had lands in or about Herfordshire. And he was foundar, as I remembar, of Goldclyve Priorye in Walles, and here, as I thinke, was his first and chefe howse.

The olde howse of Rodburne is no greate thinge, but the laste Chaundois began in the same lordshipe a mighty large howse of stone withe a wonderfull cost, as it yet aperithe by foundations of a man's height standinge yet as he left them. He had thowght to have made of his olde place a colledge.

fo. 70 b.   The Earle of Rutheland in sum old writyngs is cawlyd Lorde Turbur.

Owt of an old boke that the Erles of Ruthland hathe.

Leyland thinkithe all this to be a lye.

In the yere of owr Lorde 734. *Alfredus tertius Merc. rex* in the * yere of his reigne cam to the stronge castell of Albanac nere Grantham, and there desyryd to have for wyfe one of the 3. dowghtars of Guliam de Abanac, wherapon Gul. desired him to tary all night at his castle, and in the morninge Gul. brought his eldist dowghtar namyd Adeline starke naked in the one hand, and a swerde draune in the othar. His wyffe led the 2. caullyd Etheldred. Guliam, sone to William, led in one hand the 3. dowghtar caullid Maude, and a swerde in the othar.

Guliam the father then said to the Kynge Alfrid: Sir, heire be my 3. doughters, chese to wyfe whiche ye liste; but rather then ye shuld have any of them to your concubine I wold sle her with my owne hands. The kynge answerid that he ment to take one of them to wife, and chose Etheldrede that had fat bottoks, and of her he had Alurede that wan first all the Saxons the monarchy of England.

Leic. Linc.   *Ex antiquo Codice monasterii de Bello viso.†*

Beavoure.   *Robertus de Toterneio, fundator monasterii de Beauvoir, jacet in capitulo.*

Et juxta eum Gul. de Albeneio 1. scilicet Brito, in parte boreali.

[* Year omitted.]
[† Belvoir, on the edge of two counties.]

Item in veteri eccl. ante crucem jacet Gul. de Albeneio 2. scilicet Mechines. Et juxta eum Adeliza uxor ejus in parte australi.* Et 2. uxor ejus Cecilia jacet sub muro veteris eccles. Gul. de Albeneio 3. jacet apud Novum locum, et cor ejus sub muro contra summum altare de Bever in parte boreali.

Gul. 4. jacet ante summum altare de Bever, et cor ejus apud Croxton.

Odonellus de Albeneio jacet in occidentali † parte capituli. fo. 71 a.

Et juxta eum jacet Matildis de Unframville, mater ejus.

Et juxta eam ‡ jacet Albreda Biseth uxor Gul. 4.

Robertus de Ros jacet apud Kirkham. viscera autem ejus ante summum altare de Bever juxta corpus Gul. 4. de Albeneio, ex parte austr. qui obiit 16. die Kal. Junii anno Dom. 1285.

Isabella, uxor Roberti de Ros, jacet apud Novum locum juxta Staunford, obiitque anno Dom. 1303.§

It. Gul. de Ros, filius ejus, jacet apud Kirkham.

Item Matildis Vaus, uxor dicti Gul. jacet apud Penteney, et viscera ejus in capella S. Mariae, scilicet in pariete.

Matildis, uxor Jacobi Domini de Ros, jacet in pariete inter Capell. b. Mariae et presbiterium.

Anno Domini 1459. nata fuit Margareta, filia Thomae domini de Ros, apud Blakeney 1. die Jul.

Anno Dom. 1427. natus fuit Thomas, primogenitus Thomae domini de Ros, apud castrum de Cunnesborow.ᵃ

Anno Dom. 1429. natus Richardus, filius Thomae domini de Ros, apud castrum de Belvero.

Hic supra scriptum Henricus de Albeneio.

Robertus de Toterneio, fundator Prioratus de Belvar, obiit 2. Nonas Augusti.

Petrus de Valloniis, fundator eccl. de Byham, obiit 13. Call. Aprilis.

Prioratus de Belvero cella monaster. S. Albani.

[* *Australy*, MS.]   [† *Occidenti*, MS.]
[‡ *Eum*, Monast. Angl., tom. i, p. 328, b. 24 (ed. 1682). *Hearne.*]
[§ 1301, Mon. Angl., *loc. cit. Hearne.*]

ᵃ Conisbrough Castle.

Beds.

Inscript. tumuli in eccle. S. Pauli:

De Bello-campo jacet hîc sub marmore Simon
*fundator de Newenham.**

The prebendaries of S. Paules at Bedeford had theyr howsys round about circuite of S. Paule's churche.

There remayne yet in Bedeforde howses of prebends now longynge to Lyncolne Churche.

Roisia, wyfe to Paganus de Bello-campo, and mothar to Simon, convertyd the Chanons irregular of Bedford into Chanons regular.

Symon de Bello-campo translatyd them to Newnham.

fo. 71 b.   Paganus de Bello-campo had the barony of Bedford gyven to hym aftar the Conquest.

Bothe the hospitalls in Bedford were of the towns men foundations. They of late dayes, for bringinge theyr fee-ferme frome XL. pound to 20. pound, gave the title and patronage of one of them to Ser Reynald Bray.

Roisia was founderes of Chiksand in Bedfordshire, and there was she buried in the chapter howse.

Cawdewell Priory,[a] a litle without Bedford, was of the foundation of the Beauchamps.

The barony of Bedforde was devided at the last emongs 3. dowghtars of the last Beauchaump.

Mowlbray had the eldest.

The Lord Latimer bought the lands of the 2.

The third was maried to one Straunge.

Straunge's parte cam to 2. dowghtars. Pigot maried the one, and Pateshul the othar. A pece of Pateshul's parte is come to S. John.

Fol. 72. vacat.

In navi ecclesiae Warwike.†

fo. 73 a.   *Johannes Rouse capell. cantuar. de Gibclif,[b] qui super por-*

[* See vol. i, p. 100.]

[† See vol. ii, p. 151. Most of the notes on this fo. 73 will be found as utilized by Leland in Part V (vol. ii), pp. 42-44; see the note on p. 43.]

---

[a] Caldwell Abbey.   [b] Guy's cliff.

ticum australem hujus eccl. librariam construxit, et libris Warwicks.
ornavit. Obiit 14. *die mensis Januarii anno Dom.* 1491.   1491.

This Rowse was of the howse of the Rousis of Ragley by Alcester, as it is supposed.

He bearethe 3. crouns in his armes.

William Barswelle,* Dene of Warwike, and one of the executors of the testament of Erle Richard Becham, that saw the new buyldynge of the college, and the buyldynge of owr Lady Chapell finishid, that were begon in Richard Erle of Warwyke tyme.

Johannes Tunstall, miles.

In australi insula navis eccl.

Power armiger.

Hungfordi 3. *avus, pater, filius,* heires† of Edmund's-Cote ᵃ halfe mile or more by este out of the towne.

Bewfo‡ an esquier, to whom parte of Hu[n]gford's lands descendyd.

In transepto eccl.

Thomas de Bello-campo, comes Warwike.

Gul. Peito dominus§ de Chesterton et ejus uxor.   Peto.

Richard Erle of Warwike lay wher Alestre, Deane of Warwike, lyethe at the west ende of the Lady Chaple without.

Haseley, schole-mastar to Henry the 7. and Deane of Warwyke. He translatid Erle Richard, and he lyeth ther also buryed.

In owr Lady Chapell.

One of the Lorde Latimers at the west end of it without stone, or writynge. Kylled at a feld; some say Egcote ᵇ by Banberye.

[* Berkswell, Dean of the collegiate church; see Dugdale's Warwickshire, 1656, p. 353.]
[† Stow seems to have intended "lorell," but the word is "heires" in vol. ii, p. 42.]
[‡ Beaufort, see vol. ii, p. 42.]   [§ *Obus*, MS.]

ᵃ Emscote.   ᵇ Edgcott.

Warwicks.

Epitaphium* Richardi comitis Warwyke.

Pray devoutly for the sowle, whom God asseyle, of one of
the moaste worshipfull Knyghts in his dayes of manhod
and connynge, Richard Beauchampe, late Erle of Warwike, Lord Dispenser of Bergeveny, and of many othar
great Lordships, whos body restithe here under this tombe
in a full fayre vaulte of stone, set in the bare rocke: the
whiche visyted with longe sycknes in the Castle of Rohan
therin deceasyd full christianly the last day of Aprile in the
1439. yere of owr Lord God a 1439. he beinge at that tyme
Livetenaunt Generall of Fraunce, and of the Duchye of
fo. 73 b. Normandye, by sufficient auctoritie of owr Sovereigne Kynge
Henry the 6. The whiche body with great deliberation
and worshipfull conducte by sea and by land was browght
to Warwyke the fowrthe of Octobar the yere abovesayde,
and was leyde with full solempne exequies in a fayre chest
made of stone in the west dore of this chapell, accordynge
to his last wylle and testament, therin to rest tyll this
chapell by hym devisid in his lyfe wer made. All the
whiche chapell foundyd on the rocke, and all the members ther of his executors dyd fully make and apparail by
the aucthorytie of his sayde last will and testament; and
thereaftar by the sayde autoritie they dyd translate wor-
shipfullye the sayd body into the vault above saydc.
Honoryd be God therefore.

Owt of the glase wyndowes in owr Lady Chappell.

Elisabethe, dowghtar and heyre to Thomas Lord Berkley
et de Isle, first wyfe to Richard Beauchamp, Earle of Warwyke. This woman had by hym 3. dowghtars:

Margaret that was maried to John Earle of Shrewsbery,
cawlled Lord Talbot and Furneval.

Alienor the 2. maried to Edmond Beauforte and of
Somerset.

Elisabeth the 3. maried to George Nevile Lord Latimer.

Isabell 2. wyfe to Erle Richard Domina de Spencer, de
Glamorgan and Morgannok.

[* *Epitaphie Richardy*, MS.]

Henry Duke of Warwyke, sonne and heire to Richard **Warwicks.**
and Isabell the first Duke of Warwyke, the whiche maried
Cecile, dowghtar to Richard Nevile, Earle of Salesberie.

Anne, dowghtar to Erle Richard and Isabell, maried to
Richard Nevill, sonne and heire to Richard Neville, Erle of
Saresbyry.

In choro.

*Thomas de Bello-campo, comes Warwike, pater Thomae
comitis et avus Richardi; et uxor Thomae ibidem in eodem
tumulo.*

*Catarina, primogenita ejusdem Thomae, jacet sub plano
marmore ad ejus caput.*

Olde Erle Thomas, grauntfathar to Richard Erle of Warwyke, was cawser that [the] new quier of the Collegiate
Churche of owr Lady in Warwyke was newly reedified by
the executors of his testament. The mansyon of the olde
denry and colledge stode where the est southe est parte of
the churche yarde is now.

The new is of a latar buyldynge.

V. prebendaries and a deane.

Seint Marie the chefe parishe churche collegiatid, and no fo. 74 a.
mo within the towne. The chapell of Seint Peter over the
est gate a prebend to Seint Marie's.

The chappell over the west gate of Seint [James], a
prebend.

A fraternitie of Seint George, and a litle college with
priests on the northe syde of the west gate. Sum say that
Richard Bechamp was a setter forward of this; and the same
Earle Richard convertid the hermitage of Gibclif,ᵃ into
2. cantuaries, and erectid a new chapell there.

The northe gate at Warwyke is faullen downe.

The bridge servithe for the southe gate. It hathe xii.
arches.

Bereford ᵇ wher is a greate stone bridge over Avon a 2.
myles lower.

The castell stondethe harde by the bridge of the towne,

[* *Casta,* MS.]

ᵃ Guy's cliff. ᵇ Barford.

154 LELAND'S ITINERARY

Warwike Castle was rased downe by H. the 3. in the 48. yere of his reigne.

Warwicks.

it is set on an huge mayne rokke. The est front hathe 3. towers. The kepe stondithe in ruines by weste. There be a 3. towers besyde in the castle. The Kynge now buildith strongly on the southe syde, and there is all the fayre lodgynge of the castle. Kynge Richard the 3. began a stronge peace for artelerie on the northe syde of the castle. There be 2. goodly stretes in Warwyke. The Highe Strete (wherin is a goodly crosse) is est and west. The othar strete from northe to sowthe. The suburbe by este is cawled Smithes Streate, and at the ende of it was an hospitall of Seint John. The suburbe without the bridge by southe is cawled the Bridge Ende; and here is a chapell of Seint John, that longed to Seint John's at London. The suburbe be west is cawlled the West End. Ther is a suburbe by northe, in this was a master and bretherne of an hospitall or colledge of Seint Michell. Now it is muche in ruine, and taken for a fre chapell. There is also in the southe syde of the towne witheout the walls a parishe churche of Seint Nicolas, annexid as a prebend to Seint Maries. Rogerus de Bello-Mount, Earle of Warwike, translatyd the colledge out of the castle to Seint Maries. The Blake Friers stoode in the suburbs of the towne. Ther is a parke hard by Warwike longynge to the castle.

From Warwike to Coventrie viii. myles, 4. miles to Kyllyngworthe, and 4. to Coventrie. From Warwyke to Lichefilde xxiiii. myles by Coleshille. From Warwyke to Stratforde upon Avon 7. miles. From Warwike to Hanley a market towne, where be ruines of a castell, a vi. mylls. From Warwyke to Dudley Castle 20. myles.

fo. 74 b.
Stowre River.

Stowre in Warwykeshire within a 3. miles of Charlecote.

Chesterton, Peito's maner, a 4. myles from Warwyke.

The lordeshipe of Sudeley in Glocestershire longed to the Botelars that were western men.

Sudley Castle.

One Rafe Boteler Lord Sudeley buylded the castle of Sudeley aboute the tyme of Henry the 6. and Edward the 4.*

Butlar Lorde Sudley was emprisoned in Edwarde the 4. dayes, wherupon he resignid his castle into the hands of

[* See vol. ii, pp. 55, 56.]

Kynge Edward. This castle cam aftar to Gaspar Duke of **Warwicks.**
Bedforde that kept howshold in it.

The hawle of Sudley Castle glased with rownd beralls.

The Tracyes hold Todington lordshipe and othar lands
by the gyfte of the Botelers.

Bovy Thracy in Devonshire * longged to Thracyes of
Toddyngton, but it was sold to the Erle of Devonshire. Ther wer
One told me that the Lorde Suddeley was Lorde of Hanley 2. Partes at
a marke towne and castle in Warwykeshire,† and that Hanley.
Mastar Belknape muche laboryd to have it restoryd unto
hym as his heire.

The Lord Sudleys and Mountforts were taken for foundars
of the Blacke Friers in Oxforde.

Wedenok ᵃ Parke nere to Warwik by northe, and longynge
to Warwyke Castle.

Grove Parke thereby, and Haseley Parke also.

Edmonds Cote ᵇ bridge of stone about halfe a myle above
Warwyke on Avon.

Berforde ᶜ bridge of viii. arches ovar Avon.

Fulbroke Parke on the northe syde of Berford, about
halfe a myle of on the ryght banke of Avon. Ther was in it
a castlet of stone and brike, wherin, as I hard say, sometyme the Duke of Bedforde lay; and a litle lodge callyd
Bergcincy Gate. This castell stoode bremlye in the sight of
Warwyke Castle, and was a cawse of harte-brinynge.

Compton of late dayes rasyd muche of it, bringynge parte
to Commeton toward buildynge of his howse, and some
parte he gave awaye.

Telesforde ᵈ a priorie of Maturin Friers Order Seint Tri-
nite of the foundation of the Lucies, wherein divers of them
wer buryed.

Marke that the moaste parte of Warwykeshire that
stondithe on the lefte hond, or banke, of Avon, as the ryver
dessendethe, is called Arden, and this contrye is not so fo. 75 a.
plentifull of corne, but of grasse and woode. Suche parte of

[* Stow wrote " Dorset," a later hand corrects it.]
[† This seems to be an error for Worcestershire.]

ᵃ Wedgnock.   ᵇ Emscote.   ᶜ Barford.   ᵈ Thelsford.

Warwikeshire as lyethe by sowthe on the lefte hand, or banke, of Avon is baren of woode, but plentifull of corne.

Ther is a priory of nonnes 3. myles from Warwyke.

Gloucester. *Ex inscriptionibus in occidentali parte Glocester Churche.*

681. *Osricus rex primus* foundator of that monastary *in anno Domini* DCLXXXI. for nuns.

Saynt Arild Virgin, martired at Kinton, ny to Thornberye, by one Muncius a tiraunt, who cut of hir heade becawse she would not consent to lye withe hym. She was translatyd to this monasterye, and hathe done great miracles.

The great southe ysle of Gloucestar churche was made by oblations done at the tombe of Kynge Edward the Second.

Roger Lacye Erle of Hereford.

Roger Lord Berkley.

Hugo de Portu. Helias Giffard.

Mastar John Mangeant, Chanon of Herford, wer monks of Gloucestar.

Bernulf, Kynge of Merche, bringethe in seculer chanons and clerks, gyvynge pocessions and lyberties to them.

Kynge Canute for ill lyvynge expellyd seculer clerks, and by the counsell of Wolstane Bysshope of Wurcestar bringethe in monkes.

Aldred, Bysshope of Worcester, translatyd to Yorke, takynge a great parte of the lands of Glocestar to reedyfie the same.

A noble lord, callyd Wolphin Lekne, for 7. pristes kylled, had penaunce to find 7. monks at Glocestar.

William Conquerar gave Glocestar Abbay * decayed to his chaplen Serlo.

Osrik first under kynge and lorde of this contrie, and the Kynge of Northumberland, with the licens of Ethelrede, Kynge of Mercia, first foundyd this monasterye.

Osrike by the counsell of Bosel firste Bysshope of Worcester putteth in nunes, and makethe Kineburge his sister abbas.

[* I have made several corrections in these notes on Gloucester Abbey from the narrative founded on them in vol. ii, pp. 60, 61.]

3. noble wemen, Kineburge, Edburge, and Eva Quenes of Merchie, and only abbesses for the tymes of nunes, the whiche was 84. yeres. The nunes wer ravyshed and dryven away by warres betwixt Egbbert and Kynge of the Marche.

Albredus, B. of Wircestar, dedicated the Church of Glocestar, whiche he had builded from the foundation to S. Petar, and by the Kyng's licens obteyned, constituted Wulstan abbot there.*

Kynge William Conquerar gave, and his sonns also, liberties and pocessions to the monastarie of Glocestar.

Thomas Archebysshope of Yorke restoryd the land, the whiche Aldrede wrongfully dyd withhold.

Hanley † and Farley abbats made owr lady chapell.

Horton Abbas made the northe syde of the crosse isle.

The sowthe syde of the crosse isle made by offeryngs at the tombe of Kynge Edward the 2.

Abbote Sebroke made a great peace of the belle towre in the midle of the quiere.

Abbate Froncester buryed at the west ende of the quiere made the cloistar.

Abbate Morwent made the new west end of the churche, and the goodly porche by north.

Gamage a knight of Wales and his wife wer buried at the southe west side witheout the qwere.

Osburne celerar made a late a sqware towre by northe west the churche yarde in Abbate Malverne, *alias* Parker's tyme.

Robert Courthose is buried in the Presbitere.

Some thinke that Stranbowe's a wyf Countis of Pembroke lay where Abbot Malvern had his tombe.

Sudeley Castell sold to Kynge Edward the 4.

From Winchelescombe b to Twekesbyrie 7. myles.

To Worcester 14. mils.

To Persore ix. mils.

[* This paragraph is written on the margin at bottom of fo. 75 a.]
[† Hanley, Hamley, or Hauley; his name is uncertain. Abbot in 1447.]

———————————

a Strongbow.   b Winchcombe.

To Cirencester 15. miles.

To Glocester xii. myles.

To Eovesham 7. miles or 8.

To Southam 3. mils.

Sowtham longed to one Goodman, nowe to Hudelstan.

From Southam to Chilteham [a] market 5. miles. It longed to Tewkesbcrye. A broke; 2. brokes more.

To Glocestar vi. miles.

fo. 76 a. In Glocestar ar 11. pariche churches. Seint Ewines without the suburbe. The abbey churche. Seint Oswalde. The Graye and Blake Friers within the towne. The White Frers. Seint Margaret, and Seint Magdalen's hospitales without the towne, Seint Margaret's bettar endewed. Bartolome's hospital beyond one of the bridgs, 30. poore folke. One Pouncevolt [b] lythe in the bodye of the church there, a greate benefactor to it.

K. Henry the 3. and Stephen de Harnshull * knight foundyd the Blake Frers *anno dom.* 1239.

Lorde Barkley foundyd the Whit Friers.

vii. arches in the first bridge; one in a gut bridge beyond; v. arches in a bridge upon a pece of Severne; 4. in the cawse; 3. in a nother place, beside othar viii. at the ende.

Northe gate. Ailes gate by est. South gate. West gate beyonde the 2. first bridges new builded. Lands gyven by Henry the 8, Belle, and othar men to mayntayne the cawsies and bridges at † Glocester.

Howsys longginge to the Abbat of Glocestar.

Pinkenes [c] 3. miles of by est with a goodly parke.

The vinyarde by west at the cawsey's end.

Hartebyriby [d] northe-west [4] miles of.

[* Stow has here a blank, but he copied "Harnshull" in the narrative, vol. ii, p. 58.]
[† MS., "and."]

---

[a] Cheltenham.   [b] Pancefoote, see vol. ii, p. 59.
[c] Prinkness, now Prinknash Park.
[d] Hartpury.   See also vol. ii, p. 62.   Erroneously confused with Hartbury in my Index to that vol.

Gloucester.

No bridge on Severne byneth Glocestar.

Newenham [a] village 8. miles bynethe Glocestar *ripa dextra* in the forest of Dene. There the watar at full se is halfe a myle over. A 2. myls lower the water at full se is a myle more ovar.

Barkeley an 18. miles from Glocestar, somewhat distaunt from Severne.

Thorneberye [b] a 22. myles, not very farre from Severne on a creke goynge up to it.

From Glocestar to Brightstow 30. myles by land, 40. by water and more.

No bridge from Glocestar to Twexberye. Ther a bridge. To Avon a litle above the towne.

Fowre myles above Twekexberye a stone bridge, but none on Avon.

Inscriptiones in capitulo * *Glocester eccle.*

Hic jacet Richard Strongbowe, filius Gilberti Earle of Pembroke.

Hic jacet Philippus de Fox † *miles.*

Hic jacet Bernardus de Novo Mercato.

Hic jacet Paganus de Cadurcis.

Hic jacet Adam de Cadurcis.

fo. 76 b.

Hic jacet Robertus Curtus.

Froncester a lordshipe of a c. marke a yere 8. miles from Glocester, a myle beyond Standeley priory.

These howses of whit monks were made and erectid of houses of a religion cawllid *fratres grisei*, an order that was afore the conquest.

[Seven Cistertian houses.— L. T. S.]

Buldewas [c] in Shropshir apon the right banke of Severn hard by it. It is 7. mils from Shrobbesbyri.

Neth in Wals.

Basinge Werke in Flintshire.

Bukfast. [d]

[* *Capta*, MS.]   [† *Foye.* See vol. ii, p. 61.]

---

[a] Newnham.   [b] Thornbury.   [c] Buildwas.
                      [d] Buckfastleigh.

Bordesley in the forest of Fekenham in Worcesterschere.
Stratforde Langethorn in Est-Sex.

Gloucesters. Rogerus Erle of Hereforde founder of Flaxley in the Forest of Deene. There was a brother of Rogers Erle of Hereford that was kyllyd withe an arow in huntynge in the very place where the abbay syns was made. There was a table of this matier hanggid up in the abbay churche of Flexeley. There was a bysshope of Hereford that holp muche to the building of Flexley.

Herefords. Matildis Walerie founderes, as some say, of Acornbyry, a priorie of nuns in Acornbyry ᵃ Wood, 3. miles by sowth from Hereforde.

Hereford. Fercher and Coryn, fathar and mothar to Seint Brendane the abbate, were buryed of olde tyme in the very place where now is made a new churche for the whole towne. Ther is yet in the west end of the pariche churche a token of the olde tombe.

Owen Tuder. Owen Meridek, corruptly cawlled Owen Thider, fathar to Edmund Erle of Richemount, and graund-fathar to Kynge Henry the seventhe, buried in the Grey Freres in the northe syde of the body of the churche in a chapell.

Richard Stradel, Doctor of Divinitie in Oxforde, and Abbat of Dowre, wrote Omelies upon the Pater Noster, and upon the whole text of the Evangelystes. He flowrished in the tyme of Edward . . .*

fo. 77 a. There cam in the tyme of Ser Thomas Cantelope 3. friers prechars to Hereford, and by the favour of William Cantelope, brothar to Bysshope Cantelupe, they set up a little **Portfild is in** oratorie at Portfelde, but Bysshope Thomas toke that place **the In[n]e** from the friers. Then one Syr John Daniell havynge a litle **Gate Suburbe** place in the northe suburbe, let them have the use of it. **of Heriford.** Then the Bysshope of Hereforde gave them a plot of ground hard by Daniel's place, and ther they began to builde, and make a solempne pece of work, Daniell helpynge them. But then the Barons Warrs by Thomas of Lancastar began agayne Edward the 2, and Daniell was taken and beheadyd in Hereford by Edward the 2. and his body was buried at the great

[* Edward III. Straddel was living in 1330, according to Dugdale, Mon., v, 553.]

ᵃ Aconbury.

crosse in the minstar cemiteri of Hereforde. Then ceased **Herefords.**
the worke of the Blacke Friers colledge for a while, and *BlakeFriars*
then Kynge Edward the third holpe it, and aftar was at the *in Hereford.*
dedication of it with many noble men, at the whiche tyme
one Alexandar Bagle, Bysshope of Chestar,* dyed at Heriford,
and the kynge cam to his funeralls there. The bysshope was
buried in the quiere of the Blake Freres undar a goodly flate
stone.

Episcopi Hereforden.

Thomas de Cantilupo sedit annis 7. *obiit* 1282.
Richardus Swinfeld sedit annis 34.
Ade Orleton natus in Hereforde, sedit annis 10.
Thomas Chorleton (Tresurar of England) *sedit annis* 14.
Johannes Trillek sedit ann. 16. *et dim.*
Johannes Gilbert sedit ann. 13. *fuit et translatus in Meneviam.*
Ludovicus Chorleton † 8 *ann.*
Guiliam Corteney 5 *et dim.*
Johannes Tresvaunt.‡
Robertus Marshall.
Edmundus Lacy but elect, and translated to Excestar 1420.
Thomas Polton sedit an. uno et quar.
Thomas Spoford sedit ann. 26.
Richardus Beauchampe sedit 2. *ann. et quart.*
Reginaldus Bulers.
Johannes Stainbyri.
Thomas Myning.   fo. 77 b.
Edmund Audeley, translated to Salysbury 1502.
Hadrianus Castellensis cardinalis.
Richardus Mayew sedit ann. 11 *et dim.*
Carolus Bothe sedit ann. 18. *et* 5. *mens.*   1517.
Edwardus Fox.   1535.
Edmundus Bonher.§
Joannes Skip.‖   1539.

[* There seems to be some error here; I do not find this bishop in
either Le Neve or Stubbs.]
[† *Choleto*, MS., *i.e.*, Charlton.]
[‡ Trefnaunt probably in Leland's original.]
[§ Bonner was elected Bishop of Hereford in 1538, but before he
could take possession was translated to London. Dr. J. Gairdner in
Dic. Nat. Biog.]
[‖ *Scipio* in margin.]

V.   M

Herefords.   *Thomas de Cantilupe theologiae doctor Oxon. archid. Sta-*
forden. et cancellar. Henry 3. sedit ann. 6. menses* 11. dies
1282.   *8. obiit 8. calend. September anno Dom. 1282. Vacavit sed.*
3. moniths and 6. dayes.
Swynfilde doctor theologiae, consecratus 7. die Marche anno
1316.   *Dom. 1282. Obiit Ides of Marche Anno Dom. 1316. Prae-*
fuit ann. 34. mens. 3. dies 13.
1317.   *Sext. Non. Jul. anno Dom. 1317. Adam Orleton, natus*
Heriford: decret. doctor, consecratus † episcopus Heriford:
26. die mensis Septembar sedit annis 10. mens. 2.

De episcopis Herefordensibus tempore W. Conquerar.

Anno Domini 1077.‡ tempore William Conquerar obit Wal-
terus episcopus Hereforden: quinto anno regni Guillelmi.
Anno Dom. 1055. combustio ecclesiae cathedralis per Gri-
phinum, et Algarum, filium Leofrici comitis Merc.
1079.   *Anno Dom. 1079. Robertus de Loreing factus est episcopus*
1094.   *Hereford; qui obit anno Dom. 1094. 6. Calend.§ Julii, cui*
1102.   *successit Gerardus. Obit Gerardus anno Dom. 1102.*
Successit Reynaldus, alias Reynelmus, ut inscribitur sepul-
chro. Gulielmus Malmesbiriensis dicit Gerardum translatum
fuisse ab Herford ad sedem Eboracum.
1115.   *Reynaldus obiit anno Dom. 1115. 5. Calend. November,*
cui successit in episcopatu Richardus de Capella.
Galfridus de   *Sed secundum Guilhelmum Malmesbiriensem successit Rey-*
Cliva.   *naldo Galfridus, et Galfrido successit Richardus Clericus*
privati sigilli.
Richard hic   *Anno Dom. 1127. 17. Call. Septembar obit Richardus de*
de morte   *Capella, cui successit Galfridus de Clive.*
Galfridi.   *Robertus de Betune factus episcopus Hereford, ante Prior*
fo. 78 a.   *de Lantonie prima, anno Domini 1131.*
1131.   *Obiit Robertus Betune anno Domini 1148. 10. Calend.*
1148.   *Maii. Successit Gilbertus Folioth abbas Gloucestriae.*
Translatus est Gilbertus Folioth ad sedem London. anno
1163.   *Dom. 1163. Et electus est eodem anno Robertus Melun in*
episcopum Hereford.

[* *Mense,* MS.]   [† *Doctori cons cor,* MS.]
[‡ Stow got wrong here with dates, and corrected the first from 1077
to 1070 instead of the second, which he made 1078 and then 1055. The
last is right; Walter died in 1079 according to Stubbs.]
[§ *Callend.,* MS.]

Anno Dom. 1167. *obiit Robertus de Melun. penul. Febr.* 1167.
alias 3. *Calend. Mart., cui successit Robertus Folioth, qui* Herefords.
ecclesiam abbat. de Wigmore, per nobilem virum Hugonem de
Mortimer fundatam, dedicavit, et diversa jocalia dedit eidem
ecclesiae die dedicationis * *ejusdem.*

Obiit Robertus Folioth episcopus Herforden: nono † *die*
Maii anno Dom. 1186. *Successit Gul. de Ver. Obiit Guliam* ‡ 1186.
de Vere 24. *die Decembris anno Dom.* 1200. 1200.

Successit Aegidius de Bresa, quo anno obiit S. Hugo
episcopus Lincolne.

Anno Dom. 1215. 17. *die Novembar, id est* § 15. *Calend.* 1215.
Decembar, obit Aegidius episcopus Herforden. Successit Hugo
de Mappenor. Obiit Hugo de Mappenor anno Dom. 1219. 1219.

Successit Hugo Folioth. Obiit Hugo Folioth anno Dom. 1234.
1234. 7. *Calend. August. Successit Radulphus de Maydene-* Radulphus
stan. Dictus Radulphus Maidenston 6°. *anno episcopatus sui* ante decan.
factus est fratar Minor anno Dom. 1239. *et supervixit annis* Herforden.
5. *diebus* 35. *Successit Petrus de Aqua Blancha Saubaudus.* 1239.
Anno Dom. 1268.|| *die November Petrus de Aqua Blancha*
obiit.

Successit Johannes Brueton. Obiit Brueton anno Dom.
1245.¶ 12. *die Maii, id est* 4. *Idus Maii.* ** 1245.¶

Successit Thomas de Cantilupo. Thomas de Cantilupo
consecratus à Robert Kylwarbye archebysshope of Cantor-
berye at Cantorbery in the Feaste of the Nativitie of owr
blissed Ladye, *anno Dom.* 1275. *Obiit Cantilupus ad urbem* 1275.
veterem †† *crastino Barptolemaei, cujus ossa delata ab ecclesia*
S. Severi in urbe veteri Herefordiam. Successit Richard
Swinesfild, *qui ossa Cantilupi transtulit à capella beatae*
Mariae Hereforde ad capellam S. Joannis Baptistae ejusdem
ecclesiae. Tandem rursum translatum corpus Cantilupi à
Joanne Trilleke episcopo Hereford. in capellam S. Maryae 8.
Calend. Novembar anno dom. 1349.‡‡ *et ab obitu Cantilupi* 67°.

[* *Decationis,* MS.]
[† *Nono,* supplied by Hearne to Stow's blank.]
[‡ *Gullam,* MS.] [§ *Il est,* MS.]
[|| Stow wrote and then crossed out this date, which is, however,
correct.]
[¶ Error for 1275.]
[** *Ide May,* MS.] [†† Hearne says *In Hetruria.*]
[‡‡ Stow wrote 1349, doubtless following Leland, then crossed it out.
Writers differ as to the date of Cantilupe's post mortem translation.]

1316.
Herefords.

Richard Swinsfeld obiit anno Dom. 1316. die 5. Gregorii Pont. Ro. apud Bosburie. Sedit annis 34. Sepultus est pompa max. in Herifordensi ecclesia.

fo. 78 b.

Anno Dom. 1317. Johannes 22. Pont. Romanus contulit in magistrum Adam de Orleton, natum Hereforde, decretorum doctorem, episcopatum Hereforden.* Consecratus est Avinioni Id. Maii. Translatus est Wigorn. et postea Winton. Obiit 18. Jul. anno Dom. [1345].†

Translatus fuit Orleton ad Wigorniam per Pont. Ro. qui Herefordensem ecclesiam dedit Thomae Chorleton anno domini

1327.

1327. Obiit Chorleton 11 Januarii 1343.†

Ex schedula episcopor. Hereforden.

Petrus de Aqua Blancha et alii alienigenae expulsi sunt de Angl. per Barones apud Dover anno Domini 1262.

1262.

Radulphus de Maydenstane ex episcopo Hereforden. factus fratrum Minorum.

Ex chronico Antonini de Radulpho Maidestan.

§ Constructio
collegii fra-
trum Mi-
norum Oxon.

In tantum autem ‡ fratres illi fuerunt in partibus illis sanctitate famosi, ut monachellus ille, qui fuit ibi primus receptus ad ord. Minorum, sed et dominus Radulphus episcopus Heriforden. et quidam abbas cum multis aliis ordine intrarunt, et tam humiliter conversati sunt, ut et ipse episcopus et abbas lapides portarent pro constructione conventus.

Hactenus ex Antonino.

Stetit autem Radulphus Maidestan tandem in conventu Glocestriae. Ibi obiit et sepultus est.

1265.

Anno Dom. 1265. obiit Dominus Gualterus de Cantilupo episcopus Wigornii, et frater ‖ D. Gul. de Cantilupo militis et seneschalli illustrissimi regis Angliae.¶ Henrici 3. ac patris S. Thomae Hereforden. episcopi.

[* *Contulit i magestar Adam de Orleton natus Hereforde decretorum doctori episcopi Hereforden*, MS.]
[† Dates supplied by Hearne, from Godwin's *De Praesulibus.*]
[‡ *Ante*, MS.] [§ *Construxtio, Mynorum*, MS.]
[‖ See Godwin, p. 512.] [¶ *Reges Angli*, MS.]

Edwardus Senior, filius Alfredi regis, construxit Her- ~~Heriford~~
fordiam. *foundyd.*

Anno Dom. 1079. *combusta est Herford ab Wallensibus* *Alias*
cum ecclesia Seint Ethelberti martyris; quo tempore multi 1055.
illius ecclesiae ministri gladiis funestis occubuerunt pariter Herefords.
cum episcopo.

Robertus Lotharingus episcopus Herefordensis defloravit
Chronicon Mariani, teste Guli. Malmesbery. Gelbertus
Folliot ex abbate Glocestri: episcopus Herforden.

Gilbertus adversabatur maxime Thomae Beketo archi- fo. 79 a.
episcopo Cantuar. Thomas Beket discipulus* in scholis Ro-
berto de Melun.

Mention is made of Robert Folioth *in vita* Thomas
Beket, *ubi numeratur inter eruditos.*

Guliam Vere episcopus Herforden. plurima aedificia in
episcopatu construxit.

Hugo Folioth, Bisshope of Herford, made 2. cantuaries
in Seint Catarinc's Chapell of the southe syde of Herford
Churche cloister, and the Hospitall of Seint Catrine at
Ledburie.

Thomas Cantilupe bought lands, and gave them to his
chirche. Thomas Chorleton *episcopus* Heryford: Treasurar
of Yngland.

Orleton gave Shiningfeld[a] parsonage in Barkeshire to the
fabrike of Hereford Churche.

Alicia mater Gulhelmi Ver episcopi Herford.

Ex libro Martyrologii ecclesiae † Herifordensis.

The xviii. *Calend. Februarii obitus Wuluivae et Godivàe,* 4. *ista maneria*
quae dederunt ecclesiae Hereford: Hopam,[b] Prestonam, Pioniam *vicina oppido*
et Northonam. *Herforden.*

Radulphus Maidestan[c] primus appropriavit ecclesiam de
Beysham, alias Cellach, in comit. Herford. eccl. Herfordensi,
hac lege ut quilibet ‡ canonicus praesens in suprema missa
pecuniolam reciperet.

[* *Discipulis,* MS.]
[† *Ex libri matyr olegii eccli,* MS.]   [‡ *Quilibus,* MS.]

---

[a] Shinfield.   [b] Hope.
[c] R. Maidestone, bishop 1234.

READING
FREE PUBLIC
LIBRARY

S. Mary
Mounthaunt,   *Radulphus Maidestan emit aedes de Mounthaunte prope*
Broken   *Broken Warth London: et dedit episcopis successoribus suis.*
Wharfe, in   *Eynno* Herforden: habet jus patronatus ecclesiae S. Mariae*
London.   *de Mounthante.*[a]

Herefords.   *Johannes Trillek episcopus Herforden: max. impensis*
transtulit ossa Thomae Cantilupi.
Johannes Gilbert translatus ad sedem Meneven.
Gul. Courteney translatus ad London.
Johannes Tuefnaunt † episcopus Heriford., ante Canon.
ecclesiae Assaphi. et auditor causarum camerae apostolicae.
Robertus Maschal episcopus Herford. ante Carmel. Hic
Whit Friers.   *aedificavit chorum fratrum Carmelit. et presbiterium apud*
London. Aedificavit ibidem campanile eccl. Carmel. et multa
fo. 79 b.   *oratoria ‡ eidem eccl. contulit, et ibidem in lapide alabastrite*
sepultus.
Edmundus de Laceie, electus tempore schismatis, translatus
1420.   *ad sedem Excestrensem* in the yere of Christ 1420. in the
8. of H. the 5.
Thomas Polto[n] translatus ad § . . .
Thomas Spoford episcopus Hereforden. primo abbas Seint
Marie Eborac. dein episcopus Rofensis electus, sed ante con
secrat. translatus ad Hereford. Sepultus est Spoford Ebor. in
Mariano monasterio.
Richard de Bello-campo translatyd from Heriford to
Salisburye.
Reginaldus Butler translatus ab Herford ad Chester.
Johannes Stanbury Carmel. translatus à Bangor ad Her-
ford.
Thomas Milling‖ doctus theologus, et linguae Graecae
gnarus, ex abbate Westmonaster: factus Herforde: episcopus.
Fuit compater Edwardi principis filii Edwardi 4. et ei à con-
siliis. Fuit magnus amator sacrorum musicorum, quorum
numerum doctum alebat.

[* Is this a contemporary member of a border family, Einon? See
Leland in Wales, p. 38.]
[† Trevenant, bishop in 1389.—Stubbs.]   [‡ *Oraterea*, MS.]
[§ First to Chichester, and afterwards to Worcester; he held all three
bishoprics within six years.]   [‖ Thos. Milling, bishop 1474.]

-----

[a] St. Mary, Mounthaw.

Edmund Audley* primum† Rofensis, postea Herforden.　Herefords.
novem circiter annis demum translatus ad Sarisberye. Aedifi-
cavit sacellum adjunctum capellae S. . . . in Herforden. eccl.
et cantuariam in eo fundavit.

Hadrianus Castellensis cardi: translatus ab Herford: ad
Bath.

Richard Maiew,‡ Archedecon of Oxford, Chauncelor of
Oxford, *praeses colleg. Magd. Oxon. elemosinarius Henrici 7.*
orator in Hispania pro Catarina uxore Arthurii.

Charles Bouth § Archedeacon of Buckyngham, and Chaunselar of the Marchis of Wales, aftarward Bysshope of Herforde.

Edmunde Bonher translatyd to be Bysshope of London.‖

Ex vita S. Osithae Virgin and Martir, autore Vero　Essex.
Canon. fani S. Osithae¶ in Estsex.

Ositha filia Fredewaldi regis, et Wilburgae Pendae regis
filiae. Ositha adhaesit doctrinae Edithae et Edburgae, qua-
rum neptis erat.

Fredewaldus rex paganus.

Editha domina de Ailesbiric, quam villam non ex patris　fo. 80 a.
dono, sed extortam matris adepta gaudebat.

Ositha famulabatur Edithae in Ailesbiry.

Edburga, soror Edithae, habitabat apud Edburbiry, quae
à nomine virginis, quae vico praevidebat, nomen hoc sortita
est, ab Ailesbyri [a] *decem stadiis interfluum habens amnem, qui*
saepe turgidus inundatione pluviarum et ventorum inpulsione
itinerantibus molestum facit transitum.

Ositha, quae secreto virginitatem deo voverat, inperio patris
nupsit Sihero Christiano** regi orient. Anglorum.

Eccha et Bedewinus presbyteri designati ab Wilburga regina
curae Osithae.

Siherus rex instituebat Eccham et Bedewinum tanquam

[* Bishop of Hereford, 1480-1492.]　　　　　[† *Primis*, MS.]
[‡ R. Mayew, Bishop of Hereford, 1504 to 1516.]
[§ C. Booth, bishop 1516 to 1535.]
[‖ See before, p. 161 *note*.]
[¶ William de Vere, brother of Aubrey, first Earl of Oxford.]
[** *Christiatio*, MS.]

---

[a] Aylesbury.

Essex. *episcopos aut parochiales presbyteros à Chelmeresforde*[a] *usque ad Chic, et alibi postea late per provinciam suam.*

Editha* et Bedewinus baptizabant in eccl. apostolorum Petri et Pauli, publica tunc temporis ejus regionis sepultura propter eccl. penuriam in coemitrio Petri et Pauli.

Siherus rex ardet rem habere cum Ositha, sed illa recusando† rem habere distulit.

Dum Siherus venationi studet, Ositha absente viro velo caput consecrat.

Gaiesdine in litore‡ Tamisini maris apud Est-Saxones.

Locus qui dicitur Gaiesdine ex re nomen habens, quia dicunt ibi Gaium applicuisse. Siherus rex exoratus votum virginitatis, quod voverat Ositha velo induto, aequo animo fert.

Siherus rex donavit Osithae villam suam § de Chic.[b]

Ositha diutinis laboribus et multiformi inpensarum inpendio in Chic fabricari fecit ecclesiam in honorem apostolorum Petri et Pawli, necnon et aedificia sanctimonialium usibus commoda, miro lathomorum opere distincta. Gens de Northumbria et de Halmeresfolke.

Inguare et Hubba spoliant monasterium || Osithae in Chic.

Osithae caput amputatum tyrannide Ingwer et Ubbae ad fontem prope Chich, ubi solebat se cum virginibus lavare.

600. *Passa est anno Dom. 600. 2. Non. Octobris. Corpus Osithae sepultum ante introitum chori eccl. Petri et Pauli.*

fo. 80 b. *Mauritius episcopus London. transtulit corpus Osithae in orient. partem mag. altaris ¶ eccl. apostolorum Petri et Pauli in Chic.*

Gul. Corboile archiepiscopus Cantuar. fabricata Cantuaria argentea theca transtulit in eam partem reliquiarum Osith. Hic Gulhelmus archiepiscopus ante fuerat institutor Canonicorum non Regularium in Chic, et primus Prior eorundem.

Successit Mauritio episcopo London. Richard de Beaumeis Normannus natione, et peritus legis humanae secretorum Domini regis conscius, et caussarum et administrationum** rei pub. non segnis executor; ita ut domino rege in remotis

[* *Eccha* seems intended.]   [† *Recaussando*, MS.]
[‡ *Lito*, MS.]   [§ *Ositha villa sua*, MS.]   [|| *Monasteri*, MS.]
[¶ *Altario*, MS.]   [** *Caussarium et administratiorum*, MS.]

---

[a] Chelmsford.   [b] St. Osyth, Chich.

terrae partibus agente ipse partes suas episcopo committeret, et   Essex.
maxime terram Wallensem conquirendam, et conquisitam
custodiendam suo committeret* examini, et comitatum Salope-
shir terrae illi contiguum † illius dominio manciparet.

     Richard Beaumeis pervenit ad Chic, quod tunc temporis   *Clachendunn*
membrum erat Clachentoniae, magni quidem ipsius domi-   *manerium*
cilii.   *episcopi*
     Quatuor in eccl. S. Osithae reperit sacerdotes, quos Mauri-   *London.*
tius episcopus, ejus praedecessor, ibi constituerat, scilicet Ed-
winum, Sigarum, Godwicium,‡ qui dictus est Menstre-Prest,
qui et ipse decanus erat provinciae, et Wulfinum, quibus ad
vitae necessaria constituerat unicuique 60. *acras terrae praeter*
decimationes et altaris obventiones, quae multifarie provenie-
bant eccl. Richard episcopus missis ad Chic Nicolao et
Ranulpho Batin clericis spoliat presbiteros S. Osithae ob-
lationibus.

     Gul. de Wochenduna, Mauritii olim episcopi London:
alumnus, oravit § ut Richardus jam agrotans ‖ redderet pres-
byteris S. Osithae sua jura; id quod convalescens fecit.

     Richardus de Belmeis ¶ tertius episcopus London: nepos
Richardi, qui Mauritii successor, consilio Radulphi archi-
episcopi Cantuari: coenobium Canon. regul. constituit in
Chic.

     Habebat tum quidem Richardus episcopus clericum insignem   fo. 81 a.
Gul. de Curbuil, totius literaturae communis peritum, quem
ob probitatem morum, et literaturae et secularis prudentiae**
ad se vocaverat.

     Hic Gul. Curbuil factus est Prior Canon. de Chic.

     Gul. Curbuil vocatus ad concilium à rege designatus est
archiepiscopus Cantuari:

     Richardus, successor Mauritii episcopi London: villam,
quae Chic dicitur, solventem 20. *libras in firma Clachentonia,*[a]
usibus Canon: profuturam instituit, necnon et ecclesias de

[* *Commisisset,* MS.]
[† *Contituum, et mox mancipasset,* MS.]
[‡ *Sic.* Perhaps Godricum was intended.]
[§ *Orator,* MS.]   [‖ Hearne. *Opiotas,* MS.]
[¶ *Belumeis,* MS.]
[** Hearne suggests *literaturam et secularem prudentiam.*]

---

     [a] Clacton, Essex.

Essex. *Sumemster et Alechorne,*[a] *ecclesias de Clachenton, scilicet*
S. Jacobi et S. Nicolai, ecclesiam de Pelham, et de Aldebiria,[b]
et de alia Pelham.

    Rex Henricus contulit Canon. S. Osithae eccl. de Stowa et
Bliebrg, in qua sepultus quiescere dicitur Anna rex.

Fundatio   *Ecclesia de Blicburg*[c] *illustrata conventu Canon: consensu*
Prioratus de *regis et abbatis S. Osithiae.*
Blieburge in
Suffolke.   *Richard Byshope of London dedit sedi suae London: Lode-*
wik de patrimonio suo in commutationem pro Chec. Dedit
etiam sedi suae praedia * *in Meilande*[d] *in terra Ernulfi de*
Wigtot.

    Ex libro Veri Canon: S. Osithae de miraculis Osithae.

    Westemutha litus prope Chic, ubi portus.

    Hugo Haver pirata spoliavit Eadulvesnes, villam Canon:
eccl. S. Pauli London: et naves ejusdem villae perforavit et
demersit.

Ver Canon: *Hugo Haver depraedans littus Est-Sex: pepercit fortunis*
et autor libri *Canon: S. Osithae tempore Abelis Abbatis.*
vixit tempore
Abelis.   *Propter piratarum incursiones delatum fuit antiquitus*
corpus S. Osithae à Chic ad Ailesbiriam, ubi nutrita et sacris †
disciplinis adprime erudita cum matertera ‡ *Editha ali-*
Locus natalis *quandiu mansisse cognoscitur, et in eadem parochia apud*
S. Osithae. *Querendonam*[e] *in villa, quae nunc est Gul. de Mandevilla,*
originem nativitatis duxisse ab incolis praedicatur et creditur.

fo. 81 b.   *Gaufridus vir centum et* 16. *annorum in Ailesbiria.*

    Uxor fabri, servi § *cujusdam militis, habitantis in Ailes-*
byri, peperit quinque foetus.

    Uxor autem militis, Domini fabri, peperit 7. *foetus, cum*
longo ante tempore fuisset omnino sterilis.‖

    Quadraginta et sex annis, ut ajunt, Ositha natale solum
de Ailesbiri sui corporis praesentia illustrasse fertur. Quo
modo autem ad nos relata fuerit pro certo antiquitas ipsa, et

[* *Sua precdia,* MS.]   [† *Nutita et sacis,* MS.]
[‡ *Materteras,* MS.]   [§ *Servii,* MS.]
             [‖ *Sterites,* MS.]

---

    [a] Southminster, Althorne.   [b] Aldborough.
    [c] Blythburgh, Suffolk, was a cell to St. Osyth.
    [d] Mayland, Essex.   [e] Quarrendon.

diuturni nimis temporis prolapsus, notitiam abolevit. Certum tamen habemus corpus ad locum martyrii* fuisse relatum.

Ositha Eilesbiriam multis insignivit miraculis.

Aluredus presbiter Ailesberiensis, postea Prior Rofensis Monaster. Gul. filius Nigelli miles dominus de Burton prope Ailesbyri.

Lucia, filia Roberti Bever et Adelivae, nupsit Gul. filio Nigelli. Walterus de Haia miles et comprovincialis noster.

Hilaria propinqua Mauritii iuri mat: uxor Gualteri de Haia.

Galfridus Malet vir dives et potens in Cantebergia.

Adelisia mater mea, nobilis matrona, degebat in viduitate † 22. à morte mariti sui.

Fratres nostri ea temporis statione tres in Waullia militabant cum rege, primo scilicet congressu cum Wallensibus.

Ositha mater mea te praeelegit advocatricem, et relictis suis coenobiis, quae ipsa cum viro suo instituit, ad patrocinium tuum confugit.   *Verba Veri, autoris hujus libri, ad Ositham pro matre sua.*

Fulco Prior de Ledes.[a]

Henricus, filius Matildis Imperatricis, Colecestriam venit, ubi ‡ diem pacis et concordiae cum Gul. comite Warennae, filio Stephani regis, praesente Theobaldo archiepiscopo Cantuari: et reg: baronibus.

Matildis regina, mater Gul. comitis Warenniae, manerium quod dicitur comitis, quod juxta nos est, ex propria hereditate eccl: S. Osithae contulit, factum confirmante ejus marito Stephen rege.   *fo. 82 a.*

Ego tunc temporis in curia Theobaldi Cantuar: militabam, et à Colecestria ad S. Ositham § veniebam, ut matrem inviserem.

Gulhelmus episcopus Norwicen. consummatam ecclesiam novam ‖ S. Osithae consecravit.

Bethelem inventioni corporis Sancti Hieronimi exultans interfuit Agnes de Gueres comprovincialis nostra, uxor Adelardi de Gueres, constabularii Gaufridi comitis senioris.   *Ver autor libelli fuit in terra sancta.*

Eustachius de Barentona forestarius regis.

[* *Marty*, MS.]   [† *Sic. Anno* seems to be omitted.]
[‡ *Deest indixit, vel quid simile.* Hearne.]
[§ *Ositha*, MS.]   [‖ *Navam S. Ositha*, MS.]

---

[a] Leeds Priory in Kent.

Gens auctoris.   *Albericus de Ver, pater meus, mansionem habens apud Bo-
nedeiam,* vir quidem mag: nominis et accepti inter homines,
regis eximii Henrici prioris camerarii, et secretorum ulteri-
orum non extremus, totius Angliae justitiarius.*

*Adeliza, uxor
Alberici Ver,
et mater au-
toris hujus
libelli.*   *Adeliza, filia Gilberti de Clare, viri nobilis et eximii inter
praecipuos regni principes.*

Boneclea distat tribus stadiis ab eccl: S. Osithae.

Adeliza de Estsexa, filia Alberici Ver et Adelizae.

*Rogerus, filius Richardi, nepos comitis Hugonis Bigot, duxit
in uxorem Adelizam, filiam Adelizae.*†

*Thomas de
Candelent.*   *Thomas avunculus Rogeri filii Richardi.*

Suffolk.   *Ex vita Edmundi Martiris, dedicata Dunstano archiepiscopo Cantuari: auctore Abbone monacho Floriacensi.*‡

*Saxones orient: insulae partem sunt adepti, Jutis et Anglis
ad alia tendentibus.*

*Morabatur Edmundus eo tempore ab urbe longius in villa,
quae lingua eorum Hegilesdun dicitur, à qua et silva vicina
eodem nomine vocatur.§ Passus est Edmundus 12. Calend.
December. Multitudo provinciae in villa regia, quae lingua
Anglica || Beodricesworth* a *dicitur, Latina vero Beodrici curtis
vocatur, construxit permaximam miro ligneo tabulatu ecclesiam,
ad quam eum, ut decebat, transtulit cum magna gloria.*

fo. 82 b.   *Oswin beata femina assidebat sepulchro martyris Edmundi.*

Theodredus, cog: bonus, ejusdem provinciae episcopus.

*Leoftanus, vir potens, filius Edgari, reseravit sepulchrum
Edmundi* ¶ *Marty: et ejus corpus vidit.*

Ex libro de miraculis Edmundi Marty: auctore incerto.

*Tempore Athelredi regis quidam clerici, perpendentes mar-
tyrem mag: esse meriti, sub ejus patrocinio autoritate Aldulphi*

[* *Sic. Bonedeia* or *Boneclea,* five lines lower. Stow may have mis-
read Leland.]
[† *Uxore Adeliza filiam Adeliza,* MS.]
[‡ *Auctor Abbote monacho Floriacensis,* MS.]
[§ *Vocat,* MS.]   [|| *Qua lingwa Anglia,* MS.]
[¶ *Edmunde,* MS.]

---

a Bury St. Edmunds.

episcopi deo se devoverunt perpetuo famulari. Horum 4. sacer- **Suffolk.**
dotes, duo vero diaconi.

Leofstanus nobilis infestus collegiis S. Edmundi.

Dani duce Swino applicant apud Geynesburg.[a]

Egelwinus monachus orator ad Sweinum missus exorare non potuit ut parceret Collegio Edmundi.

Sweinus in somnis lancea ab Edmundo percussus non diu supervixit. In regione Flegge mari proxima. Corpus Edmundi martyris London: delatum.*

Corpus Edmundi relatum ad Beodricesworth.

Canutus rex Angl. scholas per oppida jussit institui.

Elfwinus episcopus et monachus agit cum Canuto rege ut ordo monasticus in eccl: Seint Edmundi institueretur. Annuit rex. Annuit et Turkillus comes in cujus ditione eccl: Edmundi sita est.

Inducti sunt monachi in eccl: S. Edmundi anno Dom. 1020. 1020.
à passione Edmundi 150.

Haroldus et Hardecanutus reges Angliae opes Canuti patris quinquennio exhauserunt.†

Edwardus 3. *ante conquestum dedit monaster: S. Edmundi octo et semis centenaria, quae Anglice Hundredes vocantur. Unus primus abbas monaster: S. Edmundi.*

Leofstanus 2. *abbas.*

Egelwinus monachus, qui orator missus fuit ab eccl: Edmundi ad Canutum, coecus fuit ante obitum.

Osgothe Claph, superbus Danus, et contemptor gloriae S. Edmundi.

Baldewinus monachus S. Dionisii prope parissios, 3. *abbas eccl. S. Edmundi.*

Gul: cog: longus patri Gul: in regno Angliae successit. fo. 83 a.

Rodbertus de Curcenn ‡ *miles cupiebat abradere villam de Southwald, sibi vicinam, ab eccl: Edmundi. Gul: de Curceum successor Rodberti de Curcenn* 14. *anno regni Henrici* 2.

[* *Sic.*]   [† *Exhamserunt,* MS.]
[‡ Robert de Curcenn, in Abbot Sampson's Miracles of St. Edmund is Robertus de Curzun (see Horstmann's "Nova Legenda Angliae," ii, p. 621), a name which took many forms, as Curson, de Courcon, de Corceone, etc., now Curzon.]

---

[a] Gainsborough.

Chelmeresford villa.

Ranulphus Capellanus tunc regalium provisor, et exactor vectigalium, postea quoque Dunelmensis episcopus. Segeba religiosa femina in eccl: S. Edmundi.

Ex unnalibus, autore incerto.

1092. *Anno Dom. 1092. apud Sarisbiriam tectum turris eccl: violentia fulminis omnino dejecit s. die postquam eam dedicaverant* Osmundus episcopus Sarisbir: et Remigius episcopus Lincoln.*

1101. *Anno Dom. 1101. Wintonia conflagravit 16. Call. Jun.*

Eodem anno 13. Call. Jun. Glocestria cum monasterio arsit.

1113. *Anno Dom. 1113. Owen fuit Powisiae regulus.*

1121. *Anno Dom. 1121. Glocestriae pars magna iterum cum monasterio arsit.*

1151. *Anno Dom. 1151. fundata est abbat: de Morgan à Roberto comite Glocestriae.*

1158. *Anno Dom. 1158. Gul. comes Glocestriae captus est in castello de Cairdif ab Wallis.*

1166. *Anno Domini 1166. obiit Robertus filius Gul. comitis Glocestriae.*

1167. *Anno Dom. 1167. villa de Kenfik prope Nethe ab Wallis combusta in nocte S. Hilarii.*

1216. *Anno Dom. 1216. Gilbertus de Clare suscepit 2⁸. comit: Glocester et Herford: quorum heres fuit.†*

fo. 83 b.   *Versus ‡ ut ferunt, Giraldi Cambrensis de Gul. de Bellocampo, episcopo Eliensi.*

Tam bene, tam facile, tam mag: negotia tractas,
Ut dubius reddar si deus es vel homo.

[* *Dedicaverat*, MS.]   [† Half a page blank follows here.]
[‡ These epigrams refer to William Longchamp (not Beauchamp) Bishop of Ely, 1189; they occur in Girald's "Vita Galfridi archiep. Ebor.," which is printed in Opera Giraldi Cambrensis, vol. iv, p. 427 (Rolls Ser.). They are there linked by short remarks, which may have led Leland to separate them by his extraneous notes, as copied by Stow and printed by Hearne, vol. viii, p. 47, but I incline to think that he copied them on the *margin* of his notes about Dour. Leland may have found Girald's work in Dour Abbey.]

Tam male, tam temere, tam turpiter omnia tractas,
   Ut dubius reddar bellua sis vel homo.

Sic cum sis minimus temptas majoribus uti,
   Ut dubius reddar simia sis vel homo.

The castell of Kilpek[a] 3. miles bynethe the hede of Worme,[b] **Herefords.**
banke *sinistra*. No notable thinge on Worme besyde Kilpek.

Sum say that it is called Diffrin dore, *i.e., vallis aurea, à fertilitate*.

The lowe grownd where Dules runnithe is called Diffrin Dule.

Ther was at Dour afore, the edification of the maner called Blak Berats Haulle.

The lordshipe selfe of Ewis Harold, wher it is narowest, is a myle in bredthe, and moste in lengthe 2. mile. It hath good corne, gresse and woode.

Dowr Abbay[c] vi. mills from Hereford flat sowth, x. miles from Monemuth by west north west, ix. from Abergeveny by playne northe.

The broke of Dour runneth by the abbay of Dour, and there it brekethe a litle above the monasterie into 2. armes, whereof the lesse arme rennethe thorowghe the monastery. The bygger arme levith the abbey a bowe shot of on the right hond or banke. The confluence is againe hard bynethe the abbey. The place where the confluence of Dour and Monow is, is 8. myles from Monemuth toune.

The valley[d] where Dour renneth betwin 2. hills is caullid Diffrine dor, *id est, aurea vallis;* but I thinke rathar *à duro flu*.

Wormes brooke cumythe into Dour † river 3. quartars of a myle bineth Dour Abbey by the left ripe. It risethe by the Haye Wood 3. miles by south southe est from Herford. It rennythe 5. myles *à fonte*.

Dulesse[e] broke comythe halfe a myle benethe this con-

[* *Honis*, MS.]   [† Here called the Dove.]

---

[a] Kilpeck castle.   [b] Worm r.
[c] Abbey Dore; see vol. iii, p. 49.   [d] Golden valley.
            [e] Dulas r.

Herefords. fluens into Dour by the right ripe. This broke risethe by west a 2. miles above his confluence with Dour, and rennethe thrwghe Ewrs Harald.[a]

fo. 84 a.
Dorstone.   Dour riseth a litle above Dorston. Dorstone is a litle village about a 6. miles from Dour Abbay west northe west *ripa dextra*.

Dour 2. myles byneth Dour Abbay enterith into Monow by the lift ripe. There is a castell a mile and more benethe Dorston apon the right ripe of Dour.[b] It is called Snothil,[c] and ther is a parke wallyd, and a castle in it on an hill Snothill caulled Sowthill, and therby is undar the castle a quarrey of Castle. marble. The castle is somewhat in ruine. Ther is a Fre Chappell. This castle longyd to Chandos. There was dyvers of the Chandos in the Grey and Blake Friers at Hereford.

The towne of Hereford West * of sum is caulled in Walche Trefawith of multitude of beeches, and of some cauled Hereford of an ould forde by the castle of Heriforde.

The abbey of Dour foundyd in Kynge Stephen's dayes by one Robertus Ewias, so caullyd bycawse that he was lord of parte of Ewias. The fame goethe that Kynge Harold had a bastard namyd Harald, and of this Harold part of Ewis was named Ewis Harold. This bastard had yssue Robert foundar of Dour Abbey; and Robart had yssue Robert. The 2. Robert had one dowghtar caullyd Sibille Ewias, maried to Sir Robert Tregoz a Norman. Robert Tregoz had issue John Tregoz. This John Tregoz maried Lord *William Can-* William Cantelupe's dowghtar caulyd Julia, sistar to Thomas *telupe senes-* Cantilupe, Bysshope of Herforde, Chancelar to Henry the *callus to* third.
Henry the
third.   John Tregoz had by Julian 2. dowghtars, Clarence maried to John Lorde de la Warc, and Sibille maried to Guliam de Grandesono.

John de la Ware had by Clarence Nicholas that sone dyed.

Guil. Graunson had Peter by Sybille. This Peter was buried in owr Lady Chapell of the Cathedrall Churche of

[*   "Este" is written above the line by another hand.]

---

[a] Ewyas Harold.   [b] Dore r.   [c] Snodhill.

Snothill
Castle.

Hereford *juxta* Thomam de Cantilupo *episcopum* Here-   Herefords.
forden:

Peter had John and Catarine.

John Graunson was Bysshope of Excester.*

Catarine his sister was maried to Ser Guy Brien Lord of Theokesbiri.

Guy Brien had a doughtar by her maryed to the Lord Percy.

The fame is that the castell of Mapherald † was buildid of   fo. 84 b.
Harold afore he was Kynge, and when he overcam the   *Mapherald*
Walsche men Harold gave this castle to his bastard. Great   *Castle.*
parte of Mapheralde Castell yet standinge and a chapell of
Seint Nicholas in it. Ther was sumetyme a parke by the
castell. The castle stondythe on a mene hill, and on the
right banke of Dules broke hard in the botom by it.

There is a village by the castle caullyd Ewis Haralde, in
the whiche was a priorie or cell of blake monkes translatyd
from Dulesse ᵃ village a myle and upper on the broke.
Dules village longed to Harald. *Filius Haraldi* foundyd
this at Dules.

Richard Brute lord of Bradwarane, *nobilis hîc Bruti
requiescunt ossa.‡*

Robertus Tregoz translatid it from Dules to Mapheralt.
It was a cell to Glocestar.

Tregoz and Graunson were the last that were men of any
greate estimation that dwellyd in Mapheralt.

Joh[a]n Beauchamp Lady of Bergeveny bowght of De la
War and Graunson Mapeherault Castell.

Matild de Bohun wife to Ser Robert Burnelle, foundar
of Bildevois ᵇ Abbey, (thowghe some for the only gifte of the
site of the howse toke the Bysshope of Chester for founder,)
was buryed in the presbitery at Dour.

Henricus de Pott *alias* Bruge. John Bruton knight and
his wyfe, fathar to John Bruton Bysshope of Hereford,
buryed in Dour.

[* See Leland's notes on the Grandison family in vol. i, pp. 236-8.]
[† See vol. iv, pp. 166, 167.]
[‡ Marginal note in MS. *Requiessent ossa*, MS.]

ᵃ Dulas.   ᵇ Buildwas.

Herefords. Ther lay of the Botears buried in the Chapitre at Dour.*
Giraldus in his Itinerarie showethe how Harald, a sonne
of Kynge Harold, dyd nex the shores of Walls accompanied
with the Norways.

Noble men buried in Dour Abbey.

Sir Robert Ewias the foundar, and Robert his sonne.
William Graunson and Sibil his wyffe.
Sir Richard Hompton lorde of Bakenton halfe a myle
from Dour Abbey.
Caducanus,† sumtyme Bysshope of Bangor, aftar monke
of Dour, and there buried, *scripsit librum omeliarum, quem
ego vidi. Scripsit etiam librum cui titulus,‡ Speculum
Christianorum. Obit anno Dom.* 1225.
The first Alanes lorde of Alanes More. The second was
lorde of Kilpeke by his wyfe.

fo. 85 a. Sir Roger Clifford the yongar and the elder lords of Can-
terceley and Broinllese Castelle.
Syr Alane Plokenet lord of Kilpek Castle.

Ultimus Alanus de Ploknet hîc tumulatur.
Nobilis urbanus vermibus esca datur.

Walerianus. Waleranes lords of Kilpek,§ doughters; and Kilpek
maried one of the Waleranes heyres, and had the castle.
Kilpek had John by Walerane's doughter. This John maried
one Joan, Bohuns Erle of Herford dowghtars.
Johan, doughtar to Bohun, foundid our Lady Messe in
the Minster of Hereford.

Ex vita S. Gundlei regis.||
Gundeleus filius regis australium Britonum.

[* These last two paragraphs are written in the margin.]
[† Martin or Cadogan was bishop of Bangor, 1215-1236. He died in
1241, Leland giving the wrong date (Tout in "Dict. Nat. Biog."), but
the above seems to be the only notice of his writings.]
[‡ *Intitulus*, MS.]   [§ No figures given.]
[|| All these lives of saints on the following pages, Gundleius to
Willebrord, p. 181, and Aidan, p. 199, to Fremund, p. 208, are notes
from John of Tynemouth's *Sanctilogium Britannia*, Cotton MS. Ti-
berius, E. 1, printed by Dr. C. Horstmann "Nova Legenda Anglia,"
Oxford, 1901. A comparison with the variants given by Dr. Horstmann shows that Leland used Tynemouth's work itself, not Capgrave's
epitome of it.]

Gunde[leus] ex Gladusa uxore Cadocum genuit.

Gundelei sex fratres cum eo tanquam principe regnabant.

Obiit Gundeleus juxta ecclesiam quam construxerat, prae-sente Dubritio episcopo Landavensi, et Cadoco 4. Cal. Aprilis.

Griphini regis milites * tempore Gul. senioris regis Angl. Gundelei eccl. diripiunt.*

Ecclesia Gundelei spoliata à militibus Haraldi tempore Edwardi Confessoris.

Ex vita Henrici Heremitae.

Henricus Heremita de Coquet insula à Danis originem duxit.

Ex S. Hildae vita.

Hilda suis precibus vertit serpentes in lapides, servata serpentum forma.

Et vita Hugonis.

Anno Dom. 1255. Judaei Lincolnia Hugonem puerum 8. annos natum, crucifixerunt. 1255.

Ex vita Ywii.†

Iwius, filius Branonis, et Egidae, educatus à Cuthberto Lindisfarnae, obiit in Minori Britan. Corpus relatum in [ab]batiam ‡ Wiltoniae quiescit.

Ex vita Justiniani martyris

Justinianus natus in Minori Britan. Justinianus pervenit ad insulam Lemeneiam, in qua vir Deo devotus Honorius, regis Thefreauci filius, relicto mundo totum se deo commendabat. Ramsey insula.

Honorius peregre profectus Lemeneiam insulam Justiniano tradidit. David episcopus Justinianum ad se vocat.

Justiniani caput à servis quos alebat amputatum. Ipse vero in sua insula sepultus est.

[* *Milite,* MS.]
[† See Horstmann's Nova Legenda Angliae, " de Scto. Ywio," ii, p. 92, which relates that *Apud Wiltoniam aiebus nostris* [John of Tynemouth, 1366] *corpus eius sanctum quiescens in magna veneratur habetur.*]
[‡ *Batiam,* MS.]

fo. 85 b.

*Ex vita S. Keinae.**

Keinesham.

Keina Brethani filia. Keinewir, id [*est*] *Keina virgo; locos ubi Keina habitabat serpentibus liberavit, et serpentes in lapides* [*vertit*], *servata etiam serpentum forma.*
Ecclesia Caine à Danis vastata. Cudocus materteram suam Keinam sepelivit.

Ex vita S. Maglorii.

Maglorius, ortus in Britannia Majori, S. Sampsonis consors fuit.

Ex vita S. Melori.

Melorus, filius Meliani, ducis Cornubiae. Melori reliquiae† *tandem Ambresbyriam* ᵃ *delatae.*

Ex vita Oswini regis et martyris.

Gedling ubi.

In Gedlinge, modo Gillinger ᵇ *vocato, non procul ab urbe Richemondiae sito, regina Eanfleda, Oswii regis uxor, et regis Oswini propinqua, in expiationem necis ejus, impetrata à rege Oswio licentia, monasterium construxit, in quo orationes assidue pro regis occisi, et ejus qui occidere jussit, animae salute quotidie domino deberent offerri; et virum devotum, nomine Trumher, nat: Angl. à Scotis ordinatum et edoctum, regis occisi propinquum, constituit abbatem. Qui postea sub rege Merc: Wulphero in provinc: Merc: et mediterr. Angl: episcopus effectus, gentium multitudinem ad fidem convertit.*‡
Coenobium ad ostium Tinae flu: spoliatum et dirutum à Danis.

Ex vita S. Paterni episcopi.

Paternus natus in Minori Britannia.

Lanbatern-vaur prope Aberostewith urbem mariti-mam.

Paternus monasteria et ecclesias per totam Kereticam regionem, quae modo Cairdiganshir vocatur, aedificavit.

[* Hearne's suggested corrections of words in these lines between brackets, also *locos* for *locres*, and *liberavit* for *liberata* of Stow's MS., agree with Tynemouth's Life of Keyna in Horstmann, ii, 103.]
[† *Cornubia . . . reliquia*, MS.]
[‡ Quoted *ipsissima verba* from Nova Leg. Ang., see Horstmann, ii, p. 270.]

ᵃ Amesbury.   ᵇ Gilling.

Monasterium Paterni[a] *prope urbem.   Obiit Paternus* 12.
Cal. Jul.

Ex vita Petroci.

Petrocus genere Camber.
Petrocus 20. *annis studuit in Hibernia.*
Petrocus Romam petiit.
Petrocus Roma reversus est ad suum monaster: in Cornubia.
Petrocus obiit prid. Non. Jun.

Ex vita S. Richardi episcopi.

Richardus factus est cancellarius Cantuar: ab Edmundo.
Richardus fit episcopus Cicestren: Obiit Richardus 3. *Non. Aprilis.*

Ex vita Roberti abbatis.   fo. 86 a.

Robertus monachus Fountanensis.
Robertus postea abbas primus novi monasterii prope Morepath.

Ex vita Thomae Cantelupi.

Thomas Cantilupus filius Guliel: Cantilupi.
*Melicenta mater Thomae, quae à comitissa Eboracensi**
orig. duxit.

Ex vita Willebrordi.

Wilgis homo Northumbrorum regionis pater Willebrordi.

In australi insula chori.   Hereford.

Gul. de Vere episcopus Hereforden: praefuit 12. *annis.*
Obiit 9. *Call. Januarii anno Dom.* 1198.   1198.
Dominus Robertus Foliot episcopus Hereforden.   [1148.]
Robertus de Melun sedit annis † . . . *tempore Henrici*
2. *filii.*‡ *Hic fuit in omni genere literarum insigniter eruditus.*
Obiit anno Dom. 1147.†   [1167.]

[* *Eburavicensi* or *Ebroice, Evreux ;* Millicent's first husband was
Almeric de Montfort, Count of Evreux.]
[† Three years and two months, 22nd Dec., 1163—27th Feb., 1166-7
—Le Neve. The date, 1147, for death is erroneous, see before, p. 163.]
[‡ This word must be an error.]

---

[a] Llanbadernfawr.

Hereford. *Dominus Robertus Betune* episcopus Hereforden.*
Dominus Reinelmus episcopus Hereforden.

Reparavit eccl. Hereforden. *Dominus Richard Maiew episcopus Hereforden. doctor theologiae, rector turbae Magdalenensis, archedecon of Oxford, Chunselar of Oxforde, eleemosinarius Henri the 7. praefuit Hereforden: eccl: 11. annis et amplius. Obiit 8. die April.*
1516. *anno Dom. 1516.*

In transepto occidentali eccl. ad austrum.†

Dominus Joannes Trefnant episcopus Herifordensis, canon. Assaphensis, et in camera apostolica causarum auditor.

In transepto occident: ad boream.

Dominus Thomas Chorleton episcopus Hereforden: Treasurar of England.

In Presbiterio.‡

Johannes Trillek doctor of Divinitie, *cujus frater Thomas Trillek fuit episcopus Rofensis, et coadjutor fratri jam admodum seni.*

In orient: transepto ad boream.

Richardus de Swinesfeld in Cantia natus, successit Thomae Cantilupo, cujus testamenti executor fuit.

In bor: insula Chori.

Robertus de Loreine episcopus Heriforden.
Dominus Galfridus de Clyve episcopus Herefordensis.
fo. 86 b. *Dominus Hugo de Maggenore§ episcopus Herifordensis.*
Petrus de Aqua Sabaudia Francus episcopus Herefordensis.
Dominus Aegidius de Brusa episcopus Hereforden.
Johannes Stanbury Carmelita episcopus Bangorensis 5. annis; translatus Hereford praefuit 21. annis. Obiit anno
1474. *Dom. 1474.*

Ther is a Bisshope of Heriford beried in owr Lady Chapell.
Petrus de Grandisono miles in sacello S. Marye sepultus.

[* *Beture,* MS.]   [† *Austri,* MS.]   [‡ *Presbiteris,* MS.]
[§ *Mapenore,* according to Le Neve and Stubbs.]

Edmundus Audeley episcopus Hereforden: et postea Sa- Hereford.
resbir: adjecit sacellum et cantuar. australi parti* sacelli
S. Mariae.

The chefe of the Lord Chorletons founders of the Grey
Freres in Shrobbesbirie.

In navi ecclesiae.

Johannes Bruton episcopus Hereforden. custos Garderobe
Dom. regis.

Gulielmus Devereux miles.

Carolus Bouth doctor legum Bononiae archideaconus Buk-
ingam, et cancellarius marchiarum Walliae tempore Henrici
principis.† Bouthe reparavit palatium suum London. voca-
tum Mounthaut, et Bisshop Castelle, alias Treescop.‡

Pembridge miles.

Radulphus Maideston emit domum de Mounthault London.§ Mounthalte.

Gul. Porter primo Gard: Novi Collegii Winton: Oxon:
postea cantor Hereforden: eccl.

Nomina episcoporum Hereforden.

Putta; Trutere, alias Tirde; Torhtere; Walhstode; Cuth- ‖ *Portneren*
berht; Podda; Acca; Eadda, vel Cedda; Ealdberth; Ceol- *antiquis*
mon; Esne; Utel; Thulfhwarde; Beonna; Eadwulf; *praeponitur.*
Cuthulf; Mucel; Daeorlath; Cinemund; Eadgar; Tidelm;
Thulfylin; Thulfric; Adulf; Adestan; Tremerin; Leofe-
gar; Aldred; Walter; Rodbertus de Loregon; Girardus,
qui postea archiepiscopus Ebor. Malmesbiriensis hic introducit
Rogerum Lardarium electum tantum Herforden. Reinelmus
fundator ecclesiae Hereforden. Gaufridus de Cliva; Richar-
dus de Capella; Rodbertus de Betunia; Gilbertus de Foliot; fo. 87 a.
Robertus de Melun; Robertus Foliot; Gul. de Ver; Aegi-
dius de Breosa; Hugo de Mapenor ¶; Hugo Foliot; Radul- Maidestone
phus de Maidenstan; Petrus de Aqua Blanca; Joannes le ** *postea*
Franciscanus.

[* In this sentence Stow writes *postia, cantur*, and *parte* for the
corrected words.]

[† *Camcillarius* and *tempori Henrico princeps*, MS.]

[‡ Or Treestop, as Stow wrote it in another place. See vol. ii, p. 79.]

[§ See before, p. 166, St. Mary Mounthaw.]

[‖ *Sic.* It is not evident to whom this refers.]

[¶ *Napenor*, MS.]   [** *Postia Fraciscanus*, MS.]

Hereford. *Breton; Thomas de Cantilupo; Richard de Swinesfeld; Adam de Orleton, natus in Hereforde; Thomas de Charleton; Joannes Trillek; Ludovicus Chorleton.*

Hugo de Foliot episcopus Hereford construxit hospitale S. Catarinae aput Ledebirie, quae non multum distat à montibus Malverniae.

Palatia episcopi Herforden.

Sugwas a flite shot, or more, of Wy ryver on the lifte ripe of it 2. miles *dim.* It stondithe in the roots of an hillet, and a park by it now without dere. Colwel [a] Park longed to the Bysshope of Hereford by Malvern Chace, and a pece of Malvern* is the bysshops, fro the crest of the hill, as it aperithe by a dyche.

Bosberie [b] x. miles by north est from Hereford at the head of Ledon [c] reveret, and therby is a place longginge to Seint John's in London caullid Upledon. [d]

Gul. Ver episcopus, ut patet ex ejus epitaphio, multa egregia construxit aedificia.

Whitburne [e] 7. miles from Worcester. It is in the very extreme parte of Herefordeshire on the right banke of Temde [f] ryver.

Johannes filius Alani, Dominus de Arundel, cepit Byssops Castell, et constabularium castri fide data interfecit anno regni 45. Henrici 3. et inde tenuit pene 6. annis.

There was a faire mansion place for the bysshope at Ledbyri xii. miles by est northe est from Hereford, and vii. myles or more from Rosse. This hous is all in ruyne. The convict prison for the Bysshope of Heriford was at Rosse, now at Hereford.

Rosse at the veri west end of the paroche churche yarde of Rosse, now in clene ruynes.

Bysshops Castle a 23. miles by north northe west from Hereford in Shropshire. It is xii. miles from Shrowsbirie.

fo. 87 b.   Prestebyri 5. miles from Glocester hard by Clife. [g] Ther is a parke hard by Prestebyri.

[* Stow spells it " Malvenn."]

---

[a] Colwall.   [b] Bosbury.   [c] Leadon r.   [d] Upleadon.
    [e] Whitbourne.   [f] Teme r.   [g] Cleeve.

Joannes le Breton episcopus Hereforden. fuit aliquanto tem- Hereford.
pore vice-comes Hereford: custos maner: de Abergeveney, et
trium castrorum.

Breton episcopus custos Garderobe domini regis.

Kilpek Castelle a 5. mils from Hereford by southe west
very nighe Worme * brooke.

Sum ruines of the waulls yet stonde. Ther was a priorie of
Blake Monks suppressyd in Thomas Spofford's Bysshope of
Herford's tyme, and clerly unitid to Glocester.

The priory stood from the castle a quartar of a myle.

The fathar of Thomas Cantelupe Byshope of Herford was
Seneshall of England, and his mothar Melicent was Countis
of Ebroice[a] in Normandie.†

Walterus uncle by father to Thomas Cantelupe bysshope
was Bysshope of Worcestar, and gave beneficis to Thomas
his nephew aftar Bysshope of Hereford, and to Hughe
Cantilupe, Thomas brother Archidcacon of Glocestar.

Ex vita Ethelberti martyris ‡ autore Giraldo Cam-
brensi Canonico Herifordensi.§

Athelbertus, Adelredi regis Orientalium Anglorum filius‖
et Leoverinae reginae. Qui et ipsi atavis editi regibus ex
Orient. Saxo: regali prosapia, Anna videlicet Enni filio, et
Etheldredae virginis patre, Adelhero et Athelwaldo, Adulfo
et Alfwoldo, quos Beda¶ in Angl. historia commemorat.

Ethelbertus unicus heres Adelredi regis.

Guerro comes solicitat Ethelbertum de uxore ducenda, vide-
licet Seledriada Egeonis australis Britanniae regis filia.

Egeon rex infidelis Adelredo Ethelberti** patri.

[* See before, p. 175.]
[† See note on Thomas Cantilupe before, p. 181.]
[‡ *Piarti*, MS.]
[§ These few notes from the Life of St. Ethelbert by Giraldus Cam-
brensis, the original of which appears to be now lost, are of the more
interest as Leland must have taken them from an undoubted manu-
script or copy of that book. See "Giraldi Cambrensis Opera," edited
by Prof. Brewer (Rolls Series, 1863), vol. iii, pp. xlv, 409.]
  [‖ *Delredi, Orientali Angli filio*, MS.]
  [¶ *Bedē*, MS.]   [** *Aderedo Atherberti*, MS.]

_____

    [a] Evreux.

Terrae-motus denotavit desolationem reg. Ab obitu enim Ethelberti multis annis sub regulis et tyrannis ad regis Edmundi tempora duravit.

Alftrida Offae filia apparatum Ethelberti ad Offam* venientis collaudat.

Grimbertus olim etiam Ethelberto familiaris.

fo. 88 a.

Ethelbertus occisus consilio uxoris Offae à Grimberto familiari Offae 13. Call. Junii.

Alfrida filia Offae Anachoreta facta apud Croilande.

Offa praecepit corpus Ethelberti cum capite occulte sepeliri in ripa flu: quod Lugge dicitur.

In loco primae sepulturae nunc est ecclesia parochialis de Maurdine[a] *in sinistra ripa Luge flu. 4. millibus passuum† ab Herefordia.*

Castellum de Kinggett Southton non longe distat à Maurdine, ut neque à Luga. Extant ad huc usque vestigia hujus castri, ubi Offa rex convenit Ethelbertum. Nunc appellantur Southtoun Waulls.[b]

Offa poenitentia facti ductus Romam petit.

Ethelbertus Brichtrico praediviti viro nocte apparuit, praecipiens ei ut corpus suum effossum‡ ad locum qui Status waie dicebatur efferret, et juxta monasterium eodem in loco situm illud cum honore reconderet. Egmundus socius Brichtrici in transferendo corpore Ethelberti. Et sic procedentes usque ad locum praesignatum ibidem corpus sanctissimi honorifice sepelierunt, in loco videlicet qui Anglice Fernlega,[c] *Latine interpretatum saltus filicis dicebatur; nostris vero diebus à comprovincialibus Herefordia nuncupatur.*

Milfridus Merc.

Milefridus Merc. rex sanctitatem viri dei fama vulgante cognovit, qui et quendam episcopum suum virum sanctum ad locum destinavit, jubens de morte martyr: et caussa cognoscere.

Milefridus quanquam id temporis in remotis regni sui partibus ageret, transmissa ad locum eundem pecunia multa ecclesiam egregiam lapidea structura ad laudem martyris à fundamentis incepit, primusque regum omnium eodem episcopum in loco constituens ecclesiam eandem cathedrali dignitate § sublimavit. Terris quoque plurimis et praediis amplis, palliis

[* *Offa venientes*, MS.]   [† *Passis*, MS.]   [‡ *Effossu*, MS.]
[§ *Ecclesie eadem cathedri dignit:*, MS.]

---

[a] Marden.   [b] Sutton, near Hereford.   [c] Fernhill.

holosericis et ornamentis egregiis, regia quoad vixit munificentia ditare quidem ac dotare non cessavit.

Egfridus, Offae regis filius, vix per annum et centum quadraginta dies pro patre regnavit.

Unde et huic nostrae paginae quod Asser historicus, verax * relator gestorum regis Alfredi, de hac generatione perversa conscripsit, eisdem interserere verbis non indignum reputavi. fo. 88 b.

Edwinus, vir potens in finibus Ledburie et montibus † Gomerici,[a] *liberatus à paralysi dedit Ledburiam eccl. Herefordensi. Ledburie North et Bisshops Castell idem manerium, et in antiquis chartis ‡ nominatio est castri de Ledburie.*

Offa rex terras plurimas circa Herefordam, martyri contulit. Est vicus in Orientalium Saxonum provincia, cui nomen Bellus Campus interpretatio dedit, in cujus praedio antiquitus lignea quaedam est basilica in honorem Ethelberti martyris.§

Ex vita Ethelberti martyr:‖ autore Osberto de Claro, monacho Westmonaster. ad Gislebertum Hereforden. episcopum.

Anna, Ethelredus, Ethelwaldus, fratres et reges Est Anglorum. Adelherus rex ex Hereswida sorore S. Hildae genuit Aldulphum et Alfwodum.

Adelherus rex una cum Penda rege in bello interfectus ab Oswio rege Northumbriae.

Aldulphus successit patri in reg. Successit Aldulpho Alfwoldus ejus frater in regno.

Berno de sanguine Alfweddi rex Est Anglorum. Berno rex.

Successit ejus filius Adelredus. Successit Adelredo Ethelbertus ejus filius, postea martyr.

Seledrida, filia et heres Egeonis mortui regis, in australibus Majoris Britanniae partibus destinata à Guerrone consule thoro Ethelberti, sed Ethelbertus eam recusavit.

Ethelbertus venit in reg: Merciorum ad vicum regium, qui villa australis dicitur. Southtoun.

[* *Veraxii*, MS.]   [† *Monts*, MS.]   [‡ *Castris*, MS.]
[§ This passage " Est—martyris " is from Girald's Life of Ethelbert in a Cotton MS., *Opera* (Rolls Ser.), vol. iii, p. 425. *Bellus Campus* seems to be Beauchamp Roding in Essex.]
[‖ Written about 1150, not yet printed; MS. at Cambridge.]

---

[a] Montgomery.

Hereford.   *Godescaleus miles, in cujus territorio Ethelberti martyris eccl: fuerat antiqua fabricatione constructa.*

Pons Here-
fordensis.   *Pons factus super Vagam*[a] *apud Herefordiam tempore Hen-rici* 1. *ipso rege in perante et piis eleemosinam ad tam utile*

fo. 89 a.   *opus erogantibus. Facta haec partim consilio domini Richardi episcopi Herefordensis, qui praecessit Roberto Betune episcopo.*

Curatores operis aut pontifices primo Alduinus de Malvernia, deinde Aldredus monachus, postremo Alvericus.

In solo namque ecclesiae Norwicensis episcopio plures quam 24. *ecclesia sancto Ethelberto martyri* * *antiquitus dedicata.*

Ex vita Roberti de Betune episcopi Herefurden: auctore Gul. Priore Lantonensi ad Reginaldum Weneloke.†

Robertus Betunensis ex militari prosapia orig. duxit.
Gunfridus praeceptor et frater Roberti.
Hatyra mons prope Lanhondeny monasteri: Waulliae.
Robertus fit canonicus apud Lanhondeni in Wallia.
Hugo de Laceio fundator et patronus eccl: Lanhondenen:[b] *in Waullia moriens sepultus est apud Wibeleiam in parte fundi quam in extremis agens eccl: donaverat.*

Cum desivissent fratres locum religionis ibi fundare missus est Robertus tanquam operis procurator.

Ermsius Prior Lanhondenensis fit anachoreta, et ei in Pri-oratu successit Robertus.

Robertus procurantibus Pagano, filio Joannis, et Milone Constabulario, ab Henrico rege fit episcopus Herefforden: quo tempore vacaverat sedes quinque annis.

Radulphus decanus Herefordensis adversabatur Roberto episcopo Herefford: Canonici Lanhondenenses ‡ *semel atque iterum* § *spoliati tempore regis Stephani.*

Robertus ad se accersivit conventum Canon: Lanhonden-sium, et aliquanto tempore in suis aedibus aluit. Interim

[* *Martii*, MS.]
[† In the margin, *Alias ad Henricum episcopum Winton.*]
[‡ Here and in the next instance the word is spelt with initial "H" instead of "L."]
[§ *Seme . . . iteru*, MS.]

---

[a] Wye r.   [b] Llanthony.

quaesivit* et invenit eis locum habitationis† apud Glocestram sub Milone Constabulario.

Expensas dedit ad aedificandum. Secundo anno transtulit illuc conventum. Ad supplementum quoque subsidii dedit eis eccl: duas Frome et Prestebyri.‡

Robertus episcopus ecclesia et possessionibus ad tempusculum spoliatus.

Episcopus Robertus cum pace restituta in sua redisset ecclesiam suam reformavit, hostica de foris munimenta diruit clerum dispersum revocavit.

Venit ad Robertum conventus unus fratrum desolatorum fo. 89 b. *numero 20. quos maledictio sterilis terrae de secessu § nemoris post quinquennium expulerat.*

Obiit Robertus episcopus in Remensi [a] urbe, eo ad concilium vocatus, quod Eugenius pontifex Ro. ibidem celebrabat.

Odo Remensis abbas, hospes Roberti episcopi. Corpus Roberti relatum Herefordam, et ibidem sepultum in ecclesia sua, quam ipse multa inpensa et solicitudine consummavit.

Cle [b] Hills.

Cle Hills be holy in Shropshire. Tende [c] river devidethe **Shropshire.** them from sume parte of Worcestershire, but from Shropshire by the more parte of the ripe.

No great plenty of wood in Cle Hills, yet ther is sufficient brushe wood. Plenty of cole, yerth, stone, nether excedinge good for lyme, whereof there they make muche and serve the contre about. Cle Hills cum within a 3. good myles of Ludlow. The village of Clebyri [d] standythe in the *Clebery.* rootes by est of Cle Hills 7. myles from Ludlow in the way to Beaudeley.[e] There was a castle in Cleberie nighe the churche by northe. The plote is yet cawled The Castell Dike. There be no market townes in Cle Hills.

The highest parte of Cle Hills is cawlyd Tyderstone.[f] In it is a fayre playne grene, and a fountayne in it. There is anothar hill a 3. miles distaunt from it caulyd The Browne

[* *Inter inquestivit*, MS.]   [† *Habitatioris*, MS.]
[‡ *Brestebyri*, MS.]   [§ *Selcessu*, MS.]

---

[a] Rheims.   [b] Clee.   [c] Teme r.
[d] Cleobury Mortimer.   [e] Bewdley.   [f] Titterstone.

Cle. There is a chace for deare. Ther is anothar cawllyd Caderton's Cle, and ther be many hethe cokks, and a broket, caulyd Mille Brokcet, springethe in it, and aftar goithe into a broket cauled Rhe,[a] and Rhe into Tende by neth Tende Bridge. There be some blo shopps to make yren apon the ripes or bankes of Mylbroke, comynge out of Caderton Cle or Casset Wood.

Ex registro quodam.

Hereford.   *Fowelppe* [b] *manerium domini Richardi de Chaundos.*
Prebenda de Whitington.
Asscheton Boterel.
Ecclesia S. Crucis de Acornbyrie. [c] *Canonici Regul: de Abbatia Wigmore, filia S. Victoris Barisiensis.*

fo. 90 a.   *Nomina Monaster: Herforden: dioec.*

Major ecclesia Herefordensis.
Prior: S. Guthlaci Herifordensis.
Abbatia Canon. de Wigmore.
Prior: de Wenloke Clun: ord:
Prior: Leonminstre.
Prior: de Chireburie. Canon.
Prior: Canon: de Wormesley.
Abbat: * *de Dowre Cisterc: ord:*
Abba: * *de Flexley in Foresta de Dene.*
Moniales de Acornbyri.
Moniales de Lingebroke. [d]
Prior: de Clifford, Clun.
Prior: de Kilpek.
Prioratus de Newente.
Prior: de Bromefeld.
Prior: de Alberbury. Grandimontenses.†
Dudelebyri an howse of Grandimontenses in Cornedale, now unitid to the Churche of Hereforde.
Acle Lyra [e] *maner. Prioris de Lyra in Normannia cellula.*

[* *Abbot, Abbo,* MS.]   [† Or Bonhommes.]

---

[a] Rea r.   [b] Fawnhope, co. Hereford.   [c] Aconbury.
[d] Limbrook.   [e] Lire (Eure dept.).

Fuit ibi tantum capella. Acle 4. mile from Hereford: *versus* **Hereford.**
Bromyard.

Nulla ecclesia collegiata sacerdotum in Dioecesi Hereforden:
praeterquam Herefordia.

Castell From apon From ryver. From commythe into
Luge *ripa sinistra*, about a myle above Mordeford Bridge.

Limites Dioecesis Herford.

Herefordshere integer.

Et pars de Shrobbeshir usque ad med: Tam flu: prope op-
pidum Shrobbesbyri: et foresta de Dene in com: Glocestriae.

Castellum Richardi [a] a 2. miles from Ludlow by sowthe,
where is a paroche churche of the same name by it. The
castle standythe on an hill. It is about a myle *dim.* from the
right ripe of Temde. It was the Lord Vaulx lately. Pope
bowght it. Now the Kyng's.

Ecclesi: parochialis Castriae * *Isabella.*

Ex libello incerti autoris de comitatibus, episcopatibus et fo. 90 b.
monasteriis Angliae.

Autor erat in Cantia natus.

Jam comperi ipsum Gervasium hoc opusculum scripsisse
postquam absolverat historiam, quam scripsit de regibus
Angliae, et archiepiscopis Cantuar.†

Gervasius monachus Cantuar: scripsit praeter Chronicon,
opusculum de regibus Angliae, et archiepiscopis Cantuar.

Anglia habens 34. Shires olim habuit tantum 32. Ad

[* *Sic.*]

[† These two paragraphs were written in the margin by Leland (and
so copied by Stow) after he had found who was the unknown author.
The *libello* is the Mappa Mundi of Gervase, and is put by Dr. Stubbs,
the editor of his works, at the end of his other writings as the last
written ("Gervase of Canterbury," Rolls Series, vol. ii, pp. viii, 414).
The copy used by Leland varied from that given by Stubbs; his lists
are not so long or so full as those of the printed edition; it may have
been a copy made for the monastery of St. Saviour's Canterbury. See
before vol. iv, p. 70, where lists of the sweet and salt waters are extracted from the *Mappa*, which I had not then recognized.]

---

[a] Richard's Castle, *cf.* vol. ii, p. 76.

Mappa Mundi. *legem West-Sax. pertinebant* 9. *ad legem Merc.* 9. *ad legem Danorum* 14.*

Domus religiosae in Cantia.

Archiepiscopatus ubi eccl. S. Trinitatis.
Rovecestre, S. Andreae.
Abbatia Sancti † *Augustini.*
Abbatia Feversham S. Salvatoris.
Abbatia Boxley Monachi albi.
Abbat. Lesnes S. Thomae.   Canon. nigri.
Abbat. Coumbwelle, Mar. Magdalen.
Abbat. La[n]gdon, S. Ma. et S. Thomae. Canon. albi.
Abbat. Brades[ol]e, S. Radegundis.
[Abbat.] Mallynge S. Mariae. Monial. nigrae.
Prior. Dover S. Martini.
Prior. Horton S. [Johan.] Evang.
Prior. Folkstan S. Mariae.
Prior. Lewesham. Mon. nigri.
Prior. S. Gregory.
Prior. Ledes. S. Nichol: Can. nigri.
Prior. S. Sepulchri.‡
Prior. Shepey, S. Mariae.
Prior. Blakwase, S. Nicol[ai] Can. albi.
Prior. Lillechirch, S. Mar. Mon. nigri.§
Prior. Daventre,[a] *S. Mariae. Mon. nigri.§*
Hospitale S. Gregorii, S. Lawrence, [S. Jacobi, S. Nicolai,] S. Thomae Dovor, S. Joannis in Blekbakechilde,|| Roffe.
Aquae dulces in Cantia. [Medewaie,] Stura, Brooke, Derent,¶ aqua de Bregge, aqua de Ospringe, aqua de Cray.

<h3 style="text-align:center">In South-Sax.</h3>

Abbat: de Otteham, S. Laurentii. Can. albi.
Prior: Arundell, S. Nicolas. Monachi nigri.
fo. 91 a.   *Prior: Atesele,*[b] *S. Petri. Monachi nigri.*

[* Stow carelessly wrote 9, Gervase has 14.]
[† *Saint*, MS.]   [‡ *Sepulchre*, MS.]   [§ *Nigre*, MS.]
[|| Gervase has *S. Johannis in Blen, Bakechilde, i.e.,* two places.]
[¶ *Derent, nunc forsan Derte,* in the margin. Darent r.]

---

[a] Davington, Kent.   [b] Sele, near Steyning.

Prior: Boiegrave,* S. Martini. Mon. nigri.   **Mappa**
Tortington, S. Mariae Magdalenae.† Can. nigri.   **Mundi.**
Prior: Hastings, S. Trinitatis. Can. nigri.
Prior: Remsted. Moniales nigrae.
Prior: Lulleminster. Moniales nigrae.‡
Prior: Rospere.§ Moniales nigrae.
Decanatus Stening: Clerici Secul. Hospitale S. Jacobi: le-
prosi Cicestriae. Haling insula.
Aquae dulces in South-Sex: Limene, Medeway, Ichene,
Chiern, aqua de Kneppe, aqua de Bradeham.
Castle at Bodiam.

In Southreia.

Prior: Horslege. Moniales nigrae.
Goseforde castellum, Blechinlegen. Aquae dulces: Emene,   *Goseforde,*
Wayes.‖   *forsan Cul-*
                                                 deford, alias

In Southampton-Shire.   *Culford.*

Abbat: de Quarraria in Wight.[a]
Prior: de Cairbroke. ibidem.
Prior: de Hamell, Sancti Andreae.¶ Monachi Grisei.
Prior: Brumor.[b]
Hichene[c] *aqua dulcis.*

In Barkshire.

Prior: Hame. Moniales nigrae.
Prior: Bromhaul. Monial: nigrae.
Prior: de Poyhele.[d] *S. Marg. Can. nigri.*
Hospitalia S. Joannis apud Abingdon, et S. Joannis apud
Wallingford, et S. Bartolemewi apud Newbyri.

[* Gervase has *Boisgrave.* Now Boxgrove.]
[† *Magdelini,* MS.]   [‡ *Moniali nigri,* MS.]
[§ Rusper. The two preceding names in Stubbs' Gervase stand as
Remisted and *Lillemenster.*]
[‖ Stubbs' copy gives these rivers as *Cwene, Waie.* ? The Wandle,
and Wey.]
[¶ *Seint Andre,* MS.]

---

[a] Quarr, I. of Wight.   [b] Bromere. See Wiltshire, p. 194.
[c] Itchen r.   [d] Poughley.
v.   O

In Wiltshire.

Abbat: Stanlege S. Mar. Monachi albi.
Prior: Fernlege. Monachi nigri.
Prior: Briontune. Can. nigri.
Prior: Bromhore, S. Mar. et S. Mich: Can. nigri.*
Hospitale † de Bradelege, S. Mariae Magda. leprosi.

In Dorsetshire.

Prior: Camestern. Moniales nigrae.‡

fo. 91 b.   ## In Sumersetsher.

Prior: Stoke, S. Andreae. Monachi nigri.
Prior: Bearew, S. Mariae.§ Monachae nigrae.
Aquae dulces: Bedret, Fenifle,‖ Aven, Briu.

In Devonshir.

Abbat: Bukfester.
*Prior: Cuich,ᵃ S. Andreae. Monachi nigri de Becco extrae
Excestre.*
Prior: Bernestaple.
Prior: Plintune.
Prior: Berdlescombe. Can. nigri.

In Cornwalle.

Prior: Tywardraith. Mon: nigrae de Angiers.
Prior: S. Cyriaci. Mon: nigri.
Prior: S. Antonii. Mon: nigri de Angiers.
Prior: S. Mariae del Val. Mon: nigri de Angers.
Prior: S. Nicolai, Core in Sylley.

[* This description answers to that of Bromere in Hants, which was, perhaps, erroneously put here in Wilts.]
[† In Stubbs this hospital is placed under Somersetshire.]
[‡ *Albae* in Stubbs.]
[§ *Mariae* omitted in MS.]
[‖ *Pedret, Jenfle* or *Genfle*—Stubbs, and see Leland's "Itinerary," vol. iv, p. 71. The known rivers seem to be the Parret, Avon, and Brue.]

ᵃ Cowyke, near Exeter.

In Est-Sax.   Mappa
                                                     Mundi.
Abbat: Chic, Petri, Paul: et S. Osithae.
Prioratus Ginge-Hestan,* vulgo Ingerstone.[a]
Aquae dulces: Heaghbridge, Hobridge.   Stura flu. dividit
Est-Sax à Southfolke.   Aqua salsa,† Huolne.   *Vlna flu.*

In Midlesex.

Prior: Keleburne.

In Southfolke.

Abbat: Sibbetune.[b]
Prior: de Eia[c] *S. Petri.   Mon: nigri de Berney.*
Prior: Clara vel Stoke, S. Joan.   Mon. nigri de Becco.
Prior: de Wangford.   Monachi nigri.
Prior: Romburgh, S. Mich.
Prior: Suthbyri,[d] *S. Barptol: Mon: nigri de West-*
minster.
Prior: Waulton, S. Felicis.[e] *Mon: nigri de Roffa.*
Prior: Leistune, S. Mariae.   Can. albi.
Liegate Castell.[f]   *Liegate Castel.*

In Northfolke.

Prior: Horsham, S. Fides.‡   Mon: nigri de Conchis.
Prior: Wirham, S. Winwallae.§   Mon: nigri de Mus-
terell.
Prior: Welsingham.   fo. 92 a.
Prior: Cogesforde.[g]

In Grantebrigeshire.

Prior: Snaveshith.   Mon: nigri.
Prior: Swafham.   Monach: nigri.
Castellum de Herwoydi.‖   *Herwordi*
                                                     Castellum.

[* *Gingettestane*—Stubbs.]   [† *Salva*, MS.]
[‡ MS. has *Fidis.*]   [§ Wereham.   MS. has *Wiwalle.*]
[‖ *Herewardi*—Stubbs.]

---

[a] Ingatestone.   [b] Sibton.   [c] Eye.
[d] Sudbury.   [e] Felixstowe.   [f] Lidgate Castle.
                       [g] Cokesford.

Mappa
Mundi.

In Lincolnshire.

Abbat: Brunne.
Abbat: Simplingham.[a]
Abbat: Heverholme.
Abbat: Sixle,[b] *S. Mariae. Can: albi et moniales.*
Abbat: Bulingtune.[c] *Can: albi et moniales.*
Abbat: Tupeholme.
Abbat: Stikeweld.[d]
Prior: Grisetum. *
Prior: Torholme.[e] *Can: nigri.*
Abbat: Catteley.[f] *Can. albi et moniales.*
Castellum de Cliford.
Castellum de Swinesheved.

In Leircestreshire.

Prior: Berewedune.[g] *Can. nigri.*
Prior: Calc: Can: nigri.
Prior: Osuluestune.[h] *Can: nigri.*
Prior: Stane.[i] *Moniales nigrae.*

In Northamtunshire.

Abbat: Bitlesden,† *S. Mariae. Mon: albi.*
Abbat: de Withory.‡ *Mon. nigri.*
Prior: Luffeld, S. Mariae. Monachi nigri.
Prior: Cateby, novus locus monialium de Semperhingham.
Hospitale S. Joannis de Northampton.
Castell: de Alderington.[k]

In Hertfordshire.

Prior: de Bello loco.[l] *Mon: nigri.*
Prior: Chille. Mon: nigrae.
Prior: Chiltre. Mon: nigri.

[* Perhaps *Fristune*, now Freston, is intended.]
[† MS. has *Bihesden*.]   [‡ *Withrop* in Stubbs.]

---

[a] Sempringham.   [b] Sixhill.   [c] Bollington.
[d] Stikewold, or Stixwold.   [e] Torkesey.   [f] Catterley.
[g] Bredon.   [h] Owston.
[i] ? Stone, in Staffordshire.   [k] Alderton.   [l] Beaulieu.

In Bedfordshire.

Abbat: Helenestoke,[a] *S. Mariae. Mon: nigri.*
*Prior: Harwood,** *S. Petar. Mon: nigri.*
Prior: Beauliu, S. Mariae Magda. Monachi nigri de
S. Albano.
Prior: de Prato, S. Mariae. Mon: nigri S. Albani.
Hospitale de Bedford, S. Joannis Baptistae.

In Bukynghamshire.

Abbat: de Paretresdune.
Abbat: de Lavendene. Can: albi.
Prior: de Bradewelle, S. Mariae. Mon: nigri.
Hospitale de Buckyngham, S. Joannis.
Laundene Castelle, Hamslepe[b] *Castelle.*

In Oxfordshire.

Abbat: Briwere.[c]
Prior: Coges. Mon: nigri.
Prior: Nortune.[d] *Can: nigri.*
Prior: Garingey,[e] *S. Mariae. Mon: nigri.*
Prior: Brakeley, S. Mariae. Can: nigri.
Hospitale de Nortune.
Castellum de Bukeby. Castellum de Darington.

In Wirecestreshire.

Prior: Elnecester.[f] *Can: nigri.*
Prior: Cochelle.[g] *Mon: albae.†*
Hospitale S. Oswaldi.

In Herefordshire.

Prior: Bertune. Mon: nigri.
Prior: Monemuth, S. Mariae, et Florentii. Mon: nigri.
Hospitalia: Bertune, Salopesbyri, Bruge.

[* *Hanwood*, MS.]   [† Stubbs has *nigrae.*]

---

[a] Elstow.	[b] Hanslope.	[c] Brucrne.
[d] Cold Norton.		[e] Goring.
[f] ? Alcester, Warwick.		[g] Cokehill.

Mappa
Mundi. *Castellum, Cnucin, Blancmister.* *
Fluvii, Tirne, Mele, Blodwelle, Cunet.†

fo. 96 b.

* In Warwikeshire.

Prior: Wrokeshale. Mon: nigrae.
Prior: Hinewode. Mon: nigrae.
*Abbat: Merivaus.*ª

In Staffordshire.

Prior: Lappele, S. Remigii. Mon: nigri.
Prior: Fairwel. Monachae ‡ nigrae.
Prior: Briuern,§ S. Mariae. Mon: nigri.
Prior: Briuern,§ S. Leonardi. Mon: albae.

In Derbyshire.||

*Prior: Derlege,*ᵇ *vel Greslege. Can: nigri.*
Prior: Dereby S. Jacobi. Mon: nigri.
Prior: Dereby. Mon: nigrae.

In Yorkeshire.

Castles: Sceltun, Kuninghburgh, Ferneltun.¶

In Richemontshire.

Abbat: Eglestune, S. Mariae: Can: albi.
Prior: Woderhale sanctorum trium. Mon: nigri.

[* *Blancmustier* in Stubbs. All these hospitals, castles, and rivers "in Herefordshire" are under Shropshire in Stubbs' Gervase.]
[† In the margin of the MS. here is noted, "Quaere reliqua folio sexto subsequenti," which appears to refer to the leaf further on, where Leland (whose writing was larger than Stow's), apparently finished copying from the *Mappa*, in the midst of his notes from the lives of saints. I have, therefore, transferred this last portion between *—* from Stow's fo. 96 b, so as to bring the same subject together.]
[‡ *Moniales* in Stubbs.]
[§ Brewood. The "Black ladies" were in Stafford, the "White ladies" over the border in Salop.]
[|| MS. has Dorsetshire in error.]
[¶ Stubbs' copy has *Cerveltune.*]

ª Wroxall, Henwood, and Merivale.   ᵇ Darley Abbey.

Prior: Ingelwde, S. Mariae.   Mon: nigrae.
Prior: Marrig, Mon: nigrae.

In episcopatu Dunelmensi.

Prior: Mai vel Segelbreg.   Mon: nigrae.
Prior: Brenkeburgh.[a]   *Can: nigri.*

In loeneis reg: Scot:

Abbat: Mailros S. Mar: Mon: albi.
Abbat: Drieburgh.[b]   *Can: albi.*

In Waullia: provinc. Landaven.

Prior: de Basselle.[c]

In Banchoren: dioecesi.

Prior: de Enisenae.†   Monac: albi.

In episcop. S. Asaphe:

Abbat: de Hudham.   Mon: albae. ＊

Forsan Tgnm＊ortane, nunc Whitland, aut non longe ab eo loco.

Ex vita Aidani abbatis, autore incerto.

fo. 92 b. contd.

Sedia ex regione Connactorum, pater S. Aidi, sive Aidani.
Venit Aidanus ‡ ex Hibernia in Britan. ad S. David episcopum.§

Beda scripsit vitam Aidani pontif: Lindifarn.

Ex vita S. Albani.

fo. 93 a.

Heraclius quidam miles coecus oculis restitutus precibus Albani martyris. Passus est Albanus 10. *Cal. Jul. anno Dom.* 286.

286.

Anno Dom. 723.‖   *Offa rex Merc: transtulit corpus S. Albani, et monasterium in ejus gratiam construxit.*

723.

[＊ *Sic.*]   [† Stubbs has *Emisenoc.*]
[‡ *Aidani*, MS.]
[§ See before, p. 178, note ‖, and Horstmann's " Nova Legenda," i, p. 18.]
[‖ John of Tynemouth has this date 793 (Horstmann, i, p. 35).]

---

[a] Brinkburne, Northumb.   [b] Melrose, Dryburgh.
[c] Basselech, or Bassaleg, Monmouths.

Anno Dom. 914. regnante Ethelstano Dani rupto scrinio reliquias S. Albani in Daniam ad monaster. Owense transtulerunt, et aliquandiu ibi servaverunt donec Egwinus monachus S. Albani in Angliam caspio furto reduxit.

Reliquiae S. Albani ob metum translatae in Ely insulam anno Dom. 1066°.

Dubium num remiserint Helienses vera ossa Albani. Herbertus Duke et miles.*

Ex vita Aldelmi.

709. *Obiit Aldelmus anno Dom. 709. ab anno 9ᵘᵒ. factus est abbas Maildunens. 34. et episcop. sui anno 4,† 50. fere passuum milibus Mailduno.ᵃ Translatum est corpus Aldelmi anno Dom. 949.*

Ex vita Alredi abbatis.

Alredus abbas de Reuesby,ᵇ postea Rievallensis abbas.

Alredus scripsit vitam Davidis regis Scotiae, et vitam Edwardi Confessoris, Margaretae reginae Scotiae, 33. omelias super onus Babilonis in Esaiam, 3. libros de spirituali amicitia, de natura animae et quantitate et subtilitate libros 2. Multas quoque scripsit epistolas.

Ex vita Amphibali.

Amphibalus Verolamii flagellatus, postea jactu ‡ lapidum occisus.

Amphibali corpus à quodam Christiano § tecte ablatum, ac sepultum ‖ à Roberto nomine plebeio villa S. Albani prope Radeburne, 3. vico Albani miliaribus, inventum est.

fo. 93 b. ### Ex vita Anselmi archiepiscopi Cantuari:

Anselmus ex nobilibus parentibus in Augustana civitate Alpium natus. Monachus Beccensis sub Herlwino abbate. Anselmus invitatus ab Hugone ¶ comite Chestrensi venit in Angliam. Exulat ab Angl. Anselmus.

[* *Myles*, MS.] [† **Tynemouth** says "anno quinto."]
[‡ *Jactum*, MS.] [§ *Christianus*, MS.]
[‖ Stow forgot the *l*, so the word looks like *sepitum* in MS.]
[¶ *Invitata ab Hogone*, MS.]

ᵃ Malmesbury. ᵇ Revesby, Linc.

Ex vita S. Audoëni archiepiscopi Rothomag.

Reliquiae Audoëni translatae in Angliam tempore Edgari regis.

Ex vita Barptolomei Monachi.

Barptolomeus ex provincia Whiteby ortus.
Barptolemeus Norwegiam petiit.
Barptolemeus fit monachus Dunelmensis, et postea Prior.
Barptolemeus obiit in insula Farnen: "Ha[n]c insulam *Farnensem vetusta longaevitas quasdam perhibet aves in colere quae aves S. Cutheberthi ab incolis appellantur. Tempore nidificationis ibi conveniunt, et tantae mansuetudinis gratim à loci sanctitate possident, ut humanos contactus et aspectus non abhorreant. Quietem amant. Secus altare quaedam ovis cubant, nullusque eas laedere praesumit. Ova sibi et ceteris hospitibus fratres apponunt. Cum masculis in aequore victum aves illae quaerunt. Pulli cum creantur, matres sequuntur, et patrias undas semel ingressi, ad nidos non revertuntur."* *

Ex vita S. Benigni.

Benignus relicta Hibernia Glastoniam venit.
Anno Dom. 1091, translatae sunt reliquiae Benigni Glastoniam.

Ex vita Bernaci episcopi.

Bernacus Romam petit, deinde Minorem Britanniam.
Bernacus venit in Demeticam provinc. id est, Southe Wals. Obiit 7. Id. Aprilis.

Ex vita Birini episcopi.

Birinus in Britanniam ab Honorio pont: Ro: missus.
Birinus applicuit apud Occident: Saxones.   fo. 94 a.
Birinus Kinegilsum regem West-Saxonum,† ac Oswaldum regem Northumbr: baptizavit.
Kynegilsus dedit Dorchester S. Birino.
Birinus anno Dom. 635. Canon: seculares instituit apud 635.

[* *Hanc insulam . . . revertuntur*, quoted from John of Tynemouth. Horstmann, "Nov. Leg.," i, p. 104.]
[† *West-Saxones*, MS.]

Dorchestar. Sedes translata à Dorchester Lincolniam per Remigium episcopum.

Alexandar episcopus Lincolne instituit Canon: regulares apud Dorchester. Obiit Birinus 3. Nonus Decembar.

Ex vita Bonifacii episcopi.*

Bonifacius fit monachus in Exancestre,[a] et postea petiit Huntscel † monaster: ubi venerabilis Winbertus abbas praefuit.

Bonifacius Thuringiam petit, et postea in Frisia factus adjutor Willebrordi episcopi.

Bonifacius Saxones et Hessos petit. Bonifacius Orthof monasterium construxit.

Multi ex Anglia confluunt ad Bonifacium.

Construxit Bonifacius 2. monasteria, unum in Frideslare[b] in honorem Petri, alterum in Amanaburgh[c] in honorem S. Michaëlis.

Bonifacius senex episcopus Willebaldum et Burghardum facit episcopos in intimis Orient. Francorum partibus.

Occisus Bonifacius Non. Jun. anno peregrinationis suae 45. episcop. sui 36. mensibus et dies 6.‡

Fuldense monasterium.   *Lullo episcopus corpus ejus perduxit ad Folde monaster: quod ipse construxerat juxta Moguntiam[d] prope flumen.*

Ethelbaldus rex Merc: à Beornredo occisus et apud Rependon sepultus.

Ex vita Saint Botulphi.

Botulphus et Adulphus "natalibus germana nativitate et charitate" ex gente Saxonica.

Adulphus fit episcopus Trajectensis.[e] Botulphus in Bri-

[* Compare these notes from Tynemouth's life of Boniface with those from Grandison's "Legenda sanctorum," Leland, vol. i, p. 232.]

[† "Nutscelle, Nuselle" (Horstmann, "Nov. Leg. Ang.," i, 122). Sir E. M. Thompson has Nutshalling or Nursling, near Winchester ("Dict. Nat. Biog.").

[‡ The dates of death of Boniface according to Tynemouth's Life should be, "peregrinationis suae 40, A.D. 755, episcopatus sui 36, mensibus 6, diebus 6." (Horstmann, i, p. 127.)]

---

[a] Exeter. [b] Fritzlar, in Hesse.
[c] Amöneburg, on the Ohm r. [d] Fulda, Mentz on the Rhine.
[e] Utrecht.

tanniam rediit. Botulphus Icanno locum construendo mona-
sterio aptum ab Ethelmundo rege accepit, ubi ad temporis*
heremus erat.

Obiit Botulphus in Icanno 15. *Cal. Jun. et ibidem sepultus* fo. 94 b.
est.

Icanho[a] *monaster: ab Inguaro et Hubba destructum.*

Ulkitellus monachus jussu Ethelwoldi episcopi Winton:
transtulit corpora Botulphi et Adulphi Thorneiam.

Erat tunc temporis in Icanho sacellum in quo solus pres-
biter sacra faciebat.

" Construxit S. Ethelwoldus non longe à monasterio
Thornensi in loco ubi beata virgo Christi Thoma†ᵢ inclusa
fuerat, lapideam ecclesiolam delicatiss: cameratam cancellulis
et duplici area, 3. *dedicatam altaribus permodicis undique*
usque ad ejus muros vallatam arboribus diversi generis.
Sedem ibi heremiticam si permisisset deus sibi elegit."

*Ex vita S. Bregwini*archiepiscopi.*

Bregwinus in Saxonia ortus. Bregwinus relicta patria in
Angliam venit.

Seint Bregwinus successit Cutheberto Anglo in archiepisco-
patu Cantuari:

Cuthbertus ex illustri Anglorum: familia ortus ecclesiam
in orientali parte majoris ecclesiae, eidem pene contiguam, in
honore Joannis Baptistae " fabricavit, ut et baptisteria et ex-
aminationes judiciorum pro diversis caussis ad correctionem
scelerum inibi celebrarentur, et archiepiscoporum corpora in ea
sepelirentur, sublata de medio antiqua consuetudine, qua eat-
enus in eccl: apost: Petri et Pauli corpora antecessorum suorum
tumulari solebant."‡

Bregwinus expletis in archiepiscopatu 3. *annis obiit* 7. *Call.*
Septembar,§ et in ecclesia S. Joannis sepelitur.

[* *Sic*, but "longo tempore" were the words probably intended to
be copied.]
[† *Toua* in Tynemouth, from whom this passage is copied. (Horst-
mann, i, 133.)]
[‡ Tynemouth (Horstmann, i, 134).]
[§ Aug. 24. Godwin, says Hearne.]

---

[a] Icanhoc, or Ycanno, Lincolns.

*Ecclesia Cantuar. cum ecclesia S. Joannis igne consumptae.** *Lanfrancus postea ecclesium "reparavit, et in ecclesiam novam corpora sanctorum episcoporum in aquilonari parte super* fo. 95 a. *voltam sub singulis locellis decenter collocavit. In illa enim conflagratione quanta damna locus ipse perpessus sit, nullus edicere potest: scilicet in auro, in argento, in libris divinis et secularibus." Privilegia regum et episcoporum ex integro corrupta † sunt.*

Ex vita S. Brithuni.

Brithunus Anglus institutus abbas Deirwald, ubi nunc Beverlege. à S. Joanne episcopo Ebora: sepultus est Beverlaci.

Ex vita Caradoci.

Caradocus ortus in provincia de Brekenauc.

Caradocus vixit in Ari insula, quam Norwegenses abducto eo spoliabant; sed postea insulae restituerunt.

Richardus, Tancredus et Flandrenses missi ‡ in Walliam infesti Caradoco heremitae. Obiit anno Dom. 1124. Caradocus, et in Menevensi ecclesia sepultus est.

Ex vita Karatoci.

Carantacus, filius Roderici regis. Carantocus fuit in Hibernia 30. annis ante nativitatem S. Danielis.

Ex vita Cedd episcopi.

Successit Saberto regi Swithelinus filius Sexbaldi, qui ab ipso Cedd baptizatus est.

Cedd recepit § ab Ethelwaldo, filio Oswaldi regis Deirorum, Lestingey ᵃ locum monaster: condendo in montibus arduis et remotis, in quo monasterium secundum ritum Lindifernensis ecclesiae instituit.

Cedd episcopus Orient: Sax: obiit in Lestingay tempore pestis. Successit Cedd in monasterio Cedda ejus frater.

[* The original words are "ecclesiam . . . vorax flamina consumpsit," utilized for the abstract.]

[† *Consumpta*, in Tynemouth.]   [‡ *Missim*, MS.]

[§ The MS. has *inperecepit*; it should be *accepit* (*accipere* in Tynemouth) or *recepit*.]

ᵃ Lastingham, Yorks.

Fratres 20. *venientes ex monaster: Cedd in regione Orient:*
Saxonum venerunt Lestingey, et omnes praeter unum peste
mortui.

Ex vita Ceddae episcopi.

Cedda agente Wulphero Merc: rege, et Theodoro archi-
episcopo Cantuar: fit episcopus Mer: et Lindispharorum.

Vixit Cedda in episcop: Lichefeldensi 2. annis et dim. fo. 95 b.
Barwe* in provincia Lindispharorum locus 50. *familiarum*
datus ab Wulphero Ceddae construendo monasterio. "*Habuit*
autem Cedda sedem apud Lichefeld, ubi sibi mansionem fecerat
non longe ab ecclesia remotiorem, in qua secretius cum 7. *vel*
8. *sociis, quotiens à labore et ministerio verbi vacabat, orare*
et legere solebat." † *Owinus primus olim ministrorum S. Ethel-*
drede monachus postea apud Ceddam.

Ex vita S. Clari.

Edwardus ‡ *tempore Edmundi regis Angliae fuit in Or-*
thestria, et Clarus mare petit, et apud Caesaris burgum ᵃ *in*
Normannia applicuit.

Clarus monasteriolum construxit in nemore juxta Heptam ᵇ
flu: in pago Wlcassino. § *Clari captum abscisum tyrannide*
potentis, quam ‖ *ille turpiter cum* ‖ *amante fugiebat.*

Ex vita S. Clitanci.

Clitancus Southe-Walliae regulus inter venandum à suis
sodalibus occisus est. Ecclesia S. Clitanci in Southe-Wallia.

Ex vita S. Eanswidae, filiae Edbaldi, regis Cantiae,
et Emmae.

Elegit Eanswida locum à vulgi frequentia remotum Fulke- ¶ *Fulkstane*
stan nominatum, ubi et pater ejus Edbaldus in honorem Petri *in Kent.*
apost: ecclesiam construxit.

[* Stow has *Warwe* as catch-word at bottom of fo. 95 a, but the name
in Tynemouth is *Barwe*, "terram 50 familiarum donavit" rex Wlferus.]
[† Horstmann, "Nova Legenda," i, 186.]
[‡ *Edwardy*, MS.]
[§ Wells interlined above *Wlcassino* in MS.]
[‖ *Qua, eum*, MS.]   [¶ Not in Stow's hand.]

ᵃ Cherbourg.   ᵇ Epta r.

READING FREE PUBLIC LIBRARY

" *Ibi ergo ex parte maris quo remotior dicitur esse ab ipsis ruricolis hujusmodi competentem fundavit ecclesiam cum officinis sibi suisque comitibus professioni ejus necessariis, à pleno tamen maris gurgite septem jugerum latitudine, i.e.* 20. *perticarum,* * *distantem, quae hodie nusquam apparet. Terra namque à mari paulatim consumpta, post longum seculum corruit, et ripa maris coemiterium hausit.*"

o. 96 a. *Ex vita S. Ebbae.*

Ebba filia Ethelfridi regis Bernisiorum.

Eanfridus et Oswaldus tantum filii Ethelfridi ex Acca, filia Ellae regis Deirorum.

Oswi, qui postea rex, filius Ethelfridi ex concubina.

Cadanus † *Scottus Ebbam amavit.*

Ebba abbas Coludi urbis, i.e. Coldingham. Duo lympidi fontes in Coludi urbe. Coludi urbs 6. (8.) ‡ *milliaribus distat à Berwico boream versus.*

Ex vita S. Eadburgae.

Cantuariae vero in coenobio scriptum reperi quod anno
1085. *Domini* 1085. *ab archiepiscopo Lanfranco fuerunt de tumulis sanctarum Mildredae et Edburgae in Thanato insula elevatae reliquae, et in eccl: beati Gregorii, quam paulo ante Cantuariae ad pauperum solamen constructam ditaverat, collocatae.*

Ex vita Edmundi martiris.

Edmundus et Edwoldus filii Alkmundi ex Siuara. §

Offa rex Est-Angl. peregre proficiscens ad cognatum suum Alkmundum, in Saxonia commorantem, pervenit, ibique Edmundum ejus || *filium in heredem adoptavit.*

Ex vita Edwoldi fratris Edmundi.

Edwoldus vitam heremiticam duxit apud fontem argenteum in Dorsetshir.

[* Tynemouth and Capgrave say 28 perches. (Horstmann, i, 297.)]

[† John of Tynemouth has *Adamnanus* (Horstmann, i, p. 304). Capgrave (says Hearne) has *Eadanus*.]

[‡ The figure 8 is interlined over 6 in the MS., no doubt following a correction by Leland, but Tynemouth has 6.]

[§ *Est Siuarae*, MS., Stow's error.]   [|| *Eis*, MS.]

Ossa S. Edwoldi translata Cernelium[a] *procurante comite Almaro tempore Dunstani.*
Almarus comes fundavit monasterinm Cerneliense.

Ex vita Elfledae.

Elfleda filia Ethelwoldi et Brightwinae nata in Clara municipio. Brightwina mortuo marito Claram dedit tempore Edgari regis monaster: Rumesiensi.[b]

Clara, Kingsclere in Southamptonshire.

Elfleda autore Edgaro rege fit monacha Rumesiae sub Merwenna abbatissa. Successit Merwennae Elwina, Elwinae vero Elfleda. Elwina cognito adventu Swani Dani fugit cum fortunis Wintoniam. Rumesia à Swano depraedata.

Ex vita S. Erkendwaldi.

fo. 96 b. contd.

Erkenwaldus et Ethelburga, ejus soror, nati in castro, seu villa, de Stallingeburg in Lindesiea ex prosapia Offae regis East-Angliae.
Erkenwaldus filius Offae regis Est-Angliae.
Erkenwaldus abbas Ceortesey, deinde episcopus London.

fo. 97 a.

Erkenwaldus foundator monasterii de Ceortesey et Berkinge, quae suo patrimonio ditavit.* *Hildelitha transmarina prima abbatissa de Berkynge, et institutrix Ethelburgae.*

Seint Erkenwaldus obiit apud Berkynge. Conflagravit Londinum tempore Mauritii episcopi London. Ignis incepit à porta occident: et pervenit ad portam orientalem.

From the west to the est.

Mauritius novae ecclesiae Paulinae inceptor. Richardus episcopus Mauritii successor, muros ecclesiae mirabiliter auxit. Richardus coemiterium Paulinae † ecclesiae muro sepsit.

Gilbertus Universale ex Altisiodoro civitate Galliae vocatus fit episcopus London. Gilbertus tectum novo operi Paulinae ecclesiae London superimposuit.

Translatum est corpus Erkenwaldi anno Dom. 1140. 14. die Novembris.

1140.

Ex vita S. Ethelwoldi episcopi Vent.

Ethelwoldus Wintoniae natus.

[* *Distavit*, MS.]   [† *Pawliae*, MS.]

---

[a] Cerne Abbas.   [b] Romsey, Hants.

Ex vita S. Fiacrii.

Fiacrius in Hibernia natus.

Ex vita Finani episcopi.

Finanus, qui et Winninus, Caprei et Lasarae filius, in media provinc: Hiberniae natus.

Ex vita Fremundi.

Fremundus Offae regis et Batildae filius.

Fremundus uno anno et dim: successit patri suo Offae viventi in regno.

Fremondus relicto reg: ad quandam insulam heremiticam* acturus vitam navigavit, sumptis secum 2. presbiteris, Burghardo, qui ejus † vitam conscripsit, et Edbritho.

Inguar et Hubba in Angliam venientibus, Offa Fremundum late quaerit et invenit.

Fremundus divino consilio Danis se opponit et vincit.

Oswy dux exercitus Offae invidens gloriae Fremundi, caput ei in sicliis ‡ amputavit quinto Id. Maii circa annum Dom.

866. 866. inter Uchington[a] et Hareburebyry. Fremundi corpus
fo. 97 b. sepultum apud Offa-churche intra domus regiae septum. Sepulchrum Fremundi inventum in loco § quo confluunt Charwelle et Brademere. Ecclesia S. sacerdotum in ripa Charwell prope sepulchrum Fremundi; unde à quodam Adelberto translatus est una cum S. Presbyteris ad Redicum,‖ ubi ab eo facta est ecclesia.

Ex Collectaneis ¶ Gervasii monachi Cantuari:
de regibus Angliae.

Mylthrudis, quae et Mildritha, monialis de Minstre in insula Thanet.

[* *Heremitam*, MS.]   [† *Eis*, MS.]
[‡ *Ejus insidiis.—Hearne.*]
[§ A place not far from Banbury (Horstmann, "Nov. Leg. Ang.," i, 454, note 10).]
[‖ Stow writes *Reditu*, but no doubt here, as sometimes elsewhere he hastily misread *c* for *t*.]   [¶ *Collectum*, MS.]

---

[a] Long Itchington, Warw.

Successit Osredo in regno Northumbar: Ethelbertus, qui et Etheldredus dictus est. Fuit filius Mollonis; qui Mollo et Ethelwoldus dicebatur.

Cedwalla rex dedit S. Wilfrido quartam partem insulae Vectae, et villam quae dicitur Paggenham.

Ethelwolphus rex West-Sax. qui et Adulphus dictus est.

In hac nova foresta postmodum duo ejus filii Richardus in collo, Guhelmus in pectore sagittis confossi.

Monasterium de Wiltune captum à * *Roberto comite Glocestr: quod incastellatum fuerunt à contra Stephani rege †
et fratre ejus Henrico episcopo Winton. etc. ut Stephanus cum fratre, relictis vasis argenteis, turpiter fugerit.*

Confirmata pax inter Stephanum et Henricum opera Gul. comitis Arundele.

*" Unde Eustachius, regis Stephani filius, pro pace inita iracundiae felle commotus recessit à patre, et cum in patrimonio S. Edmundi in die S. Laurentii saeviret indignans ad mensam sedens [in]sanus effectus vitam finivit, et apud Faversham sepultus est, sicut et mater " ‡ Gul. filius regis Stephani junior §
de equo corruit super Berhamdune, et tibiam fregit.*

Coenobium de Boxley consensu Stephani à Gul. de Ypra fundatum est.

Rex Henricus 2. applicuit in Penbroke, inde cum classe in Hiberniam iturus. ||

Johannes rex cum Huberto archiepiscopo Cantuariae navim ¶ apud Shoreham conscendit habiturus colloquium cum rege Fraunce.

Hactenus ex collectaneis Gervasii.

fo. 98 a.

Ex annalibus incerti autoris.

Anno Dom. 1290. *Gul. de Breosa senior obiit apud Findon, et sepultus est in monaster: de Sele.*[a]   1290.

[* à added by Hearne.]
[† For this passage Hearne suggests the better reading, " quod incastellatum fuerat contra eum à Stephano rege," etc.]
[‡ Quoted, see "Gesta Regum," Gervase of Canterbury, Rolls Series, vol. ii, p. 76.]
[§ *Junitr*, MS.]   [|| *Inturus*, MS.]   [¶ *Cantuare navi*, MS.]

[a] Sele, Sussex.

V.   P

Anno Dom. 1291. *Joanna, filia regis Edwardi primi, et comitissa Glocestriae, Gilbertum filium suum primogenitum peperit apud Theokesbyri.*

1292.   *Anno Dom.* 1292. 15. *Cal. Apri. obiit apud Chilham. Domina Isabella de Dovora, comitissa de Assele. Sepulta est Cantuar: in ecclesia Christi.*

Anno Dom. 1292. *Non: Februarii obiit Ananias episcopus Assaphensis. Fuit de ord. Praedic. Eodem anno* 8. *Id. Apri: Leulinus de Bronflite* [a] *electus in episcopum Assaphen: Fuit ante can: Assaphensis.*

1294.   *Anno Dom.* 1294. *rex Edwardus* 1. *constituit Gull. de Leyburne capitaneum navium suarum.*

742.   *Anno Dom.* 742. *Cuthbertus archiepiscopus Cantuari: celebravit concilium apud Clovesho, praesente rege Ethelbalde.*

694.   *Anno Dom.* 694. *Withredus rex Cantiae, et Brightwaldus archiepiscopus Cantuar: celebraverunt concilium in Bakechild.* [b]

Werburga regina uxor Withredi. Alricus filius Withredi.

Kent.   *Ex libro Gervasii monachi Cantuar. de vitis archiepiscoporum Cantuar: ecclesiae.* *

Augustinus praepositus monasterii quod est ad clivum Scauri Romae à Greg: pont. Ro: 14. *anno imper: Mauritii Augusti in Britan: cum aliis monachis missus sociis ante omnibus circiter* 40. *Applicuit Augustinus in Thaneto.*

Augustinus Doroberniam veniens permissu † *Ethelberti regis ecclesiam S. Martini celebrat, oratorium tunc temporis Berthae reginae.*

Augustinus jussu ‡ *Gregorii consecratus in episcopum ab Eleutherio Arelatensi episcopo.*

Augustinus in ecclesia Salvatoris Dorobern: monachos instituit.

Ethelbertus instinctu § *August: monasterium Petro et*

[* Gervase, Rolls Ser., vol. ii, p. 325, etc.]
[† *Permissa*, MS.]
[‡ Hearne. The word is imperfectly written by Stow.]
[§ MS. has *instructu*.]

---

[a] Leoline Bromfield.   [b] Bapchild, Kent.

*Pawlo extra muros Dorober:** construxit, locum videlicet* **Kent.**
sepulturae regum et archiepiscoporum Cantiae.

Tria pallia tempore August: in Britan. à Gregor. pont.
Ro. missa.

August: sedit annis 16. *Sepultus est in ecclesia Petri.*   fo. 98 b.

Successit Laurentius, qui tyrannidem Edbaldi filii Ethel-
berti metuens, relicturus Cantiam erat: sed divino oraculo
monitus in Britan. permansit,† et Edbaldum regem ad
Christianismum revocavit.

Sedit annis 5. *Obiit* 4. *No. Febru. et sepultus est in*
ecclesia S. Petri Dorobern:

Millitus primus London. episcopus successit, vir pedibus
aeger, animo valens. Praefuit annis 5. *Obiit* 8. *Call. Maii.*
Sepultus est Dorobern. in ecclesia S. Petri.

Successit Justus prius ‡ episcopus Rofensis. Sedit annis 3.
Obiit 4. *Id. Novembar. Sepultus Dorobern. in ecclesia S.*
Petri.

Successit Honorius. Hic misit Felicem Burgund. at evang:
praedicaret provinc. Orient. Angl.

Sedit Honorius annis 19. *Obiit* 2. *Id. Octobar. Vacavit*
sedes anno uno, mensibus 6. *Sepultus in ecclesia S. Petri.*

Successit Deus dedit de gente West-Sax. oriundus. Sedit
ann. 10. *Obiit* 2. *Id. Jul. Sepultus est in ecclesia S. Petri.*
Vacavit sedes annis 3.§

Successit Theodorus.‖ Hic Adrianum ab Ebroino dimissum
fecit abbatem in monaster: Petri Dorobern. Omnes Britan:
episcopi submittebant se Theodoro. Sedit annis 22. *Obiit*
anno aetatis suae 88. *Sepultus est in monasterio¶ Petri et*
Pawli Dorobern.

Successit Brightwaldus abbas Raculf monasterii, quod est
*juxta flu: Gearland.** Consecratus est à Godwino Galliarum*
metropolitano. Sedit annis 37. *et mensibus* 6. *Obiit quinto*
Id. Januarii.

[* Dorobernia or Durovernum, apparently the name of the Roman
town which preceded Canterbury. Leland refers to the church and
monastery of SS. Peter and Paul ("extra muros," the first place of
Christian burial) as at Dorobernia throughout; he continues the name
even after the time of Cuthbert, who built a special chapel of St. John the
Baptist near the cathedral, in which the archbishops should be buried.]

[† *Primansit*, MS.]   [‡ *F. Primus.*]   [§ *Anno* MS.]
[‖ *Theodorius*, MS.]   [¶ *Monasterie*, MS.]
[** *Geanlade*, Gervase, ii, 343.]

Kent.   *Successit Tatwinus presbiter monasterii Briudun in provinc. Merc. Sedit annis 3. Obiit 3. Calend. August.*

Successit Nothelmus * presbiter London. et monachus Sedit annis quinque. Obiit 16. Cal. Novembris. Sepultus est Doroberniae in ecclesiae Petri et Pawlli.

Successit Cuthebertus prius episcopus Hereforden : Hic aedificavit sacellum S. Joannis in orient : parte ecclesiae Petri, et sepulchrum sibi suisque successoribus. Sedit annis 17. Obiit 7. Cal. Novembris. sepultus in ecclesia S. Joannis quam ipse construxit.

fo. 99 a.   *Successit Bregwi[n]us. Sedit annis 3. Obiit 8. Call. Septembar. sepultus in sacello S. Joannis.*

Successit Jambertus † abbas ecclesiae S. Augustini Doroberniae. Sinodus celebrata apud Chealchite. Sedit Jambertus annis 5. Obiit 4. Decembris. Sepultus est in ecclesia S. Joannis Baptistae Doroberniae.

Successit Athelardus quidam abbas. Hic recuperavit pallium sedi suae ab Offa rege ablatum ac Lichefildensi ecclesiae collatum. Celebravit concilium apud Clovesho. Sedit annis 13. Sepultus est in ecclesia S. Joannis Bapt. Dorobern.

Successit Wulfredus. Hic dedit quasdam terras Werebardo ‡ cognato suo, quas ille moriturus § ecclesiae Cantuar: restituit. Sedit annis 38. Sepultus est Dorobern.

Successit Flegildus ‖ abbas electus 7. Call. Maii, ordinatus v. Id. Jul. Obiit 3. Call. Septembar.

Successit Chelnothus Cantuar: ecclesiae,¶ id est, prior, decanus, electus 3. Call. Jul. consecratus eodem anno vi. Call. Septem. Hic primis episcopatus annis quinque tantum monachos habuit in sua eccl: ceteris peste consumptis.

Dani hoc tempore Cantiam vastabant. Presbyteri et clerici in missi monacus ** psallebant in choro Cantuar: Sedit annis 41. Sepultus est Dorobern :

Successit Athelredus primo monachus Cantuar: postea

[* MS. has *Nothelinus*, an easy error.]
[† Or *Jaenbert*, Stubbs.]   [‡ *Werehardo*, Stubbs.]
[§ *Morturus*, MS.]
[‖ *Feologild*, Stubbs.]
[¶ Hearne suggests for this sentence, "ecclesiae decanus, id est, prior" as the right succession of words, which agrees with Gervase, ii, pp. 348, 349.]
[** Hearne suggests "immixti monachis" as intended.]

episcopus Wiltoniensis. Sedit annis 18. Obiit anno Dom. **Kent.**
893. Vacavit sedes 2. ann. **893.**

Successit Plegemundus, qui in Cestria insula, quae dicitur ab incolis Plegmundesham, per annos plurimos heremiticam duxerat vitam.

Septem ecclesias episcopis destitutas episcopis insignivit. Sedit ann. 34. Sepultus est Dorobern. in ecclesia Christi.

Successit * Wulfelmus Wellensis episcopus. Sedit ann. 13.

Successit Odo Scireburn: episcopus, qui cum esset clericus, habitum monachialem suscepit. Hic pelicem ab aula Edwini regis facie candenti ferro notavit. Hic transtulit reliquias Wil[f]ridi à Ripensi ecclesia Cantuar:

Hic tectum Cantuar: ecclesiae vetustate corruptum reparavit. Incertum quot annis sedit.

Successit Elfsins episcopus Winton. cognomento Lippe. **fo. 99 b.** Obiit inter eundum Romam in Alpibus.

Successit Brightelmus Dorsetensis episcopus. Hic parum idoneus visus postea Dorsetensem repetit ecclesiam.

Successit Dunstanus Wigorn: episcopus. Sedit annis 33. Obiit 988. anno aetatis suae 7[o]. **988.**

Successit Ethelgarus Selesigensis episcopus. Sedit an. 1. mensibus 3.

Successit Siricus episcopus Wiltuniensis. Sedit annis 5. Sepultus est Dorobern.

Successit Elfricus Shireburnensis episcopus. Sedit annis 11.

Successit Elphegus natalibus clarus monachus de Deorhurste, electus † anno Dom. 1006. aetatis suae anno 53. Hujus **1006.** tempore direpta et tota miserrime spoliata à Danis Cantuaria, ac postea concremata.

Finianus ‡ abbas S. Augustini abire permittitur. Goduinus episcopus captus, et Leofruna abbatissa monasterii S. Mildrethae.

Elphegus archepiscopus captus, et carcere septem mensibus detentus, et deinde à Thrum Dano occisus 13. Call. Maii. Sedit ann. 6. mensibus 7. Sepultus primo London. in ecclesia S. Pauli, postea translatus Cantuari:

Successit Livingus Wellensis episcopus. Sedit ann. 7.

Egelnothus decanus Cantuari: ecclesiae successit. Decani

[* Athelm of Wells, Wulfelm's predecessor, is omitted here.]
[† Dectus, MS.]
[‡ Elmarus is the name in Gervase, ii, 360.]

Kent. *nomen tempore Anselmi mutatum in nomen Prioris. Sedit ann.* 17. *Obiit* 4. *Call. Novembar. Sepultus est in ecclesia Christi.*

Successit Eadsinnus episcopus Wentanus, capellanus Haraldi regis.* Sedit ann. 11. *Obiit* 5. *Call. Novembar.*

*Successit Robertus, genere Normannus, episcopus London. ante monachus Gemeticensis.*ᵃ *Sedit ann.* 2.

Stigandus, quondam Australium Sax. episcopus, postea invasor Winton. sedis,† invasit sedem ‡ Cantuar: Roberto adhuc vivente. Sedit ann. 18. *Obiit Winton. in carcere. Vacavit § sedes* 2. *annis.*

Successit Lanfrancus abbas Cadomen: natione Longoberdus, filius Harebaldi et Rosae.

fo. 100 a. *Celebravit Lanfrancus* 6. *concilia, primum Wintonia,* 2. *London.* 3. *Wintonia.* 4. *London.* 5. *Claudia.* 6. *Glocestria.*

Lanfrancus renovavit ecclesiam Christi Cantuari:

Lanfrancus ‖ reparavit ecclesiam S. Andreae apud Rochestar.

Lanfrancus reparavit ecclesiam S. Albani.

Lanfrancus ecclesiam S. Gregorii extra Cantuari: et hospitale à fundamentis inchoavit.

Lanfrancus ecclesiam S. Nicholai ad occidentem Cantuariae, et hospitale leprosorum fecit. Sedit annis 19. *Obiit* 5. *Call. Jun. Sepultus est in ecclesia Christi Cantuar: Vacavit sedes ann.* 4.

Successit Anselmus abbas Beccensis. Natus in Augusta civitate patre Gundulpho, matre Ermenberga. Consecratus

1093. *anno Dom.* 1093. *Discordia inter regem et Anselmum pro auctoritate Ro. pont.*

Anselmus exulatus quia¶ refutavit accipere pallium à manu regis. Restitutus sedi Anselmus. Sedit annis 16. *Obiit* 11. *Call. Maii in anno Dom.* 1109. *aetatis suae anno* 76.

*Successit Radulphus Rofensis episcopus, quondam Sagiensis*ᵇ *abbas. Successit Radulpho in Rofensi sede Ernulphus abbas de Burgo. Lis magna inter Thurstanum archiepiscopum*

[* *Haraldy reges*, MS.]   [† *Seis*, MS.]
[‡ *Dedem*, MS.]   [§ *Vacuit*, MS.]
[‖ *Lanfrankecus*, MS.]   [¶ MS. has *exulātiqua*.]

ᵃ Jumièges.   ᵇ Seez, in Normandy.

Ebora: et Radulphum Cantuar. Sedit annis 8. mensibus Kent.
6. Obiit 3. Callend. Novembar.

*Successit Gul. Corbuil can. S. Osithes. Ab Honorio pont.
Ro. factus est legatus in Anglia et Scotia. Collegium cleri-
corum Dovariae suppressit, et novum coenobium monachorum
in australi parte oppidi pro eo construxit. Sedit ann.* 15.
Obiit Cantuar. 6. Call. Decembris. Vacavit sedes annis 2.

Successit Theobaldus abbas Beccensis.[a] *Tempore Theobaldi
propter litem inter eum et Henricum episcopum Winton:
fratrem regis Stephani de titulo legati, advenerunt multi
caussidici in Angliam. Tunc primus horum magister Vacarius
in Oxenfordia legem docuit.*

Lambertus primus abbas de Boxley. Claribaldus primus fo. 100 b.
*abbas de Fauresham. Exulat Theobaldus ob depositionem
Gul. Ebora: pont. in Remensi concilio.*

*Redit Theobaldus ad sedem mortuo rege Stephano. Sedit
Theobaldus ann.* 22. *Obiit* 14. *Call. Maii anno Dom.* 1161. 1161.
Sepultus est in ecclesia Christi.

Successit Thomas Bekel archiep Cantuar: sañtuar: * *et
cancellar: regis. Sedit ann.* 9. *Obiit* 4. *Callend. Januarii.*

*Successit Richardus natione Norman: monach: Cantuar:
et Prior Doverensis coenobii.*

*Godefridus episcopus S. Asaph resignavit annulum episcop:
Richardo Cantuar: in concilio Westmonaster:*

*Richardus regio edicto canon: seculares expulit ab Walt-
ham, et can. regulares induxit. Sedit ann.* 10. *mensibus* 8.
*Obiit apud Hallinges. Sepultus in ecclesia Christi in oratorio
beatae Mariae.*

*Successit Balduinus episcopus Wigorn: antea abbas de
Forda.*

Balduinus Exoniae ex infimo genere natus.

*Balduinus à Barptolemeo episcopo Exon. factus archid:
Exon.*

Baldinus fit monachus in Forda, et postea abbas.

Mortuo Rogero episcopo Wigorn: successit Balduinus.

Consilio Baldewini omnes episcopi Angliae studebant

[* This sentence must be wrongly copied; perhaps "archiepiscopi
Cantuar. familiar. et cancellar." is intended.]

---

[a] Abbey of Bec, Normandy.

Kent. *monachos ab ecclesiis cathedralibus* expellere, et clericos introducere.*

Baldewinus novam ecclesi : Cantuar : fabricavit, stnatam † ab eccle : monachorum, ubi jussit clericos suos domos ‡ 7. mansionarias facere.

Baldwinus monachos Cantuar : duriter tractat.

Ecclesia à Balduino incepta Cantuariae, et domus mansionariae eidem adjunctae § demolitae. Baldwinus lapideam ecclesiam apud Lamhith prope London : incepit, et domus mansionarias ibidem pro clericis suis fabricavit. Sedit annis. 5. mensibus 11. Obiit in obsidione civitatis Acon, et ibidem sepultus est. Capella de Hakington, opus Balduini Cantuar : jussu Celestini pont : Ro : demolita est.

Successit Hubertus primo ecclesiue Ebora : decanus, postea episcopus Saresbiriensis.

fo. 101 a. "*Hubertus Sarisberi : episcopus apud Acon in omnium oculis gratiosus, et in re militari adeo magnificus ut etiam regi Richardo esset admirandus. Erat enim statura procerus, consilio providus, ingenio callens, licet non eloquio pollens. Cum praefecto quondam Angliae Ranulpho ‖ de Glanvilla quodammodo ¶ regnum Angl. regebat, eo quod ipsius maxime consilio idem Ranulphus frueretur.*" *Sepelivit Balduinum apud Acon. Capella de Lamhith jussu pont : Ro. solo tenus complanata. Hic Hubertus Cantuar : infestiss. fuit Giraldo ** archiepiscopo Menevensi, qui pro pallio ecclesiae Menevensi †† restituendo strenue laborabat Romae.‡‡ Sedit annis 11. mens. 8. diebus 12. Obiit 3. Id. Jul. in villa de Tenham.*

Hactenus ex Gervasio.

Vacavit §§ sedes an. 1. mens. 11. diebus 16.

Successit Stephen Langton. Sedit ann. 22. diebus 23.

[* *Ecclesi cathedri*, MS.]   [† Perhaps *separatam.—Hearne.*]
[‡ MS. has *dedem*; no sense.—*Hearne.*]
[§ *Adjuncta*, MS.]
[‖ *Randulf* in Gervase; see the passage in vol. ii, 406.]
[¶ *Quodam*, MS.]   [** *Infestess: fuit Giralde*, MS.]
[†† The MS. has *ecclesia* here, redundant.]
[‡‡ *Aborat Roma*, MS.]
[§§ Gervase' "Lives of the Archbishops of Canterbury" ends with Hubert. Leland continues his notes on successive archbishops down to the death of Henry Chicheley in 1443, but I have not found his source for these.]

Hic prius erat Ro. ecclesiae presbyter Card : et ab Innocen- **Kent.**
tio 3. *Ro : pont. consecratus anno Dom.* 1227.

Vacavit sedes anno 1. *et dim. mense, diebus* 12.

Successit Richardus cog : Magnus. Sedit annis 2. *Vacavit sedes anno* 1. *ebdomadibus* 18.

Hic prius erat cancellarius Lincoln : Obiit anno Dom. 1231.

Successit Edmundus. Sedit ann. 8. *Vacavit sedes ann.* 3. *mens.* 2. *diebus* 3. *Hic prius erat thesaur.*

Successit Bonifacius. Sedit annis 26. *mensibus* 6. *diebus* 18. *Vacavit sedes annis* 2. *ebdomad :* 10. *diebus* 3.

Successit Robertus de Kilwardby. Sedit ann. 6. *Vacavit* 45. *septimanis* * *et diebus* 3.

Hic fuerat ante de ord. Praed : Factus est à Gregor : 10. *pont. Ro. archiepiscopus Cantuar : Viterbi : postea Card : Portuensis factus à Nicholao* 3. *pont : Ro.*

Johannes Pecham de ord : min : successit. Sedit ann. 13. *et* 45. *septimanis,*† *diebus* 2. *Vacavit* ‡ *sedes anno* 1.

Successit Robertus de Winchelsey. Sedit ann. 19. *Vacavit* **1292.** *sedes mens.* 9. *et sept. una. Obiit anno Dom.* 1313. *Fuerat prius. archid. Essex.*

Successit Galterus Reginalds. Sedit ann. 13. *mens.* 10. *diebus* 3.

Hic § *prius fuerat thesaur : regis Angliae, et Wigorn. episcopus similiter, et cancellar : Dom. regis. Vacavit sedes mens.* 6. *sept.* 3. *et die una usque ad* 6. *Call. Jun. anno Dom.* 1338.

Simon Mepham successit. Sedit 5. *ann.* 4. *mens. et* 17. *die-* **fo.** 101 b. *bus. Vacavit sedes* 4. *mens. diebus* 10.

Johannes de Strateford successit. Sedit 11. *ann.* 6. *mens.* 3. *sept.* 4. *diebus. Vacat eccle.* 3. *mens. et* 11. *diebus.*

Successit Johannes Ufford electus et confirmatus. Sedit 6. *mensibus et* 4. *diebus. Vacavit sedes* 2. *mens.* 3. *diebus.*

Successit Thomas Bredwardine. Sedit 5. *sept. et* 4. *diebus. Vacavit sedes* 4. *mens. diebus* 2.

Successit Simon Iselepe. Sedit ann. 18. *mens.* 4. *diebus* 13. *Vacat sedes* 6. *mensibus,* 3. *sept.* 4. *diebus. Hic prius erat can : Cicestrensis.*

Successit Simon Langham primo abbas Westmonaster: et episcopus Eliensis. Sedit annis 2. *sept.* 3. *Urbanus* 5. *pont.*

[* *Septemn̄*, MS.]   [† *Septimam*, MS.]   [‡ *Vacasit*, MS.]
[§ *His*, MS.]

Kent. *Ro. elegit hunc in card:* 10. *Call. Octobar. quo tempore resignavit archiep. Cantuar. Vacavit sedes* 7. *sept. et die* 1.

Successit Gul. de Whitlesey episcopus Rofensis, postea Wigorn: Translatus fuit Cantuar: per Urbanum 5. *pont: Ro: Sedit ann.* 5. *mens.* 8. *dies* 14.

Vacavit eccle: mens: 11. *sept.* 3. *dies* 3.

Simon de Sudbyri successit prius episcopus London. translatus per Gregorium 11. *pont. Ro: Sedit ann.* 6. *dep. h'' ** 6. *diebus. Securi percussus fuit apud turrim London. à seditiosis. Vacavit sedes* 4. *mens. et* 16. *diebus.*

Successit Gul. Courteney, filius comitis Devon. prius episcopus Hereforde, 2. *London. Sedit annis* 15. *mens.* 11. *diebus* 2. *Vacavit sedes* 3. *mensibus et* 3. *diebus.*

Successit Thomas Arundell primo Elien. episcopus. Sedit ann. 17.

Successit Henri. Chicheley legum doctor, prius cancellar. Sarum, et à Gregor. 12. *pont. Ro. episcopus Menevensis factus. Sedit annis* 29. *Obiit anno Dom.* 1443. 2. *Id. April. Johannes Stratford successit.*

fo. 107 b.†   It appearithe by the legende of S. Pandonia ‡ that she was a kynge of Scotts dowghtar, and after flienge them that would have deflowrid hir, she cam to a kynns woman of hirs, priorese of a nunrey at Eltesley in Cambridgeshire, 4. myles from Seint Neotes, and aftar dyenge was byried in Eltesley by a well cawled S. Pandonia Welle. She was translatyd into Eltesley Churche anno 1344. as it aperithe by the lessons of hir translation made by one Ser Richarde, parishe priste there.

Eltesley in Cumbridgshire.

1344.

Some say that the olde priory was by the vicarage.

Croxton is halfe a myle from Eltesle, and is in Cambridgeshire. Elnig halfe a myle beyonde is in Huntyngduneshire. Eltesley was of late yeres inpropriate to Deney ª Abbay. Syr Manok of Southfolke is lorde of that village.

One Mac William beinge a yongger brothar of a gentleman in Yrland cam to Bristowe, and there so increasyd in ryches that in continuance he bowght lands to the sume of

[* *Sept.* 5. seems intended.—*Hearne.*]
[† Fos. 102 a-107 a, on Welsh matters, are printed in vol. iv, pp. 168-180.]   [‡ See vol. i, p. 1.]

ª Denney.

a 3. or 400. markes by the yere, and so the land continuyd a certeyn while in the heires males of Mac William, and aftar cam to a dowghtar of theyrs that was maried to one of the Semars.

This land, as I remember that I have written in a nothar place, lay partely aboute Cainesham.*

There was of late one of the Mac Williams in Est-Sex, and he left heyres males.

The last Lord Grey of Codnor left 3. doughtars, whereof *Gray of* one was maried to Syr Rowland Lentalle of Notyngham- *Codenor.* shire, a nothar to Newport of Shropshire, and the third to one Souche a yongar brothar of the howse of the Lord Souches. Thes 3. had the Lord Grayes lands in copar[ti]tion, where of the lordeshipe of Ailesford in Kent and How Hundred was parte, the whiche Mastar Wyat now hathe bowght. There were some of the lord Grayes of Codnor byried at Ailesford Freres.

Lentall dyenge without isswe male lefte 2. dowghtars, whereof one callyd Catarine was maried to one of the Lord Souches, the other to Cornwale Baron of Burford, and so cam they to be copartiners in the Lord Grey of Codnor's lands.

The Lordes Souches hathe had by a good tyme parte of fo. 108 a. the Lorde Cantelupes, and the Lord S. Maures lands.

The castle of Gresby in Notynghamshire was the Lord Cantelupe's, and sum of the Cantelupes lay byried at Bew-vale a house of Cartusyans there.

The Lordes Souches had aftar this castelle.

This Lorde Souche's father lay muche at a goodly manor place caullid Marsch[a] by Bruton in Somersetteshire. This house is now in ruine.

The Lorde Souche that is now hathe a faire manor place in Devonshir caullid . . . It is a . . . myles from Excester. And this manor with othar cam to this Lord Souche by one of the 4. dowghtars and heires of the Lord Dunham of Devonshire that was his mothar.

[* Leland's only references to Cainesham, now Keynsham, appear to be in vol. iv, p. 139, and pp. 92, 102-3 of the present volume, neither of which apply to the above.]

---

[a] Marsh.

The 4. dowghtars and heyres of the Lord Dunham were maried to the Lord Souche, to the Lord Fitz-Gwarin, to Arundell, and to the Baron of Carow.

Worcester-shire.

Dowre or Stowre.

(The cource of Dour, alias Stowr, ryver in Wicester-shire.) Dowr, alias Stour,[a] ryver risethe out of the pondes of Hales Owen, a priori of Whit Chanons, and óthar springs ther about. Thence it goithe to the tounelet of Hales Owen in Wicestershire, about a myle of *in ripa super:* Then to Sture Bridge in Wicestershire a market towne about a 4. myles of.

Thens to Kinuar[b] a thorough fare a 2. myles *in ripa super.*[*] Thens to Sturton Castle (as I remembar in Staffordshire) a myle from Kinuar.[b] It stondithe on a hill a litle from the hither rype. (Bewdley is a 2. myles from Kidour.) Thens to Kidour Mynstre[c] a good market towne, and rennethe thrwghe the mydle of it, and at rages drownythe a pecc of it. In Kidour Minstre is but one churche, but it is large. The personage was inproprate to the chanons of Mayden Bradley in Wileshire. A litle benethe Kidour is a fayre manor place on Stour caulyd Candalewel. It was the Conxeys,† and now it longethe to the Winters, men of fayre lande. Stowre goythe into Severne by the hither rype of it at Stourmouthe a litle benethe Mitton 2. myles from Kidour Mynster.

fo. 108 b.

Clinte in Cowbage,[d] wher S. Kenelme was martirid, is a 2. miles from Hales Priorie.

Averey parson of Dene tolde me that he had redd that Askaperius, the murtherer of S. Kenelm, was maried to Quindred, sistar to S. Kenelme, and that he reynid a 2. or 3. yeres after Kenelme, untyll suche tyme that a kinnesman of Kenelmes put hym downe. But loke bettar for this mattar. Sens he tolde me that it is in S. Kenelme's lyfe that Ascaperius was maried to Quendrede, and reignid with her 2. or 3. yeres untyll Kenclm's uncle put hym downe. He

Gloucester-shire.

Ascaperius duxit Quendredam in uxorem.

[* Stow has *supra.*]

[† Perhaps the Cockseys (Cookseys, *Dr. Lyttleton*), an old Kidder-minster family. Camden's "Britannia" (1789 ed.), vol. ii, p. 351.]

---

[a] Stour r.   [b] Kinver, or Kinfare.   [c] Kidderminster.

[d] Clent, Cowbach, a pasture near Hales Owen.

saythe that it aperithe by Seint Kenelme's legend that Winchelcombe [a] was *oppidum muro cinctum*.   And he saythe that the towne buyldinge was muche toward Sudeley Castell, and that ther yet remayne sum tokens of a diche and the foundation of a wall, and that ther be tokens of an othar way up a praty way beyonde the highe strete above the churche where the farme of Cornedene is: so that of old tyme it was a mighty large towne. *Winchelcombe. Gloucestershire.*

The monastery was set in the best parte of all the towne, and hard by it where the pariocie churche is was Kynge Kenulphe Palace.   Winchelcombe is set in the rottes of Cotiswolde.

The ryver [b] that cummythe as the old towne stoode thorough the mydle of Winchelcombe is comonly caulyd ther Grope cunte, but aftar a litle benethe Todington, by the whiche it rennith, it changythe the name, and aftar a this syde Eovesham at a litle village caullyd Ampton [c] it rennythe into Avon.   The head of this rivar is a 2. myles above Wynchelescombe in the hill.

This riveret cummythe within a qwartar of a myle of Hayles [d] monasterie in the valley under it.

Olde Ser Umfrey Stafford's father was on the feeld, and very stiffe agayne Henry the vii. where he was taken, and after behedid at Bewdele towne aboute the wiche quarters he had muche lande. *fo. 109a.*

Sudeley Castell by Winchelcombe was buildid, as it is there comonly spoken, *ex spoliis nobilium bello Gallico captorum.*

Butlar Lord Sudeley.

The Lord Harington, a man of fayre lands in Lancastreshire and othar partes, marid the heire of the Lorde Boneville of Devonshire, by whom he had the lordeshipes of Winchecombe and Shoute [e] with othar landes.   The last lorde of the very name of the Haringtons was slayne *bello civili* betwixt Kynge Henry the vi. and Edwarde the 4. whos wife the Lord Hastinges that was beheddid by Richard Duke then of Glocester in the tour of London did marie.   Sens I hard that one Neville had * Horneby.   Harrington of *Lancashire and Dorset.*

[* *Hand*, MS.]

[a] Winchcombe.   [b] Isborne r.   [c] Little Hampton.
[d] Hayles Abbey.   [e] Shute.

Hornby. There was a yonger brother of the Haryngtons
that had in gifte Horneby Castelle: and an heire generall of
this howse was aftar maried to one of the Standeleys, aftar
Lord Mountegle, that had a child, but dead borne, as sum
saye, by hir: whereupon he required the lands for terme
of lyfe, and beinge in pocession aftar bought the inheritaunce of it to hym and his heirs.

The sole dowghtar and heire of the Lorde Harington
cawlyd . . . was maried to Thomas the first Marquese of
Dorset that favorid the cummynge of Henry the vii., and
he had by hir a 14. children, bothe men and wimen, of
excedinge goodly parsonage, of the whiche the first sune
lyvyd not longe, and then had Thomas the name of Lorde
Harington, and aftar was the second Marquese of Dorset.

Gleston
Castell.
There is a ruine and waulles of a castle in Lancastershire
cawlyd Gleston Castell,[a] sometyme longynge to the Lorde
Haringtons, now to the Marquise of Dorset. It stondithe a
2. miles from Carthemaile.[b]

**Leicester-
shire.**

fo. 109 b.
Syr John Grey that maried the dowghtar and heire of the
Lorde Ferrares of Groby was slayne *bello civili*, as I hard, at
Northampton; but I am not sure of this. That Gray whose
wyfe, dowghtar to the Lord Ryvars, was aftar maried to
Kynge Edward, was fathar to Thomas first Marques of
Dorset. The Marquese of Dorset by heires generales of the
Rivers had the fayre manor place of Graftan,[c] and goodly
parks and lands thereaboute, for the whiche he gave hym
in exchange Lughborow with parks there about, and othar
goodly lands in Leircestarshire. Lughborow was of the
Bellemounts lands, and the late old Countes of Oxforde had
it in dowre.

Luterworthe towne and lands there aboute be of en-
heritance to the Lord Marques of Dorset by the title of
Groby.

Bewmaner,[d] wher Leonard Gray by the kyng's leave
dyd dwell, was also the Lord Bellemonts, and so was the
great pasture betwyxt Leircestre and Groby caulyd Bellemonts Lease.[e]

Wolvescrofte
Priorye.
Wolvescrofte [f] Priorie of Blake Chanons about a mile from

---

a Gleaston Castle.   b Cartmell.   c Grafton.
d Beaumanor.   e Beaumont's Leys.   f Ulverscroft.

Brodegate^a was the sepulture of diveres of the Ferrares of Groby. And there was buried a late the Countis of Wicester, wyfe to the Lord Leonard Graye.

As far as I could perceyve by questioninge with the auncient servaunts and officers of the Marquese of Dorsete, suche parte of the Erle of Leyrcester launds as cam to Saerus de Quinci Erle of Wynchestar fell aftar by heires generals to the Lord Bellemonte, Ferrares and Lovelle.

Mastar Constable told me that the namẽ of his familie was notablitatyd by the Erles of Chestar, and that it was a name taken by reason of office borne. He tolde me also that one of his predicessors maried a dowghtar of the Lacys Erle of Lyncolne.

The diches and the plotte where the castelle of Mere stoode appere not far from the chirche of Mere the market toune. **Cheshire.**

The goodly gate howse and fronte of the Lorde Stourton's howse in Stourton was buyldyd *ex spoliis Gallorum.*

Sir William Parre told me that his aunclters wore men of a xx. marks of land by the yere in the marches of Wales, and that one of them beinge clarke of the kechyn with one of the Lorde Rosses fell in love with a dowghtar of his, and maried hir agayne hir father's wille, by whome the castell of Kendalle, and 300. marks by ycre of land cam to this parre, and so was the name first in the northe parte nobilitate. ** Origo familiae filii Henrici.* *fo. 110 a. Kendall was the Lord Rosses.*

Master Brudeneld told me that the Busseys of Lyncolnshire had a 1000. *li.* of lands by the yere in the tyme of Richard the second, and that a great peace of the vale and playne from Huntington to Lincolne [was] † of theyr pocessions, and that they had 2. castells in that parte, ‡ whereof one was at Fokyngham, that sins the Lorde Bellemont had, and now the Duke of Northfolke hathe it as a pece of attayntyd land in gifte. **Lincolnshire.**

Ther is a great fe gateryd abowte Bostone parts by the name of Petronille de la Corone, dowghtar by lykelihode to *Petronilla Corona.*

[* *Origio fimilia,* MS.] [† *Was* added by Hearne.]
[‡ Stow has *partes.*]

---

a Bradgate.

Friston Priorye. de la Corone, foundar of Friston^a Priorie, and buried at Croyland. This fe is now payde to the Lorde Russe, but the Richemount fee is greatar there.

There is also a nothar fee cauled Pepardine, and that the Lorde Linsey had. And the owners of these fees be lords of the towne of Boston.

Brakeley, **Northants.** Mastar Paynell told me that he saw at Brakley in the parts by Bukyngham manifest tokens that it had bene a wallyd toune, and tokens of the gates and towres in the walles by the halfe cirkles of the foundations of them. (I sowght diligently, and could find no tokens of wales or diches.) And that there hathe bene a castell, the dyke and

Hospitalarii. hills whereof do yet appere. (I saw the castle plott.) And that ther hathe bene dyvars churches in it. And that ther was of late a place of Crossyd Friers, and that one Nevill a great gentilman there was buried. And that one Neville apon a tyme kyllyd in the churche at Brakeley a priest and buried hym in his sacrid vestiments: and that this Nevill toke there an othar prist and buried hym quike.*

There is no suche booke. Mastar Paynell tolde me also that he saw an olde boke in the quier, or the vestrie, of Brakeley Churche, wherein were many things of the acts done at that churche.

fo. 110 b.
Worcester.

Nomina episcoporum Wigorn.†

Boselus episcopus Wigorn: in anno Dom. 692.
Ostoforus in anno 717.
Eugenius, alias Exwinus,‡ in anno 743.
Wilfridus anno Dom. 775.
Milredus anno Dom. 783.
Weremundus anno Dom. 791.
Thilherus anno Dom. 798.
Hetheredus anno Dom. 822. *Dedit Icombe.*

[* As to Brackley and Neville, see vol. ii, pp. 35-38.]
[† This list nearly agrees with Florence of Worcester (Hwiccia) as far as John Pagham; also, with one or two exceptions noted, with the lists given by Dr. Stubbs ("Reg. Sacrum Anglicanum") and Hardy's Le Neve ("Fasti Eccles. Anglicarum," 1854). But Leland's dates differ considerably and irregularly from those given by Dr. Stubbs.]
[‡ *Ecgwine* or *Egwinus* (Stubbs and Luard).]

---

^a Frieston.

Worcester.

Denebertus anno Dom. 846.
Headbertus anno Dom. 852. *Dedit Crole.*
Alchimus* anno Dom. 915.
Wereferthus anno Dom. 922.
Athelwinus anno Dom. 929.
Wilbertus anno Dom. 937.
Kenewoldus anno Dom. 938. *Dedit Odingley.*
S. Dunstanus ⎱ *circa an. Dom.* 969.
S. Oswaldus ⎰
Adulphus anno Dom. 1003.
Wulstanus reprobus anno Dom. 1025.
Leofsius anno Dom. 1041.
Britegus anno Dom. 1052. *praeceptor Wolstani postea†
episcopi.*
Livi[n]gus anno Dom. 1061.
Aldredus anno Dom. 1062.
S. Wolstann anno aetatis suae plus quam 50. *anno Dom.*
1095. *Hawkesbiri ante monachatum. Wolstanus natus apud
Hichenton*ᵃ *in comit. Warwike.‡*
Sampson anno Dom. 1112. *Civitas Wigorn. cum ecclesia
cathedrali, et omnibus aliis cum castello igne crematur.*
Theodwaldus§ anno 1117.
Thulphus anno Dom. 1124.
Simon anno Dom. 1139.
Johannes Pagham anno Dom. 1157.
Aluredus anno Dom. 1160.
Rogerus filius comitis Glocesteriae anno Dom. 1164. *obiit in
peregrinatione inter redeundum ab Hierosolymis.*
Baldwinus anno Dom. 1184.   fo. 111 a.
Gul. Northale anno Dom. 1189.
Robertus anno Dom. 1193.
Henricus anno Dom. 1195.
Johannes de Constantiis anno 1198. *ante decanus Roto-
magensis.*

[* *Alhwinus* in Florence of Worc.]
[† *Postie*, MS.]   [‡ Marginal note in MS.]
[§ This bishop is neither in Florence of Worc. nor in Stubbs. According to Hardy's edition of Le Neve Theobald and Theulphus were one man (vol. iii, p. 49).]

ᵃ Itchington.

v.   Q

Worcester.

Maugerius anno Dom. 1200.

Gwalterus Grey anno Dom. 1215.

Silvester anno Dom. 1217.

Ecclesia cathedr: dedicatur in honore D. Mariae, Petri, et Sanctorum Oswaldi et Wolstani.

Gul: Bleys anno Dom. 1220.

Gaulterus de Cantilupo anno Dom. 1237.

Nicolaus anno Dom. 1268.

Godefridus Giffart anno Dom. 1269. *Appropriatio ecclesiae de Grinley tempore hujus episcopi. Sedit annis* 34. *mensibus* 4. *diebus* 4.

Gul. Gaynesburge de ord. fratrum Minorum anno Dom. 1305.

Walterus Reynaud anno Dom. 1308.

Gualterus Maidestane anno Dom. 1313.

Thomas Cobham anno Dom. 1317.

Adam Horleton anno Dom. 1337.

Simon* de Monte acuto anno Dom. 1333.

Thomas Henihal anno Dom. 1337.

Wolstanus anno Dom. 1338.

Johannes Thoresby anno Dom. 1349.

Reginaldus Brian anno Dom. 1350.

David anno Dom. 1358.†

Johannes de Bernet anno Dom. 1362.

Gul. Whitlesey anno Dom. 1367.

Gul. Lynne anno Dom. 1369.

Henricus Wakefelde anno Dom. 1375.

Tittemannus de Winchecombe anno Dom. 1385.

Richardus Cliffurd anno Dom. 1401.

Thomas Peverelle anno Dom. 1407.

Philippus Morgan anno Dom. 1419.

Thomas Pulton anno Dom. 1425. *Obiit Romae.*

Thomas Bulshere‡ anno Dom. 1435.

Joannes Carpenter anno Dom. 1443.

fo. 111 b.   *Johannes Alcoke anno Dom.* 1476.

Robertus Morton anno Dom. 1496.

Joannes Giglis anno Dom. 1497.

Sylvestar de Gigles anno Dom. 1521.

[* MS. has *Thomas.*]
[† *David* is not in Stubbs nor Le Neve.]
[‡ A marginal note rightly corrects this to *Bourchier.*]

Julius anno Dom. 1522. *Resignavit episcopatum Hiero-* Worcester. *nymo, qui postea Clemens pontifex Ro. Hieronymus accepit episcopatum mense Mart:* 1522. *Hugo Latimer mense Augusti anno Dom.* 1535.

Joannes Belle anno Dom. 1539.

Godefridus Giffart* episcopus Wigorn: exornavit columnas orient: partis ecclesiae cathedralis Wigorn: columnellis marmoreis cum juncturis areis deauratis.

Thomas Cobham episcopus Wigorn: fecit testudinem borealis insulae in navi ecclesiae.

Wolstanus Brannesford Prior Wigorn: et postea episcopus Wigorn: erexit magnam aulam Prioris.

Brannesford Bridge super Tende duobus passuum milibus supra Powike.

Gul. Lynne cum equum conscenderet profecturus ad Parlamentum obiit Wigorn: correptus apoplexia.

Henricus Wakefilde episcopus Wigorn: auxit occident. partem ecclesiae cathedr: Wigorn: 2. *arcubus.*

Erexit etiam porticum ecclesiae cathedr: Wigorn: versus boream.

Erexit etiam mag: capellam in castele de Herthisbyri.[a]

Tittomannus de Winchelescumbe episcopus Wigorn: orator regis in nuptiis filiae regis Angl: et duus Hannoniae

Richardus Clifford Wigorn: episcopus, postea London. sepultus est in ecclesia cathedra: London. ad austrum prope S. Erkenwaldum.

Johannes Carpenter episcopus Wigorn: erexit magnam turrim, id est, the Gate House apud Herthisbiriam. Obiit at Northwike episcopi,[b] *et sepultus apud Westbyry prope Brightstow, ubi fuit alter fundator.*

Johannes Alcok episcopus Wigorn: erexit capellam S. Mariae in navi ecclesiae quam designaverat suo sepulchro.

Robertus Morton episcopus Wigorn: nepos Johannis Morton archiepiscopi Cantuar: sepultus est in navi ecclesiae cathedr: S. Pauli London:

[* I do not find the original of these fuller notes on Worcester bishops from Giffart onwards in Birchington or other texts given by Wharton. It may be noted that the last bishop Leland cites was of 1539, which supplies us with a date for some of his researches.]

---

[a] Hartlebury.　　　　　[b] Northwich Park.

READING FREE PUBLIC LIBRARY

fo. 112 a.   *Johannes de Gigles, i.e. de liliis, natus Lucae in Italia,*
Worcester.   *episcopus Wigorn:*
Julius Medices episcopus Wigorn: postea Clemens dictus pont: Ro:
Johannes Pagham episcopus Wigorn: dedit Bibery [a] *monaster: de Osney, et post emit Elme episcopi, et* [*] *dedit sedi.*
Maugerius Nothus ex decano Ebor: episcopus Wigorn: de quo in Decretalibus capitulo Cum Wigor[n]enses.
Joannes Carpenter voluit in titulum assumere ut episcopus Wigorn: et Westbiriensis diceretur. Hic ex veteri collegio, quod erat Westebiriae, novum fecit, et praediis auxit, addito pinnato muro, porta et turribus instar castelli.
Habent episcopi Wigornienses villam et ferarum septum apud Hendre non procul ab Westbyri: sed aedes olim amplae nunc patiuntur ruinam. †

Placis belongynge to the Bysshope of Wurcestar.

The palace at Worcestar. Herthilbery [b] Castle 7. myles from Worcestar, 4. myles to Ombresley [c] on Severn longynge to Eovesham, and 3. to Herthilberi, and 4. to Kidermister. Alechirch [d] 2. myles from Bordesley Abbey. Latimer repayred it.

Northwike *in dominio de Claynes* [e] 2. myles from Worcestar. This Northewike was one John of Wodds *in hominum memoria*, and bought of a bysshope for lake of a howse in Claynes. It is motid, and had a parke.

Whityngdon [f] in Coteshold in ruine.

Hillyngdon the paroche churche to Uxbridge, xv. myles from London.

Stroud Place at London.

fo. 112 b.   Placis belonginge to the Prior.

Batnal [g] a mile out of Worcester with a parke and pooles.
Grymley [h] a 3. miles above Worcestar *prope* Severn agayne Ombresley *in ripa dextra Sabrinae.*

[* MS. has *ad* for *et*.]   [† *Ruina*, MS.]

---

[a] Bibury, a parish in Gloucestershire.   [b] Hartlebury.
[c] Ombersley.   [d] Alvechurch.   [e] Claines.
[f] Whittington, Gloucestershire.   [g] Batenhall.   [h] Grimley.

Halow[a] a park withowt a howse a 2. myles from Worcestar. **Worcester.**

Croule[b] a 4. myls from Worcestar.

More *prope* Tende a 10. myles from Worcestar *prope fines* Herefordshire.

Urso de Abetot vicecomes Wigorn: sepultus fuit ad pedes Joannis regis, et inde translatus in borealem partem presbyterij juxta sepulchrum Eovesham Prioris Wigorn.

There is yet one of the Abetots, a man of 20. *li.* land in Worcester towne.

The names of noblemen that gave lands to Worcestar Churche be in the glasse wyndowes in the cloistrie there.

Gilbertus de Clare comes Glocestar et Hereford, et Joanna ejus uxor fieri fecerunt fossatum in summitate montium Chace de Malverne in praejudicium Godefridi episcopi Wigorn: etc.

In navi ecclesiae.

Henry Wakefeld episcopus Wigorn: obiit 11. *Mart: anno D.* 1394. *et suae consecrationis* 20. *anno.*

Joannes Beauchampe miles de familia comitum Warwici charus Edwardo 3. *et Richardo* 2. *tandem decollatus tempore Henrici* 4 This Beauchampe was owner of Holt, a praty pile a 3. myle by northe owt of Worcestar on Severne *ripa dextra* a mile above Grimley. At this Holt Kynge Richard the 2. made attorneaments.

In bor. insula navis.

Johan: Beauchaumpe de Powike et Elisabethe ejus uxor. **fo. 113 a.**

Richard Bray armiger, pater Reginald Bray, fuit medicus, **Bray medicus**
ut quidam ferunt, Henrici 6. **Henrici 6.**

In australi insula navis.

Thomas Liteltone miles et justitiarius banchi, qui scripsit **Litleton.** *Tenuras.*

Inscriptio Baptisterii in nigro marmore.

Hic fons est vitae. Mundandi quicunque venite. Suscipit ista reos, et parit unda deos.

[a] Hallow. [b] Crowle.

In Presbyterio.

Johannes rex, cujus sepulchrum Alchirch sacrista nuper renovavit.

Sacellum in quo Arturius princeps sepultus est ad austrum.

Grifith filius Rhesi in eodem sacello.

Epitaphium Alexandri* Necham.

Eclypsim patitur sapientia: sol sepelitur.†
Qui dum vivebat studii genus ‡ omne vigebat.
Solvitur in cineres Neccham, cui si foret heres.
In terris unus, minus esset flebile funus.

1101.

Of Lychefild I have left out for brivity, it is to small purpos.

William Fitz Alane foundyd Haghemon *anno Dom.* 1101. the 1. of W. Ruffus.§ Ther was an hermitage and a chapell before the erectynge of the abbey. W. Fitz Allyn and his wyffe, with Richard Fitz Allen and othar, ar ther buried, and Richard Fitz Alan a child, whiche child fell, as is sayde, by the neclygence of his norice out of hir armes from the batelments of the castle of Shrawardig.[a]

Devonshire.

Dertmouthe Castell.

Where as I have wrytten that the castell and vyllage of Stoke Fleminge stode at Dertmowthe, I made ii. errors. Fyrst the castell berithe the name of Dertmouthe in an olde evydence, and not of Stoke Flemynge, thowghe the Flemings were the auncient lords and buyldars of it longe afore or it cam to the Carews hands. Secondly Stoke Flemyng is a praty olde tounlet toward the shore about a myle *dim.* west from Dertemouthe. Dyvers of the Flemings ar buryed at Stoke. Ther is a chapell of Seint Patrike in the castle of Dartemouthe, and by some old writynges it aperithe that it was a cell of monks. Yet I hard syns some contend that it was caulyd Stoke Castle.

Acton Burnell.
fo. 113b.
Burnell episcopus.

The abat of Haghmon told me that he hathe hard that the castell of Acton Burnell or goodly manor place, where the Parliament was kepte, was first made by one Burnell a bysshope.

[* *Alexandar,* MS.]   [† *Sepeliter,* MS.]   [‡ *Gens,* MS.]
[§ This should be Henry I.]

---

[a] Shrawardine.

The Universite Churche in Oxford, alias S. Marye *Universite* Churche, was begon to be reedified in the tyme of Doctor *Churche in* Fitz-James, aftar Bysshope of London. He procuryd muche *Oxford.* mony towards the buyldynge of it. The enbatylments of it wer full of pinacles: but in a tempestious wethar most parte of them were throwne downe in one nyght.

Gualtar Erle of Sarum and Sibylle his wyfe founders of Bradenestoke, a priorie of Blake Chanons in Wyleshire.

Ther was a fayre colege in the Erls of Lancaster tyme a lytle* with Banborow in Northumbreland, now clene downe. S. George Darcy told me of it.

Roder[a] ryver rysethe, as some say, in a great poole callyd *Shropshire.* Hurmer a 6. myles from Shrobbesbyry by northe.

Ther yssuythe out of this pole a broke, and aftar resortith to an othar poole callyd Wibbemere, and here, as the moste commune sayenge is, risethe Roden ryver, that aftar a 6. or 7. myles course commythe into Terne a 2. myles above Terne Bridge.

Ther were in Oxford of auncient tyme 800. burgeses *Oxforde.* houses and mo with in the towne of Oxford, and a 400. without in the suburbes.

The seale of Oxford hathe an ox on it withe a castle, or wallyd towne, and about it is writen *Sigillum civitatis Oxoniae†* etc.

Some say that there were 24. parishe churchis and mo in the towne and suburbs of Oxford.

Kynge Henry the first somewhat restoryd the towne of Oxforde.

The towne of Oxford moste floryshed withe scollars in an huge nombar, and other inhabitaunts, in Henry the 3. tyme. Ther was an infinit nombar of writars and parchement makers in Oxford in Henry the 3. tyme.

The bowrgesis of Oxford say that Vortimer made theyr *fo. 114 a.* towne. The nombar of scolars and inhabitaunts in Oxforde were so greate in Henry the 3. tyme that they had lybertye to provyd for vitails 2. myles about.

[* *Sic.* Apparently a word or two omitted.]   [† *Oxonia,* MS.]

---

[a] Roden r.

Oxford.

Bridgs on Charwell.

Arcus 20.
in ponte ori-
entali.

Est Bridge at Oxford. To Iselep Brige of stone a 3. myles upper on Charwell by land. To Gosford Bridge a myle or more. To Emmeley [a] Bridge a 2. myles upper. To Heywood [b] Bridge a 2. miles uper etc.

Where as now the bridge of stone is ovar Charwell by Magdalen Colledge was a trajectus, or fery, in Kynge Henry the third's dayes, caulyd Steneford.

It apperithe by the preface of the donation of Kynge Edgare unto the Priory of Worcester that he was the very first Monarchie thrwghly in all regions of England and Scotland amonge the Saxon kyngs.

It aperithe also there that he had the whole homage of Scotland, and was taken for chefe Head and Governar of all the Isles about England even to Norwege.

It ther also aperithe that he was crownyd in Irland in Dubelin the chefe cite of it, and that all Ireland was subject unto hym.

The Duke of Buckyngham was lord of Hagmoundham,[c] sens the kynges, now Russel's, Lord Admirall.

Maydenhed.
Maydenhethe.

Maindenhevid in Bukinghamshire,* of old tyme cawllid Sowth-Eilington. It toke the name of Maidenhed of a hedde that they sayd was one of the xi. thousand Virgines, to the whiche offering there was made in a chapell.

Drew Baren-
tyne.

One Barentyne, a yongar brother of the chefe house of the Barentines, was a gold-smythe of London, and becam wonderfull riche and purchasid fayre lands, and dyenge, as it is sayde, without heires, gave parte of his lands to a yongar brothar of the Barentyns called Drew, and he had very many children, but in continuance they dyed, and it cam then to the chefe howse of the Barentynes.

fo. 114 b.

The parsell of lands that Drew lefte to his name was Litle Haseley in Oxfordshire, wher Ser William Barentyne now dwellethe.†

[* Leland appears to have written this in error for Berkshire.]
[† For other references to the Barentynes, see vol. i, p. 114, and vol. ii, p. 19.]

---

[a] Enslow?   [b] Heyford.   [c] Amersham, in Bucks.

Barentyne the gold-smythe buyldyd the Maner Place at *Barentyne* Litle Haseley. *Gold-Smithe.*

Barentyn the gold-smithe gave faire lands to the societie of the gold-smithes of London, and thcy kepte a very solempne obite yerely for hym.

Barentyne dwellyd in the faire place right agaynst the Gold-smithes Haule, and I thinke that he buyldyd that howse, and I thinke that he buyldyd a pece of the gold-smythe haule.

Barentine's graundfathar now lyvynge maried the Countes of Henault's dowghtar, begotten on hir by Gullim Duke of Suffolke, that first maried hir, and aftar *facto divortio* to Chaucer's heire. *Chaucers.*

Barentyn Gold-Smythe lyethe buried in Seint Zacharies churche by the Gold-Smiths Haule.

The chefe howse of the Barentynes florished in Henry the first, in Henry the 3. and Kynge Edward the 3. dayes.

The heyres of the Barentynes from Edward the 3. tyme tyll nowe were nepotes.

The Vale of Aeilesbyrie is a greate thinge in compace. *Alesberye.* One way it stretchethe from the costs of the foreste of . . . **Bucks.** alonge by Tame, and still by the rotes of Chilterne Hilles almoste to Dunstable.

It goithe also to Newporte Panelle, to Stony Stratforde, to Buckyngham, and limitethe on eche of them. Birdestane Parke and lordshipe standithe one way some what highe, and is countyd to be the mydle parte of the Vale of Ailesburye.

The well of S. Osythe at Querendune[a] bytwyxte Aeilesbyry and Querendune.

Querendune, sometyme the Spencers lands, a goode myle from Ailesberie, and an hamlet longing to Ailesbery. An howse of Grey Friers at Aielesbery.

Aeilborow,[b] of some soundyd Hilborow, a 3. myles by fo. 115a. southe from Aillesbyri. It was of late the Mounteacutes *Ailborow.* landes, and standithe on one of the Chiltren Hills.

Burton[c] a mile from Aeilesbery. Syr Antony . . . fathar *Burton.* attayntyd for comynge withe Kynge Richard to Bosworthe Field; his sonne aftar restoryd to his lands.

---

[a] Quarrendon.   [b] Ellesborough.   [c] Bierton.

APPENDIX

APPENDIX (WALES)*

Glamorganshire

P. 101.

SINGHENITH, id est, dimidia pars cantaredae. Ergen, Anglice Urchinfeld.

Kreyke yn yre,[a] id est, niveus collis, ex yra, id est, nix.

Ban, id est, locus assignatus, unde et montes excelsiores dicuntur Banne.

Bancor, id est, chorus de fama excellens.

Mor haveren, id est, mare Sabrinum.[b]

Tapha[c] fluvius habet duo brachia, quorum alter major, alter minor Tapha appellatur, et currunt in unum in principio de Singhenith adjacentis regioni Brechenioc.

Habertawe vulgo nuncupatur Swinseia.

Barth idem est quod bardus, vel poëta.

[* From Leland's MS. of "Collectanea," vol. iii, pp. 101-106 (Gough, "Top. Gen.," c. 3), printed in Hearne's "Collectanea," second edition, 1774, vol. iv, pp. 90-94. These pages of notes, chiefly on Glamorganshire, should have been placed at the end of Appendix B to the vol. iii of this edition, "Leland in Wales"; I did not then recognize that the notes relate to places in Glamorganshire, and must have been used by Leland in his narrative. See vol. iii, pp. 17-36.

These detached pages were not written by Leland, but by a very different hand; perhaps some Welsh friend may have sent him the information. Pages 96-98 in the MS. which precede them describe Anglesey (see before, vol. iii, Appendix B; pp. 99, 100 are blank); p. 107 relates to Gower land, and is in Leland's hand (vol. iii, Appendix A). There seems to be nothing else in this hand in the three volumes of Leland's MS. Collectanea. Burton appears to have placed the leaves in by the wrong edges, and to have numbered the pages before finding out his mistake; he thereupon added letters indicating the right order, which accordingly was followed by Hearne, and is continued here. They stand pp. 101, 102, 103*d*, 104*a*, 105*c*, 106*b*, and I so print the figures for reference.]

---

[a] Craig Eryri, or Snowdon. [b] Severn r. [c] Tâv, Taue r.

Ele[a] fluvius . . . currens in mare apud Penharth.

Ddaw currens per Pont vayn,[b] habens originem spatio illius passuum duorum milium in loco vocato pant Llywyth, id est, vallis collorata, et transit in mare Sabrinum illinc ad tria millia passuum in loco vocato Haberddaw.

Ewenny fluvius.

Ogmor fluvius.

Moithike, id est, Salopia.

Monmowth Cambrice Moynwess, *i.e.* Monovaga.*

Kayr vyske, alias Brynbyga.[c]

Merthyne wylht, id est, merlinus silvestris vulgariter nuncupatus.

Ewenny cellula sub monasterio Glocestriae.

Lancarovan,[d] id est, locus assignatus à cervis, distans spatio trium milliarium à Pont vayn.

Habertawe, id est, Suunsey.

Haber doye glevyth, id est, os duorum gladiorum.

Brevie, id est, mugire unde et Landdewe breve[e] dicitur, et illic sanctus David contra haereticus mugiebat.

P. 102.   Apud Pont yr heske, qui est pons super Tapham, distans a llan Taphe septem passibus milium, est alta rupis, ubi salmones saltu admirabili adverso flumine rupem conscendunt.

Peder, id est, Petrus. Patarne, id est, Patarnus.

Apud Llantoyt[f] in orientali parte cimiterii fani sancti Iltuti ferunt corpus Hoëli Da, id est, Hoëli boni, esse sepultum.

Llanllecnye, alias Lymster, id est, locus leonis.[g]

Castrum de Llan Blethian distans à Pontvayn quingentis passibus, ubi est porta quae habet septem cataractas.

Castrum de Penllyyn distans à Pontvayn mille passibus.

Colhiw[h] quidam porticulus maris prope Llan Iltute,[i] ubi transitur mare Sabrinum directe ad Dunster et Minhed in Somersetsher.

[* *Monovaga*, added by Leland.]

---

[a] Lai, Elei r.   [b] Thawan r., Cowbridge.   [c] Usk.
[d] Llan Carvan.   [e] Llan Dewi brevi.   [f] Llantwit.
[g] Leominster.   [h] Colhow.
[i] Llantwit major. See vol. iii, pp. 27, 32, 33.

Rivus de Remne originem habens in loco vocato Blayn P. 104 a.
Remne,[a] id est, caput Remne, Anglice the Poynt of Remne,
et currit in mare Sabrinum tribus millibus passuum à
Kayrdyff.

Rivus de Taffe Veghan, id est, Tapha parva, habens
originem in monte quodam in Brecnoc, et descendit in
Taffe Vawre, id est, Tapha magna, habente originem in
monte de Brecnoc vocato, ut credo, the Banne Bēghhynioc,[b]
et locus ubi cadit in Tapha magna vocatur Haber du Taffe,
*id est, casus utriusque Taphae, alterius † in alteram; qui locus
est in partibus de Singhenith sub monte vocato the Garth,
a parte occidentali ejusdem. In quo monte est castrum vetus,
quod olim fuit celebre, quod vocatur castell Morleýs, id est,
castrum sonitus maris, quia ab orientali parte ejusdem
castri currit quidam rivulus, vocatus More leys, id est,
sonitus maris propter strepitum illum, quem ‡ facit in
descensu suo per rupes, et currit in Tapha sub dicto monte
de Garth in australi parte ejusdem.

Item est in dicto Singhenyth quoddam castrum, vulgariter
nuncupatum Kair Fillye,[c] id est, castrum Fillic, quod est
castrum munitissimum, tum ex arte tum ex situ loci propter
paludes illi castri adherentes, et [distat §] à Tapha duobus
millibus et quingentis passibus, et stat ab orientali parte
fluminis, et distat à Kairdyff quatuor millibus passuum, et
stat à Kayrdiff versus septentrionem. Est et aliud castrum
in eadem plaga distans à Kairdyff duobus millibus passuum,
quod vocatur Castell Cough, id est, castrum rubrum, quod
stat in rupe rubea, distans à Tapha quingentis passibus.
Item aliud castrum vocatum castrum de Llandaffe prope
Tapham distans à Kayrdiff mille passibus. Deinde est
castrum de Kayrdiff, quod est primum et principale totius
Glamorgantiae.

Item est et alius rivus, vulgariter nuncupatus Leye, habens P. 106 b.

[* Between these two lines is a scratch plan of the Tâv and its valley.
Another of Pontvayn and its neighbourhood occurs further on, p. 241.
Hearne reproduces them.]
[† *Altera*, MS.]   [‡ *Strepidum illud quod*, MS.]
[§ Added by Hearne.]

---

[a] Blaen Remny.   [b] Bannè Brycheinog.   [c] Caerphilly.

originem in loco vulgariter nuncupato Kreyky Denas,[a] id est, in monte de Denas, qui stat prope locum vulgariter nuncupatum Pen Rise, id est, caput Resi, ab australi parte ejusdem. Iste rivus currit in mare Sabrinum in loco vocato Penarth, id est, caput ursi, et transit per valles pulcherrimas, penes quem sunt plura castra olim pulcra et ampla. Primum est castrum de Llantrissent, quod stat in orientali parte illius in monte vocato Kreyk Lantrissent, distans à dicto rivo ducentis passibus. Item inferius est castrum vocatum castell llan Peder, id est, castrum loci Petri, et stat in occidentali parte illius rivi, distans jact: lapidis ab eo rivo, et à Kairdiff quatuor millibus versus occidentalem plagam plus quam septentrionem. Est et aliud castrum, vocatum vulgariter castrum Sancti Georgii, et est prope dictum rivum ad jactum lapilli, et stat à parte occidentali ejusdem, et à Kairdiff iii[bus] millibus passuum. Est et aliud, quod vulgariter nuncupatur castrum Sancti Fagani, prope dictum rivum, et stat à parte orientali ejusdem, et distat à Kair duobus millibus passuum.

Item sunt alia nonnulla castra in illa regione, puta castrum de Dinas Powes, quod ab australi parte vertente in occidentem stat à Kairdiff, distans ab ead: quatuor millibus passuum. Est et aliud castrum de Wenvo magis tendens in occidentalem plagam, distans à Kairdiff quinque millibus passuum. Est et aliud, quod vocatur castrum de Funmoyn,[b] magis vertens in australem plagam, distans à Kayrdiff vi millibus passuum, et à mari Sabrino duobus millibus passuum.

Item est alius rivus, qui vulgariter nuncupatur Thawan, id est, Thaus, habens originem in loco vocato pant Llewyth, distans à Pont vayn versus septentrionalem plagam duobus millibus et quingentis passibus, et currit per Pont vayn[c] in mare Sabrinum in loco vulgariter nuncupato Haber Thawan, id est, casus Thawi in aliud, et habet aliqua castra prope se sita. Est castrum de Talevan[d] in orientali parte ejusdem, distans ab eodem mille quingentis passibus et a Pontvayn duobus millibus passuum. Item est aliud castrum quod vocatur castrum de Penlleyn,[e] id est, caput Lini, et stat in occidentali plaga ejusdem, et distat ab eodem ducentis passibus, et Pontvayn mille passibus, et stat ab occidentali

P. 105 c.

[a] Craig Dinas.
[c] Cowbridge.
[b] Fonmone castle. See vol. iii, p. 24.
[d] Tal y van.
[e] Penlline.

plaga ejusdem. Item est oppidum, moenibus et fossis cir-
cumdatum, cujus orientalis porta stat ad ripas rivi in occidentali plaga ejusdem rivi, et currit rivus per moenia dicti
Pontvayn, relinquendo oppidum ab occidentali et septen-
trionali plaga. Item est et aliud castrum, distans à Pontvayn
ducentis passibus, quod vulgariter nuncupatur castell Lan-
lythan,[a] id est, castrum Lithani, et stat ab orientali plaga
ejusdem rivi, distans ab illo jactu lapidis, et in illo castro est
turris, sive porta, in qua sunt loca pro septem cathar . . . et
est munitissima structura.*

Item est aliud castrum, quod vulgariter nuncupatur castrum
Sancti . . . et stat in rupe prope Sabrinum mare, distans à
Pontvayn quatuor millibus passuum versus † australem plagam
tendentem ad occidentem.

Est etiam in illa regione quidam locus, vocatus vulgariter
locus Sancti Iltuti, cujus precibus, ut fertur, obtinuit à
domino, ut nullum animal ‡ venenosum infra precinctum
illius parochiae esset, nec ut § animal huc usque visum est
aliquod vivum mortuum tamen dicitur, illic. Illic est
phanum Sancti Iltuti, quod est celeberimum, ac in cimiterio
in orientali plaga illius fani jacet corpus Hoëli || boni olim
principis Wallie, et distat a Pont vayn iii[bus] millibus passuum,
et à mare Sabrino mille passibus, et tanto spatio distat Pont
vayn ab Haberthaw,[b] ubi rivus de Thawan cadit in mare
Sabrinum, ac ubi est portus pro lembis ac carinis parvis.

Item est alius rivus qui vulgariter nuncupatur Wenny,
habens originem in loco vocato ¶ etc. . . . et currit . . .**

Item prope rivum de Wenny est cellula, sive monasterium
monachorum ordinis sancti Benedicti, quod stat ab orientali
parte rivi, et distat à Pont vayn tribus millibus passuum. Est
etiam quoddam castrum, quod vocatur castrum de Coite,
stans ab occidentali plaga illius rivi, et distat ab eodem

[* See before, p. 238.]   [† *Vestrum*, MS.]
[‡ "Animal" cannot now be seen, the margin of this leaf, being torn,
has been repaired, probably since Hearne's day.]
[§ *Sic.*]   [|| This name is gone : Hearne may have seen it.]
[¶ Vulgariter nuncupato Gelle ule oke currens in Oggor vawre in-
cipiente in loco vocato Bolgh y clauth.—*Marginal note.*]
[** The leaf here is damaged.]

---

  [a] Llan Bleðian.   [b] Aber Thaw.

V.   R

duobus millibus passuum, et à Pont vayn quinque millibus passuum. Est et alius rivus, vulgariter nuncupatus Oggure Veghan, habens originem in loco vocato Aylth y rett,* et currens in mare Sabrinum apud Haber Oggur,[a] ubi est quod-

P. 103 d. dam castrum vocatum castrum de Haber Oggur, et distat à Pont vayn quinque millibus passuum, et stat in australi parte illius rivi.

Item est aliud castrum vocatum castrum de Llan Gonoyt,[b] id est, loci gonoti, et distat à Pont vayn x millibus passuum versus occidentalem plagam, partim tendens in septentrionem, et distat à monasterio de Morgan[c] duobus millibus passuum versus septentrionalem plagam. Item est alius rivus qui vocatur Havan.[d] Item alius qui vocatur Kenfik.[e]

[* The words "Veghan—y rett" are inserted and in the margin by a different hand, the same which added the previous marginal note.]

---

[a] Aber Ogwr.   [b] Llangynwyd.   [c] Margam.
          [d] Avon r.   [e] Kenffig r.

GENERAL INDEXES

TO

THE WHOLE WORK

I

INDEX OF PERSONS AND LANDOWNERS

[The word " temp." after a name indicates that the person was living in Leland's time. Bishops in long lists are not indexed individually; the lists are given under the place-names.]

ABBO, monk of Fleury, St. Benoit sur Loire, v, 172.

Abergavenny, Edward, Lord, i, 76; Joan, Lady, ii, 47 *n.*; William Beauchamp, Lord, 67; Lord, 87; iv, 167.

Abetots of Worcester, v, 229.

Abingdon, Abbots of, i, 121; John of St. Helen's, v, 1, 2.

Achard, *Berks*, iv, 99.

Aclam, Acklam, parson of Petworth, iv, 92.

Acton, Mr., of Ripley, *Worc.*, *temp.*, ii, 88

Acton of Acton? *Worc.*, iv, 112; Robert, beheaded, 163.

Acton, Lawrence, Mayor of Newcastle, iv, 118; brothers William and Lawrence, merchants of Newcastle, v, 145.

Adam, Hugh, *Glamorgan*, iii, 31.

Ædbald, son of Æthelbert, his palace, iv, 48.

Ælphege, Ælfheah, Archbishop of Canterbury, tomb, iv, 38, 40, 57.

Æschwin, Bishop, i, 117.

Ager family of Otterdene, iv, 43.

Alan de la Corone, *alias* Alan Opendore, iv, 181.

Alan, of Alan's More and Kilpeck Castle, tomb, v, 178.

Alarde of Winchelsea, iv, 114.

Albany, Albeniacus, Lord of Belvoir Castle, etc., iv, 89; members of the family buried in Belvoir monastery, v, 148, 149; Albanys of Norfolk, iv, 119.

Albanac Castle near Grantham, William of, v, 149.

Albemarle, Earl of, i, 62.

Alcher, iv, 42, 53.

Alcock, Bishop, i, 49.

Aldborough, William and Richard, i, 85.

Aldhelm, Bishop of Malmsbury, i, 130.

Aldred and Wolstan, Bishops of Worcester, ii, 59, 60.

Aldulph of Tetbury, iv, 103.

Aldwin, a hermit, ii, 164.

Alester, Dean of Warwick, tomb, ii, 42; v, 151.

Alexander, clothier of Trowbridge, *temp.*, i, 136.

Alfred, King, and son Edward, buried at Hyde, i, 272; supposed founder of Oxford University, ii, 152.

Alfred of Beverley quoted, iv, 53.

Alington, *Camb.*, iv, 97.

Allen, Thomas, free schools founded by, in Staffordshire, v, 19.

Almaric, prior of Warwick, Patriarch of Jerusalem, ii, 158.

Anderton, Mr., *temp.*, *Lancs.*, iv, 7.

Andrews, Mr., *Oxon, temp.*, iii, 55.

Angarville, Richard de Bury, *alias*, ii, 161.

Anketill, iv, 107, 108.

245

[* *Bagle*, vol. v, p. 161, is Stow's error for Bagche or Bache. Leland's story is also obscure if not erroneous. No Alexander Bache occurs in the lists of bishops of Chester, but one of that name was Bishop of St. Asaph from 1390 to 1395, when he died. As Edward III (whose confessor he is said to have been, vol. ii, p. 67) died in 1377, this bishop cannot have been the man.]

Baillie, clothier of Trowbridge, i, 136.

Bainham, Baynham, Baynonn, Mr., of Westbury, *Glouc.*, *temp.*, ii, 64. (Perhaps George Beyneham, J.P. of co. Glouc. in 1542.) *See* Baynon.

Baldwin, John, Chief Justice, *temp.*, ii, 111.

Balsall, Dr. Thomas, tomb, ii, 49.

Bane, Mr., student in Louvain, Leland's letter to, ii, 145.

Barber or Barbour, Geoffry, merchant of Abingdon, v, 78, 113-116, 118.

Bardolph, Lord, i, 25.

Barentine, Barentyne, Barrentyne, Sir William, *temp.*, i, 114, 117; ii, 19; family of London and Oxfordshire, and *temp.*, v, 232, 233.

Bareswell or Barkeswell. *See* Berkswell.

Barkeley. *See* Berkeley.

Barnes, Lord, iv, 96, 128.

Barnard Castle, Richard of, tomb, v, 128.

Barningham family, iv, 30.

Barnstaple, lords of, i, 170.

Barow, Henry, Esquire, iv, 163.

Barre, Humfrey le, iv, 103.

Barret, *Cornw.*, i, 204.

Barwik or Barok, tomb at Wimborne, i, 257, 304.

Basset family, *Derbys.*, ii, 14; *Oxon*, 33, 103, 105; *Staff.*, 171, 172.

Basset of Treheddy, i, 189, 190; of Pencoit, *Glamorgan*, iii, 21.

Bassingburn, iv, 123.

Bath, Earl of, i, 171, 301.

Bath and Wells, Bishops of, i, 290-294.

Bawdey of Somerby, *temp.*, i, 25, 26.

Bayllie, James, of Oxford, *temp.*, i, 125.

Baynard family, *Essex*, iv, 110.

Baynon, Baynan, Inon, iv, 86, 87; William, *temp.*, 87.

Baynton, iv, 163; Sir Edward, i, 132; iv, 99; Beynton, *Dorset*, 108.

Baynton, Mr., *temp.*, i, 133, 258; v, 82.

Beauchamp, William, Lord of Abergavenny, ii, 67. *See* Abergavenny.

Beauchamps, Lords of Alcester, ii, 51; of Burford, v, 74. *See* Warwick, Earls of.

Beauchamp family, Bellocampo, iv, 159; of Bedford, Simon Paganus and wife Roisia, i, 100, 101; iv, 34; v, 150; of Holt, i, 15; v, 229; of Powick, ii, 90; tomb, v, 229; of Gloucestershire, 133.

Beauchamp, Bishop, i, 264; Thomas, knt., of Dorset, iv, 108.

Beaufort, knt., tomb in Osney, i, 124; tomb in Warwick, ii, 42; Henry, Cardinal, iv, 159.

Beaufort, Lady Margaret, i, 22, 27, 257, 299.

Beaufort, Thomas, Duke of Exeter, and wife Margaret, tomb, ii, 119.

Beaumont or Bellmont, *Leic.*, iv, 126, 127; *Devon*, 127.

Beaupie, tomb in Ludlow, ii, 77, 79 *n.*

Beaupray, i, 187; Sheriff of Cornwall, 235.

Beauvais, Beaumeis, Belmeis, Richard de, v, 168, 169.

Bec or Bek, Antony de, Bishop of Durham in 1284, i, 70; v, 60, 127, 131, 145.

Becket, Thomas, v, 165; translated, iv, 39, 40; life of, by Grim, 118, 143.

Beckington, Thomas, Bishop of Bath, i, 145, 290, 291, 293.

Becoles, ? Beccles, Alan de, ii, 160.

Bede, the "noble monk," buried at Durham, v, 128; cited, ii, 25; v, 39, 54, 185.

Boleyn, Sir Geoffry, and family,
ii, 9, 10, 112; possessions, iv,
124.
Boleyn, Queen Anne (?), i, 133;
Geoffry, Mayor of London, iv,
44.
Boleyn, Thomas, Earl of Wilt-
shire, i, 20; ii, 10.
Bolney, gentleman, iv, 78.
Bond, merchant of Coventry, ii,
107.
Bonhomes, family of Corsham and
Laycock, *temp.*, i, 134; of
Haslebury, iv, 107.
Bonner, Edmund, Bishop of Here-
ford and then of London, *temp.*,
v, 161, 167.
Bonville, Boneville family, i, 157,
208, 242, 297; William, *Dorset*,
iv, 108, 120.
Booth, Archbishop of York, i,
72.
Booth, Bouth, Charles, Bishop of
Hereford, v, 27, 161; tomb,
183; Lawrence, Bishop of Durham, v, 131.
Booth, of Dunham Massey, *Cheshire, temp.*, iv, 5; v, 27; of
Barton, *Lanc.*, 27.
Borow, Sir Thomas, and wife,
of Gainsborough, i, 33; their
grandson, Lord Borow, v, 37,
58, 63.
Borowgh, merchant of Lyme
Regis, i, 244.
Bosel, first Bishop of Worcester,
ii, 59.
Bostock of Bostock, *Cheshire*, v,
27.
Botreaux, iv, 132; Lord, and his
wife, i, 163, 176; Reginald
de, 235, 298; Margaret, tomb,
264.
Boucher, Bourcher, Sir John,
iv, 34; Thomas, Cardinal, 44;
tomb, 39; Lord, killed at Bar-
net, 162; Humfrey, son of Lord
Berners, i, 104; Henry, Earl of
Essex, 313; family, 313.
Bouth. *See* Booth.

Boville, Beville, family, i, 181,
185.
Bowelle, William, *Dorset*, iv, 108.
Bowes family of Durham, Mon-
sieur de Arches, ii, 9.
Bowes (Bowis), Mr., *temp.*, *Yorks*,
ii, 7, 9; iv, 28; Sir Ralph of
Eggleston, i, 78.
Bowmer, Sir Ralph, iv, 29.
Brackenbury, Mr., i, 76.
Bradley, William and Hugh de,
iv, 102.
Bradshaw, Mr., of Hawe, *Lanc.*,
v, 41.
Bradshaw, Henry, poet, iv, 55.
Brainton, Mr., *Herefords.*, iii, 103.
Brandesburn, Henry, tomb, i,
264.
Brantingham, Bishop of Exeter, i,
227, 235.
Braundele. *See* Bromley.
Bray, Sir Reynald, or Reginald,
i, 101, 116; ii, 8; Lord, i, 116;
v, 8.
Bray, Richard, Esq., *medicus* to
Henry VI, tomb, v, 229.
Brecknock, Archdeacon of, iii,
109; Eleanor, Lady of, iv, 125;
Humphrey, Lord of, 126.
Breose, Breuse, Brayuse, family
property, ii, 13; Reginald de,
and five others, iv, 103, 125;
William of, tomb, v, 209.
Brereton, Sir Richard of Cheshire,
v, 26; Sir Randol, *temp.*, iv, 4;
v, 30; Sir William, 30.
Breton, Bruton, John le, Bishop
of Hereford, *custos* Garderobe,
etc., v, 177, 183, 185.
Bridges, Mr., of Cubberley, *Wilts*,
temp., i, 130; v, 147; of Glou-
cestershire, ii, 5; Sir John,
Glouc., iv, 115, 131, 132; of
Berkshire, *temp.*, iv, 115.
Bridport, Giles of, Bishop of Salisbury, i, 265, 267, 268.
Brien, Briente, family of Dart-
mouth, and Guido de, lord of
Woodsford and Tewkesbury, i,
221; iv, 73, 157; v, 177.

Brigham, Christopher, merchant of Newcastle, v, 59.

Brightnel, *Northants*, iv, 124.

Brinstan (Beornstan), Bishop, his life, i, 229; image, 270.

Brocas, Isabel, of Missenden and Quainton, and father Sir Bernard-Brocas, ii, 3.

Brocas married to a Sandys with land, ii, 8.

Broke, Edward, *Dorset*, iv, 108.

Brokesby, Esq., of Leicester, i, 16; of Shoulby, 21.

Broko, ? Brocas, Lords, ii, 51.

Bromley, Sir John, of Staffordshire and his heirs, v, 29.

Brooke, Lord, i, 189, 193, 212, 217; iv, 72.

Brooke, Lord. *See* Willoughby.

Brotherton, Thomas of, son to Edward I, i, 88, 327; family, iv, 83, 90, 93.

Brough, John de, Earl of Ulster, iv, 155.

Broughton, lands of, iv, 97; John, *Flints.*, iii, 69.

Broune family, of Thrapstone, i, 6.

Brounscombe, Walter, i, 197, 226.

Browne, Mr., knt., *temp.*, ii, 52.

Browning, Bruning, of Melbury, *Dorset*, epitaphs, i, 247; iv, 109.

Bruce family, i, 63, 64, 99.

Brudenel of Dene, Mr., *temp.*, i, 12, 13, 307, 308, 313; ii, 5; v, 223. *See* Entwistle.

Brudenel, Edmund, and wife, tomb at Amersham, ii, 113; Robert, chief justice, 113.

Bruer, William, i, 223; of Bridgewater, 162, 163, 298; Alice, 266.

Bruer, William, Bishop of Exeter, i, 226, 238.

Brun, Sir Morice, and mother, Lady Brun, ii, 3.

Brut, Brutte, Richard, iv, 107.

Bruton, John, knt., and wife, tomb, v, 177.

Bryan. *See* Brien.

Buckingham, Duke of, iii, 12, 42, 49, 105, 107, 111; v, 13; how styled, iv, 24; Edward, 106; v, 100; Humphrey, iv, 160.

Buckingham, John, Bishop of Lincoln, iv, 45.

Buckingham, Humphry, Duke of, ii, 20.

Buckingham, Thomas, Earl of, and wife Eleanor, ii, 20.

Bubwith, Nicholas, Bishop of Bath, i, 145, 290, 292.

Budock, Mr., *temp.*, i, 212.

Bulbeck, Viscounts, iv, 147, 148.

Bulkeleys of Daneham parish, Eaton and Whatcroft, *Cheshire*, v, 27; and of Wales, 27, 28.

Bunbury, gentleman near Wirral, *Ches.*, v, 26.

Burgh, Thomas, knt., and wife, tombs at Gainsborough, v, 123.

Burgh, Brough, John de, Earl of Ulster (Holvester, Ultonia), i (John de Genevilla), 313; iv, 155, 156.

Burley, Sir John, tomb, ii, 67.

Burnell, Sir Robert, v, 177; Bishop Burnell and his manor place at Acton, *Salop*, 230.

Burrough, Mr., *Leic.*, iv, 20.

Burton, knt., of Nostel, iv, 13.

Burwash, Bartholomew de, and daughter Elizabeth, iv, 157, 158; Henry, Bishop of Lincoln, his brother and nephew, tombs, v, 120, 121.

Bury, Richard, Bishop of Durham, writer of " Philobiblon," ii, 161; v, 127, 131.

Bussey family of Hougham and of Haydor, i, 26; iv, 123, 124, 131; of Lincolnshire, lands, v, 223.

Bush, Ralph, iv, 108.

Butevilayne, William, iv, 103.

Butler, Earl of Ormond, ii, 10.

Butler, Boteler, *Glamorgans.*, iii, 31, 32; Mr. of Rawcliff, *Lanc.*, *temp.*, iv, 9.

Butler, Boteler, Thomas, Lord

noble warrior, iv, 110, 115, 116; family and possessions, v, 147, 148, 176, 190.

Chapman, clothier, of Bath, i, 143.

Chaucer, Thomas, Lord of Ewelme, Hook Norton, etc., *Oxon*, and Alice, family of, i, 112; ii, 5, 19; v, 74.

Chaumburne, Sir Philip, *temp.*, i, 217.

Chaumon, Sir John, of Efford, i, 176.

Chauncy, John, knt., iv, 102.

Chaveneys, family, *Leic.*, ii, 7.

Chaworth, Sir John, of Nottinghamshire, iv, 19; of Derbyshire, v, 3.

Chedder, Lord, v, 104.

Cheltenham, Abbot of Tewkesbury, iv, 136.

Chenduit family, i, 234, 235.

Cheney, Cheyney, Lord, Warden of Cinque Ports, i, 125; Sir John, 264; Warden of Dover, *temp.*, iv, 70; Cheyni, knt., 73; of Pynne, Exeter, ii, 17.

Chenies family, i, 105.

Chester, Earls of, iv, 147; Ralph or Randol, v, 24.

Chetweine, Chetwynd, of Ingestre, *Staff.*, ii, 171.

Chicheley, Henry, Archbishop, iv, 44; Bishop, 34, 39.

Chicheley, chamberlain of London, family, iv, 34.

Chideock, John, knt., iv, 108.

Chillenden, Thomas, prior of Canterbury, iv, 41.

Choke, Sir Richard, Chief Justice, v, 80, 84.

Cholmeley, Cholmondeley, family, *Yorks*, i, 62, 63; Mr., *Cheshire*, *temp.*, iv, 2; v, 30.

Chorleton family, *Salop*, iii, 66; v, 18, 183; Louis, Bishop of Hereford, 162, 181, 184; Lord Powis, iv, 76.

Clare family, iv, 154-156; Gilbert de, and wife Joan, ii, 92;

v, 102, 172, 174, 229; Sir Nicholas, 67.

Clare, Earl of Gloucester, iv, 140. *See* Gloucester.

Clare, Richard, Earl of Hereford, iv, 154, 155.

Claregenet, i, 83.

Clarelle, i, 36.

Clarence, Duke of, iv, 138, 161; how styled, 24; Isabella Neville, Duchess of, 161.

Clarivaulx, i, 328; ii, 14.

Claxton, Burnham, i, 75.

Clement of Lichfield, Abbot of Evesham, ii, 52.

Cleobury, Thomas, Abbot of Dour, *temp.*, ii, 84.

Clerk, Bishop of Bath, i, 145, 149, 291.

Clerk, Mr., of Weston, *temp.*, i, 114.

Clifford, iv, 132; of Kent, 88; Roger, 126; v, 178.

Clifton, Gervase, beheaded, iv, 162; Mr., *temp.*, i, 89.

Clinton, Lord, of Folkestone, *temp.*, iv, 64; descended from Earl of Huntingdon, ii, 17. *See* Fiennes.

Clopton, Hugh, of Stratford-on-Avon, ii, 27, 28; his works there, 49, 50.

Cobham, Margaret, i, 35; Sir John, and wife, iv, 44; Cobhams of Lingfield, Surrey, 118.

Cokkis ? Cocks or Cox, gentleman to Prince Arthur, ii, 77, 79 *n*.

Coleclough of Bloreton, *Staff.*, ii, 172.

Coleshill, iv, 73.

Colville, knt., *Kent*, iv, 66.

Colworp, Alice, ii, 2.

Compton, knt., *Cornw.*, i, 205.

Compton, Sir William, Keeper of Fulbrook, *Warw.*, ii, 48.

Compton, Cometon, Mr., *temp.* (Constable of Sudley and Gloucester Castles, ? of Hanley Castle also), iv, 135, 136, 141.

Coningsby at Hampton, *Heref.*, ii, 70.

V. S

Haly, Mr., tomb, ii, 42 (probably
John Haly, Prebendary of Wells
in 1531. *See* Let. and Pap.,
Hen. VIII, vol. v, Nos. 529-
30).
Hamelin de Barham, a Norman
founder, iii, 50.
Handley, Humphrey, beheaded,
iv, 162.
Hanmer family, *Flintshire*, iii, 68.
Hansard of Lincolnshire, ii, 12;
Mr., of Hills manor, *temp.*, v,
36.
Harbottle, lands of, in North-
umberland, v, 58.
Harcourt, Harecourt family, ii,
169; of Oxfordshire, iv, 129.
Harding, John, historian, ii, 167.
Harding, Lord Berkeley, iv, 103;
Robert and family, genealogy,
103, 104, 130.
Harman, *alias* Veysey, Bishop of
Exeter, ii, 98, 99; restores
Sutton-Coldfield, 98.
Harnhull, Stephen de, knt., ii,
58.
Harold, King, his son Harold and
family at Ewias, v, 176, 177,
178.
Harold, time of King Edward the
Confessor, ii, 65.
Harold Harefoot crowned, ii, 153.
Harpsden, *Oxon*, iv, 101.
Harrington of Rutland, ii, 5; Mr.,
temp., iv, 90; family, 122.
Harrington, Lords, of Lancashire
and Dorset, v, 221, 222.
Haseley, Dean of Warwick,
schoolmaster to Henry VII,
tomb, ii, 42; v, 151.
Haslerig, of Northumberland and
Noseley, i, 14, 21; v, 57, 58.
Hastings, Lord, i, 20, 98, 176,
206; beheaded in the Tower,
his daughter, v, 3; other kin-
dred, 4; William, Earl of Pembroke, tomb, ii, 67; John, Earl
of Pembroke, iv, 84; Earl of
Huntingdon, *temp.*, 4, 71, 103,
132; Hugh, 157.

Hastings, Richard, Chamberlain
to Edward III, tomb, iv, 23.
Hastings from Suffolk, his house
in Spilsby, v, 34; of Wilksby,
Linc., 37.
Hatfield, Thomas, Bishop of Dur-
ham, v, 127, 131.
Haughton, *Salop*, iii, 67.
Haver, Hugh, pirate, v, 170.
Hawley, John, merchant of Dart-
mouth, i, 220, 221.
Heneage of Hainton, *Linc.*, v, 37;
Sir Thomas, *temp.*, 37.
Henry le Moyne, iv, 103.
Henry IV, King, tomb, iv, 38.
Henry V, date of birth, iv, 94.
Herbert, Sir Walter, iv, 91. *See*
Pembroke.
Herbert and Finch families, iv,
114; Herbert Fitz Peter, 125.
Herbert family, *Brecknocks.*, iii,
107; *Glamorgans.*, 23, 25, 26,
42.
Hereford, Bishops Lorengo and
Kynelm (Losinga and Rein-
helm, *Stubbs*), ii, 66.
Hereford, Milo, Earl of, ii, 63;
Roger, Earl of, iv, 102. *See*
Bohun and Lacy.
Hereward, Roger, iv, 103.
Herman, John, of Rendlesham,
iv, 75.
Heron, Sir John, i, 115; his son
Giles, 116; of Ford, iv, 117.
Herring, John, iv, 108.
Heydon, family of, Norfolk and
Surrey, ii, 11, 12.
Heywood, Dean of Lichfield, ii,
100.
Higden, Dean of York, i, 43.
Hiatt, James, iv, 132.
Hill, Sir Rowland, merchant of
London, bridge built by, ii,
83.
Hill of Modbury, i, 217.
Hinmar, Mr., Chancellor of Dur-
ham, v, 128.
Hoel, Robert, knt., tomb, ii, 150.
Holbeche, David, a lawyer of
Oswestry, iii, 75.

T

Simeon of Durham, quoted, iv, 53.
Simon, Bishop of Salisbury, i, 268.
Skargill, knt., i, 43.
Skeffington of Skeffington, i, 21.
Skirlaw, Walter, Bishop of Durham, i, 52, 68, 70 ; v, 128, 129, 131, 132.
Skrimesha of Norbury, *Staff.*, a lawyer, *temp.*, ii, 170.
Skriven, *Salop*, iii, 66.
Slane, lords of, i, 299.
Smith, Mr., *Cheshire*, *temp.*, iii, 91 ; Smith, *Leic.*, iv, 20.
Snede of Broadwall, *Staff.*, ii, 172.
Somerey, Earl, ii, 17.
Somerset, Edmund, Duke of, ii, 21 ; iv, 87 ; Edmund and brother John beheaded, 162; John, Earl of, i, 257, 308; tomb, iv, 40; Sir Charles, 91.
Somerton of Drayton, *Oxon*, ii, 13.
Souch, Lord. *See* Zouch.
Spaine, ii, 15.
Speke, Mr., *temp.*, i, 157, 160, 227.
Spencer, Lord Edward, iv, 134.
Spencer, or le Dispencer, Hugh II, Earl of Gloucester, iv, 140; his wife Eleanor de Clare, 156; her death, 157; Hugh III and wife, Elizabeth, 157; family, 156-158; property of, ii, 110.
Spurstow, Mr., *temp.*, iv, 3; v, 23.
Stafford, Humfrey, with the Silver Hand, iv, 72, 73; Humfrey, knt., *Dorset*, 108.
Stafford, Sir Humphry, *Northamptons.*, family and *temp.*, iv, 78, 79.
Stafford, Ralph, first Earl, iv, 83.
Stafford, Earl of Wiltshire, i, 6; Edmund de, i, 226, 236.
Stafford of Worcester, iv, 80; of Froham, iv, 149.

Stafford, Lord, *temp.*, ii, 27; v, 13; family of knights, ii, 95; tombs and pedigree, v, 21; Sir Humphrey Stafford's father beheaded, v, 221.
Stanley, Standeley, Earl of Derby, ii, 35, 37 ; Sir William of, iv, 3; Thomas, first Earl Derby, iv, 97; family of Staffordshire, Cheshire, etc., ii, 170, 171; v, 26, 28, 30.
Stanley, Lord Monteagle, iv, 97.
Stanley, William, esquire, of Bucknell, and his wife, ii, 34.
Stanton family, *Staff.*, ii, 172.
Starky, Starkey of Cheshire, v, 26, 29.
Stapleton, Sir Brian, i, 44; knight, 227 ; bishop, 227, 236, 237; ii, 15.
Stapleton, Mr., of London, *temp.*, v, 2.
Stawel, Thomas, knight, tomb, i, 287.
Stawford, merchant of London, i, 170, 299.
Steward, James, King of Scotland, and wife, iv, 127, 128.
Stoke, Adam of Great Bedwin, *Wilts*, tomb, v, 79.
Stoner, Stoneher, ii, 19; Stoner, a judge, i, 117; Sir Walter, v, 72.
Stonnard, *Cornw.*, i, 206.
Stonor. *See* Stoner.
Storthwayt, John, i, 145; tomb, 293.
Storton or Stourton, *Staff.*, Lord, v, 20.
Stoure, Mr., i, 218.
Stourton of Stourton, Lord, *Wilts*, *temp.*, v, 106, 108, 223.
Straddel, Dr. Richard, writer and abbot of Dore, v, 160.
Stradeling, *Glamorgans.*, iii, 27, 28, 31, 32, 38.
Strange, i, 100.
Strangewaise of Harlesey, i, 68; ii, 2; Sir Giles, i, 243; of Melbury, 247, 248.

ii, 59; possessions of the Archbishops, iv, 12, 18.
Yorke, Mr., *temp.*, ii, 8.

Zouch, Souch, Lord, i, 127, 205,
218; iv, 21, 74; possessions of,
74, 131; v, 219; William and
wife Eleanor de Clare, iv, 156;
Elizabeth, 157; Edward de la,
tomb, i, 287.
Zouch, of Codnor and Derbyshire,
temp., i, 12, 13; iv, 118, 123.
Zouch, William de la, Archbishop
of York, v, 125, 135.

INDEX OF PLACES AND SUBJECTS

v.   X

READING PUBLIC LIBRARY

Môn, various places, and waters—*continued*.
   Tygai, Corse, iii, 133.
   Ynys Badrig, Little Mouse isle, iii, 132.
Mone r., iii, 45.
Monk bridge, York, i, 54; v, 17.
Monkton Farleigh, i, 134.
Monmouth, town and bridge, ii, 71; iii, 45, 47; priory, 50; Castle, iv, 167.
Monnow r., confluence with Wye r., ii, 69, 70.
Montacute, i, 157-8; cell to, 206, 324. *See* Holme.
Monteburgh Abbey, Normandy, three Devonshire cells of, i, 243.
Montford bridge, ii, 83.
Montgomeryshire, additions to, in 1535-6, iii, 54, 55.
Montgomery, iii, 11, 41, 53, 125; v, 14, 187; Welsh names, Trevaldwyn, Cairovaldwine, iii, 11; v, 13.
Morda, or Vorda r., iii, 76.
Mordiford, *Heref.*, iii, 49; iv, 165; bridge, ii, 69.
More or Ver r., *Herts*, iv, 98.
Morgan. *See* Margam, also *n.* †, p. 15.
Morganhog, Morcantuc, *Glamorgansh.*, iii, 15.
Morlaix, Britanny, merchants of, at Lyme Regis, i, 244.
Morleis, Morleys Castle, iii, 16, 18; v, 239.
Morley, *Lanc.*, iv, 6, 7, 10; Morley Hall, v, 42.
Morton Corbet, *Salop*, iii, 65; iv, 1; v, 14.
Morpeth on the Wansbeck r., v, 62, 63; Castle, 63.
Mortham Tower, iv, 28, 30.
Mortlake, iv, 86.
Morville, *Salop*, ii, 85.
Morwelham, Morwell, Morleham, i, 210, 211.
Moss and fir wood, *Ches.*, v, 30, 43.
Mottisfont priory, i, 163; ii, 8.

Moulton and Castle, in Holland, *Linc.*, ii, 147, 148.
Moulton Park, *Northants*, i, 11.
Mountferrant Castle, i, 58; *Yorks*, iv, 33.
Mountjoy Castle in Spain, iv, 132.
Mount Sorrel, i, 17.
Mousehole, *Cornw.*, i, 183, 189, 319.
Mowðwy, iii, 55, 66, 78.
Muchelney, v, 109.
Muggleswick, *Durh.*, v, 132.
Mulgrave, i, 58, 59; Castle, iv, 33.
Multon, *Northants*, i, 11.
Mumbles, Mummes, iii, 127.
Mŵd, The, Llan Boduan, iii, 84.
Myerscough, *Lanc.*, iv, 9.
Mynyð du, the Black mountain, iii, 112, 119; iv, 179, 180.
Mynyð Gelli haið, Mennith Kelthle, iii, 22.
Mynyð y Gader, iii, 110 *bis*.
Mynwy, Monnow, Mone r. (Ewias), iii, 45, 47.
Myton, *Yorks*, i, 66.

Nadder r., i, 262.
Nant Bay, iii, 122.
Nant Bran, iii, 24.
Nant Conway commote and its five parishes, iii, 80.
Nantglyn, *Denbigh*, ii, 27.
Nant Gwrtheyrn (Vortigern) in Pistill, iii, 79, 87, 88.
Nanthonddi, iii, 110.
Nant-llŷs, iii, 119.
Nantwich, iv, 4, 75; v, 23, 29.
Nappa, Nocastle, *Yorks*, iv, 28, 33, 86.
Narberth, Arberth, iii, 62.
Nare Head, i, 200, 201.
Naunton, *Glouc.*, iii, 39.
Naunton Hall, Rendlesham, *Suff.*, iv, 75.
Navy of Edward I, William de Leyburne, Captain of, v, 210.
Naworth Castle, *Cumb.*, ii, 7; v, 55.
Neasham, i, 69.

Pateley bridge, *Yorks*, i, 81; v, 143.
Patrington, i, 51, 61.
Paulet, near Bridgwater, iv, 71.
Pawlton, i, 144.
Payne's Castle, iii, 42, 109; iv, 165; v, 50.
Peak, High, Castle, *Derbys.*, v, 31.
Pebidiog, iii, 63, 64, 65.
Pecforton, *Ches.*, iv, 3.
Peder brook, i, 161.
Pedware r., iii, 20, 22.
Peebles, source of the Tweed near, v, 67.
Pembridge, *Heref.*, ii, 72, 166.
Pembroke, iii, 115, 116; cell of monks, iii, 51.
Pembro, *Cornw.*, i, 187, 191.
Penar hill, iii, 20.
Penbont, iii, 28, 29, 33, 34.
Penbrey, Kidwelly, iii, 60.
Pen brook, *Staff.*, v, 21.
Pencarreg and Gogurne lake, iii, 117.
Pencoit, iii, 21; iv, 85.
Pencombe, *Cornw.*, i, 189.
Pencrag hill, *Radnor*, iii, 42.
Pendennis, St. Ives, *Cornw.* (not Pendeen), i, 192, 193.
Pendennis Castle, i, 196, 197, 202.
Pendewr, St. David's Head, iii, 65.
Pendragon Castle, v, 146.
Pen-du-Lwyn, iii, 26.
Penfilly r., course of and bridge, ii, 73; iv, 165.
Pengarsike or Garsike, i, 188.
Pengelli, Penkelthe Castle, iii, 10, 107, 110, 111.
Penhill Beacon and Castle, *Yorks*, iv, 26; v, 134.
Penkestel creek, i, 195.
Penknek, i, 205, 235.
Penkridge, ii, 170; iv, 82; v, 21, 22; and Pillenhall, ii, 169.
Penlee, i, 211.
Penley in Chiltern, i, 105.
Penllech, iii, 80.

Penllimmon mountain, iii, 125.
Penlline, Penllyn, Castle, iii, 32; v, 238, 240.
Penllyn commote, iii, 74, 77.
Penllyn lordship, *Denbighs.*, iii, 95.
Penmachno, iii, 81, 89.
Penmaen mawr and vychan, iii, 85.
Penmon priory, *Môn*, iii, 133.
Penmynnyð, iii, 134.
Pennalun, Abbot Laurod, iv, 168.
Pennarth, iii, 22.
Penpoll creek, i, 207.
Penrice and Castle, iii, 16, 127.
Penrith, v, 2, 46, 48, 53, 54; Castle, 56, 147.
Penrhyn, *Flint*, iii, 93.
Penrhyn, *Carnarvon*, iii, 84, 89.
Penrhyn dew-draeth, iii, 88, 89.
Penrhyn dû, haven, iii, 88.
Penrhyn, Little Orme's Head, iii, 89.
Penryn, *Cornw.*, i, 196, 197, 322.
Pensford, *Somers.*, v, 103.
Pentaney priory, i, 93.
Pentewan, Pentowen, i, 201, 202.
Pentyrch, Castle Mynach in, iii, 21.
Penwith, i, 189.
Penwortham, *Lanc.*, iv, 8, 9.
Penzance, i, 189, 319, 320.
Peover r., iv, 5.
Pepper Hill, near Hampton, *Salop*, v, 18.
Perche in Normandy, iv, 100.
Pershore, *Worc.*, ii, 27; iii, 39, 40; monastery, iv, 151; bridge, v, 9.
Peterborough, quarry at, ii, 149.
Peterill r., v, 54, 56.
Peterston-super-Ely, Llanpeder, iii, 25.
Petherton, North and South, *Somers.*, i, 161; iv, 122; park, i, 161.
Petit Tor, i, 224.
Petty pool, *Ches.*, iv, 3.
Petworth, honour of, iv, 77, 78; v, 49, 50; market town, 92; the

READING FREE PUBLIC LIBRARY

CHISWICK PRESS: PRINTED BY CHARLES WHITTINGHAM AND CO.
TOOKS COURT, CHANCERY LANE, LONDON.